ORGANIZATIONAL EFFECTIVENESS
Theory-Utilization-Research

ORGANIZATIONAL EFFECTIVENESS: THEORY—RESEARCH—UTILIZATION

edited by

S. Lee Spray
Department of Sociology and Anthropology
Kent State University

published by
The Comparative Administration Research Institute
Graduate School of Business Administration
Kent State University

DISTRIBUTED BY THE KENT STATE UNIVERSITY PRESS

COLLEGE OF BUSINESS ADMINISTRATION
GRADUATE SCHOOL OF BUSINESS ADMINISTRATION
Gail E. Mullin . . . . Dean

COMPARATIVE ADMINISTRATION RESEARCH INSTITUTE
Anant R. Negandhi . . . . . . Director

Library of Congress Cataloging in Publication Data
Main entry under title:

Organizational effectiveness.

Bibliography: p.
Includes index.
1.   Organizational effectiveness—Addresses, essays,
lectures.   I.   Spray, S. Lee, 1935-
HD38.074   658.4   75–36534
ISBN 0–87338–183–1

Library of Congress Catalog Card Number 75—36534
ISBN: 0–87338–183–1 cloth bound $ 12.50

Photosetting by Thomson Press (India) Limited, New Delhi

PREFACE

Since human organizations are created and maintained by individuals for the purpose of accomplishing large-scale tasks, one would naturally assume that people concerned with understanding and/or running organizations would devote a great deal of attention to evaluating the effectiveness of various organizational arrangements. While many have been concerned with the assessment of organizational performance, the fact remains that effective organizations still resemble elephants, in the sense that they are identifiable when encountered, but very difficult to describe. There are little grounds for pessimism, however, since interest in understanding organizational effectiveness has undergone a marked growth in the past few years. Indeed, the volume of literature on this subject and its rate of increase is as impressive as the complexity of the phenomena which it tries to analyze and explain. Like other developments, however, the coming of the "golden era" of research on organizational effectiveness has created as well as resolved problems. Specifically, both the sheer volume and the multiplicity of points of view from which organizational effectiveness has been examined has led to a state of bewilderment for many individuals interested in getting a firm handle on the problem. The present volume attempts to provide some guidelines which may help those interested in organizational effectiveness more comfortably orient themselves to the labyrinth of writings on the topic. More specifically, the volume attempts to identify and examine critically some of the major approaches to the study of organizational effectiveness, indicate the ways in which such approaches are linked to each other, and suggest ways to narrow the existing gap between theoretical knowledge and practical action.

To facilitate the systematic treatment of these topics, the volume has been organized into three sections. The first section contains papers focusing on theoretical dimensions involved in the assessment of organizational effectiveness. While the papers in this section, contributed by Dubin, Evan and Campbell, explore different theoretical dimensions, they all share a common concern for integrating the study of organizational effectiveness into general organizational theory.

The second section is composed of four papers, one contributed by Srivastva and Salipante, one by Price, one by Marsh and Mannari and one by Stewart. Each of these papers contributes important substantive knowledge, as well as serving as models for the kind of theoretically informed empirical research sorely needed in the field at the present time.

The third section focuses on the critical issue of the utilization of scientific knowledge by organizational practitioners. The first chapter in this volume, contributed by Spray, also addresses itself to this problem.

The aims of this volume are clearly ambitious. The extent to which these objectives are achieved is due mainly to the contributions of others. The contributions of the authors of the papers contained in this volume stand out in this regard. Those who generously gave of their time and energy in serious discussion of these papers have also played a critical role. My role has been confined to synthesizing and organizing the excellent contributions of others. In attempting to accomplish this task I have benefited by the guidance and assistance of many others. In particular, I have benefited from the scholarly wisdom and administrative skill of Professor Anant Negandhi, the astute observations of Charles Hanna and John Roberts, and the splendid editorial and administrative support of Barbara Fisher and Judy Mazur. In a less tangible but equally important way, I have benefited from the wisdom and counsel which I have received from Professor Robert Dubin for more than a decade. While the value of this volume is directly attributable to the generosity and talents of these, and many other people, I alone am responsible for any limitations of the volume.

Kent   S. Lee Spray
1976

CONTRIBUTORS

John P. Campbell, *University of Minnesota*

Robert Dubin, *University of California at Irvine*

William M. Evan, *University of Pennsylvania*

Mark A. Frohman, *R. G. Barry Corporation, Columbus, Ohio*

Michael J. Kavanagh, *State University of New York at Binghamton*

Hiroshi Mannari, *Kwansei Gakuin University, Nishinomiya, Japan*

Robert M. Marsh, *Brown University*

Michael M. McGill, *Southern Methodist University*

James L. Price, *University of Iowa*

Paul F. Salipante, Jr., *Case Western Reserve University*

Marshall Sashkin, *Wayne State University*

S. Lee Spray, *Kent State University*

Suresh Srivastva, *Case Western Reserve University*

James H. Stewart, *Saint Olaf College*

CONTENTS

SECTION IV: ORGANIZATIONAL EFFECTIVENESS—RELEVANCE

Organizational Effectiveness: Theory, Research and Utilization
Introduction

S. LEE SPRAY
Kent State University

The importance of assessing the performance of formal organizations was widely recognized rather early in the twentieth century. Thus, Weber (1947), Barnard (1938), and members of what has come to be known as the "classical" school of organizational theorists, (Fayol, 1949; Gulick, 1937; Taylor, 1911; Urwick, 1943) all placed heavy emphasis on the determinates of organizational effectiveness or "efficiency." These early theorists, however, were concerned primarily with developing conceptual frameworks and/or a set of prescriptive principles which, if adhered to, would result in maximum organizational efficiency. The subsequent development of empirical methods in the social sciences, combined with a recognition of the increasingly pervasive influence of formal organizations, resulted in a proliferation of approaches to the study of organizational effectiveness. Consequently, theoretical pluralism is one of the defining characteristics of the extant literature dealing with organizational performance.

Since the end of World War II, the proliferation of relatively distinct models of organizational effectiveness has occurred at an increasingly accelerated rate. Thus, in recent years the case study tradition, initiated by sociologists such as Blau (1955), Gouldner (1954), Selznick (1949), and Whyte (1948) has been supplemented by a variety of approaches. These include the decision-making model of March and Simon (1958), the criterion approach of Georgopoulos and Tannenbaum (1971), the contingency approach of Lawrence and Lorsch (1967), the structural approach of the Aston group (Hinings and Lee, 1971; Inkson, Pugh, and Hickson, 1970; Pheysey, Payne and Pugh, 1971; Pugh and Pheysey, 1973), and various systems models (Evan, 1972; Katz and Kahn, 1966; Likert, 1961; Taylor and Bowers, 1972). In addition, a host of programmatic approaches, such as operations research, cost/benefit analysis, management by objectives, and various organizational development models, have recently been added to the literature on organizational effectiveness. Moreover, the present level of diversity in the field does not appear to be a transient state of affairs, since the newer approaches have been offered as additions to rather than replacements of the older models.

Organizational analysts have been preoccupied with efforts to systematize the study of organizational performance by precisely specifying the conceptual schemes and methodological techniques employed in empirical research; hence, they have devoted major attention to the differences among various approaches. Emphasizing the differences among various approaches to organizational effectiveness undoubtedly facilitates the precise specification of the range of phenomena amenable to analysis by each perspective. The diversity of specific interest manifested by organizational analysts should not, however, be allowed to obscure the consensus which exists at a general level in the field. Scanning the organizational horizon in search of similar processes which—due to competing theoretical perspectives or a variety of other influences—have escaped consensual definition is more than simply a mopping-up procedure on a lexicographical plane. Highlighting the common observational dimensions embedded in various approaches to organizational effectiveness provides a foundation for exploring the emerging task of synthesizing the multiplicity of perspectives.

The search for commonality in the diversity of approaches to the study of organizational effectiveness can be conveniently initiated by simply noting that analysts of organizational performance have been concerned largely with raising and answering the following five distinct but closely interrelated questions:

1. What alternative ways of evaluating organizational performance are conceivable?
2. What alternative ways of evaluating organizational performance actually have been utilized?
3. What are the underlying causes of various levels of organizational performance?
4. What are the consequences of various levels of organizational performance for other organizational processes?
5. What advantages and disadvantages are inherent in the various approaches to evaluating organizational performance?

While theory building should be concerned with all of these questions, the developed theory itself should contain propositions dealing directly with the third and fourth questions, *i.e.*, with the problem of causes and consequences of various levels of organizational performance. The first question is relevant to theory building, while the second is relevant to data collection and analysis relative to discovering the grounds for accepting or rejecting proposed theories. While attempts to answer the fifth question are involved in the theory-building process, the actual answers are not embodied in the theory.

Of course, not all organizational analysts have been equally interested in all of these questions. Most have been more concerned with some than with others; but as the papers contained in this volume demonstrate, analysts of organizational performance have been concerned to some degree with all of these questions and with little else. Thus, in the first paper, Dubin uses the second question as the principal organizing theme, while questions three and four serve as the basis of several important variations on the central theme. In the second paper, Evan gives careful consideration to questions two and five but, using a systems approach, organizes the thrust of his analysis around the relationship between organizational effectiveness and other organizational processes, *i.e.*, question four. In the third paper, Campbell presents a systematic analysis of conceptual and measurement developments in the area of organizational performance. In the process, he provides an insightful blend of questions two and three.

The second section of this volume contains reports on four outstanding and instructive studies of organizational effectiveness. Although sharing a common concern for sound empirical assessment of the determinates of organizational effectiveness (question three), the major contribution of each paper is quite distinct. First, Srivastva and Salipante present a much needed summary and critique of the existing empirical literature on the relationship between autonomy and individual and organizational performance. Next, Price provides us with the most comprehensive and systematic codification of existing scientific knowledge presently extant on the relationship between turnover and organizational effectiveness. In the process, he makes a major contribution to the developing systemization of the field of organizational performance. The third research paper, authored by Marsh and Mannari, contributes fascinating empirical findings on employee performance in Japanese firms and provides a much needed demonstration of how theory and field work can be meaningfully integrated in investigating effectiveness. In the final paper in this section, Stewart utilizes a multidimensional perspective of effectiveness to empirically assess the range of factors accounting for organizational performance within different time frames. This paper not only provides important substantive findings in a largely neglected area—namely, performance in voluntary organizations— it also contributes empirical support to an extremely important theoretical point: the fact that organizations give priority to different goals at different times in their histories.

The two papers contained in the third section are primarily interested in question five. Specifically, both are concerned with the problems associated with utilizing scientific knowledge to alter levels of organizational performance. McGill convincingly underscores the need for empirical assessment of the strategies designed to improve organizational effectiveness. Frohman, Sashkin, and Kavanagh, on the other hand, provide a systematic exposition of a comprehensive approach to the diagnosis and subsequent alteration of levels of organizational effectiveness. While both papers are clearly distinct in terms of the areas of neglect addressed, they both imply that the gap between organizational effectiveness and application is being reduced.

All nine papers herein contained are original manuscripts written especially for the eighth annual Comparative Administration Research Institute/Conference held at Kent State University in April 1975. The last paper in this volume, authored by Spray, is a general summary of the central theme of the conference.

REFERENCES

Barnard, C. I. *The Functions of the Executive*. Cambridge, Mass.: Harvard University
1938 Press.

Blau, P. M. *The Dynamics of Bureaucracy*. Chicago: The University of Chicago
1955 Press.

Evan, W. M. "An Organization-Set Model of Interorganizational Relations."
1972 In M. F. Tuite, M. Radnor, and R. K. Chisholm (eds.), *Interorganizational Decision Making*: 181–200. Chicago: Aldine Publishing Co.

Fayol, H. *General and Industrial Management*. London: Pitman.
1949

Georgopoulous, B. S. and A. S. Tannenbaum. "A Study of Organizational Effective-
1971 ness." In J. Ghorphade (ed.), *Assessment of Organizational Effectiveness*. Pacific Palisades, Calif.: Goodyear.

Gouldner, A. W. *Patterns of Industrial Bureaucracy*. Glencoe, Ill.: The Free Press.
1954

Gulick, L. "Notes of the Theory of Organization." In L. Gulick and L. Urwick (eds.),
1937 *Papers on the Science of Administration*. New York: The Institute of Public Administration.

Hinings, C. R., and G. L. Lee. "Dimensions of Organization Structure and Their
1971 Context: A Replication." *Sociology*, 5:83–93.

Inkson, J. H. K., D. S. Pugh, and D. J. Hickson. "Organization Context and Structure:
1970 An Abbreviated Replication." *Administrative Science Quarterly*, 15:318–29.

Katz, D., and R. L. Kahn. *The Social Psychology of Organizations*. New York:
1966 John Wiley, Inc.

Lawrence, P. R., and J. W. Lorsch. *Organization and Environment*. Cambridge,
1967 Mass.: Division of Research, Graduate School of Business Administration, Harvard University.

Likert, R. *New Patterns of Management*. New York: McGraw-Hill.
1961

March J. G., and H. A. Simon. *Organizations*. New York: Wiley.
1958

Pheysey, D. C., R. L. Payne, and D. S. Pugh. "Influence of Structure at Organi-
1971 zational and Group Levels." *Administrative Science Quarterly*, 16:61–73.

Pugh, D. S., and D. Pheysey. "A Comparative Administration Model." In A. R.
1973 Negandhi (ed.), *Modern Organization Theory*. Kent, Ohio: Kent State University Press.

Selznick, P. *TVA and the Grass Roots*. Berkeley, Calif.: University of California
1949 Press

Taylor, J. C., and Bowers, D. G. *Survey of Organizations*. Ann Arbor, Mich.: Institute
1972 for Social Research.

Taylor, F. W. *The Principles of Scientific Management*. New York: Harper.
1911

Urwick, L. F. *The Elements of Administration*. New York: Harper.
1943

Weber, M. *The Theory of Social and Economic Organizations*. Trans. by A. M.
1947 Henderson and T. Parsons. Glencoe, Ill.: The Free Press.

Whyte, W. F. *Human Problems of the Restaurant Industry*. New York: McGraw-Hill.
1948

Section I

ORGANIZATIONAL EFFECTIVENESS —THEORY—

This section consists of papers contributed by Dubin, Evan, and Campbell. In the first paper, Dubin focuses on the various perspectives utilized in assessing organizational effectiveness. The focus of the second paper, by Evan, is on the relationship between effectiveness and other organizational processes. In the third paper, Campbell presents a systematic analysis of conceptual and measurement developments in the area of organizational performance.

Organizational Effectiveness: Some Dilemmas of Perspective

ROBERT DUBIN
University of California
at Irvine

Organizational effectiveness has at least two fundamentally different meanings. It is worthwhile to sort out these meanings, with the expectation that, by so doing, our thinking can be clarified. The strategy employed in this paper is to examine some of the dilemmas that result from differing perspectives about organizational effectiveness. Once these dilemmas are recognized, we are at least halfway toward their resolution.

THE FUNDAMENTAL DILEMMA

Organizational effectiveness has a different meaning, depending on whether the organization is viewed from inside or outside. The inside perspective of an organization is a typical managerial viewpoint. The fundamental question asked about organizational effectiveness is whether the resources invested are utilized efficiently. Return on investment is a typical way to measure this type of organizational effectiveness.

A radically different view of organizational effectiveness considers the output of the organization, which is evaluated for its contribution to the larger society. Organizational effectiveness from this viewpoint is more likely to be measured by some form of cost-benefit analysis.

These are distinctly different ways of viewing organizational effectiveness. Further, there is the highly significant fact that a high level of effectiveness from one standpoint may not be correlated with a high level of effectiveness from the other standpoint. For example, the efficient production of chastity belts may still achieve low marks on organizational effectiveness when measured against the social benefits of wearing the belts in a sexually permissive society (the contemporary English manufacturer of chastity belts has just declared bankruptcy!). On the other hand, a welfare benefit distribution system which is internally inefficient may be judged to have high organizational effectiveness if it delivers large welfare payments during periods of economic crisis.

7

To my knowledge, there is no single instance when the dilemma of efficient resource utilization versus social utility is resolved by maximizing both. Inevitably, some compromise is reached so that a level of organization efficiency and a level of socially acceptable output are combined in a way that is "satisficing," to use Simon's happy phrase. In capitalist societies— at least since the justifications provided by Adam Smith—the contention that the individual pursuit of self-interest in economic behavior automatically maximizes the achievement of social goals has not been true.

Socialist-apologists argue with vigor that the pursuit of social utility is the only way to maximize internal technical effectiveness, since identifying societal interest with organizational interest is achieved through collective ownership of the means of production as Marx insisted and as Mao still proclaims. The research literature is replete with examples of the inefficiency of socialist productive enterprises, making it clear that return on investment is less than optimum. The great cultural revolution in the People's Republic of China was partially directed at eradicating the so-called neocapitalist tendencies of organizational bureaucrats who attempted to introduce efficiency into Chinese organizations at the alleged expense of realizing social goals.

This distinction between social utility of output and operating efficiency is one that pervades the economy. The counterpoint of internal efficiency and social utility of output is so fundamental that almost all contemporary social problems involving organizations can be analyzed from the standpoint of this dilemma. Indeed, whenever an organization comes under attack from the outside, its leaders will defend it on grounds of organizational effectiveness quite opposite from those used as the basis of attack. Executives of a public agency under pressure for its operating inefficiency will point with pride to the social goals to which it supposedly addresses itself and claim effectiveness in achieving such goals. A private organization condemned for failing to realize socially valued outputs will be defended by its executives with arguments about its internal operating efficiency.

The two meanings of organizational effectiveness are worlds apart. They simply cannot be reconciled. The means employed to achieve these respective forms of organizational effectiveness are not identical. Attempts to achieve consistency between the two orientations cannot, in the nature of the case, be successful. Thus, we must face squarely the fact that organizations live under conflicting demands regarding their effectiveness. Two primary analytical problems are posed by the inherent conflict between these two views. The first task is to determine how pervasive the distinction is between the two kinds of organizational effectiveness in the normal operation of organizations, especially business organizations. The second is to determine the kinds of strategies available in dealing with the fundamental dilemma of organizational effectiveness.

ORGANIZATIONAL EFFECTIVENESS IN THE BUSINESS WORLD

The dilemma of organizational effectiveness will be dealt with here in three separate areas of business operations: market and economic behavior, personnel management, and organizational structure.

Economic Activities

In economic behavior, the general phenomenon of administered prices has become a very central operating feature of American, and indeed, Western capitalism. Administered prices in the American economy have been fostered further by several states developing fair trade laws to establish minimum retail prices for many products. The fundamental argument underlying the administered price phenomenon is *not* one of profit maximization. Basically, establishing an administered price permits long-range planning of production, with special emphasis on lengthening production runs. If the individual firms must constantly respond to changes in market prices (as pure competition theory says they do), and they do this at least in part by varying the level of production, then considerable inefficiencies may be introduced into the production process as a result. With administered prices, however, it becomes possible to plan longer runs in the production cycle because the firms need not respond to constant changes in market prices. Thus, the idea of administered prices is essentially supported by arguments about the accompanying efficiencies of production.

The argument against administered prices, at least in American society, is that it is a socially undersirable form of economic behavior. It penalizes the consumer by introducing inflexibility at the lower levels of pricing, which is, of course, where the consumer is particularly interested in making the best bargain. The old populist arguments about monopoly controlled prices being a disadvantage to consumers have now become arguments that it is socially undesirable for consumers to have their options limited by administered prices.

In the realm of economic behavior, there is an even more extreme example of the conflict between social purpose and organizational efficiency. It is probably highly efficient for an organization to engage in industrial espionage, with the end view being to steal a competitor's trade secrets. The alternative for the individual firm is to engage in its own research and development, with all the attendant costs and the possibilities of failure (after all, if a competitor has something worth stealing, it must already be successful in some degree). Nonetheless, the society of businessmen (if not the entire society) is likely to condemn industrial espionage as morally reprehensible, even though it is manifestly efficient as a means of improving the operating effectiveness of the pilfering firm.

The fact that administered prices are so widespread, and industrial espionage so endemic, seems to make it clear that condemnation based on the social utility view of organizational effectiveness will not eradicate these organizationally efficient behaviors.

Personnel Management

The same fundamental dilemma can be seen in personnel practices. Consider the issue of individual productivity as it relates to work satisfaction. Viewed strictly from an efficiency standpoint, the subdivision of work—with all it entails in the way of short cycle, repetitive, simple, and undemanding personal input—is generally efficient. Subdivision of work scores high on return on investment, including investment in personnel (when the cost of low-skilled operatives is balanced against high turnover and absenteeism, for example). This very mode of organizing and staffing work stations may be accompanied by only modest levels of work satisfaction which in turn may be viewed as socially undesirable. Furthermore, it is often argued that such job dilution has permanent and undesirable consequences for the personality, if not the mentality, of the individual worker. (This is essentially the Marxist psychological-humanist argument against work simplification and job dilution as being exploitative of the individual's capacity to perform and grow.) The attack on job dilution, which is spearheaded by the gospel of job enlargement and job enrichment, is based essentially on the claim that the worker as a person will be psychologically and mentally better off, and therefore society will be better off, if the worker has the opportunity to be employed in enriched and enlarged jobs. The research literature is by no means clear on whether job enlargement and job enrichment really produce greater productivity or efficiency. The literature is even less specific about whether the modified job content does indeed produce more psychologically fulfilled or more mentally mature persons. This, of course, is the point of the illustration: that the social goal of bettering the individual worker's psyche may be at odds with the efficiency that derives from subdivided work tasks.

It is one of the proud claims of many companies that they reward long and loyal service to the organization, principally through continuity of employment. At the same time, most firms are faced with very rapid technological changes in manufacturing processes and the products turned out. In order to provide long-service personnel with continuity of employment, it may be necessary to invest considerable time and money in their retraining as technology changes. I believe it can be demonstrated that it would, in fact, be more efficient to fire the old employees and hire new, more highly skilled and trained workers as their replacements. The fact that many firms do not do this is one indication that they are willing to apply to themselves the social utility test of organizational effectiveness and override the productive efficiency test. This, by the way, is not something often credited to American business firms, although many do sacrifice operating efficiency to the larger social purpose of providing continuity of employment. Companies have been encouraged in this practice, of course, by the requirements of union contracts which provide seniority protection for workers.

We also can see the fundamental dilemma operating in the most recent innovation in personnel practices, namely that of affirmative action. The social utility underlying affirmative action is very clear: to provide reasonable and effective employment opportunities to those who are socially disadvantaged by race or sex. There may be a deliberate setting aside of skill and merit in favor of realizing the social goal when choices are made to hire or promote. Such choices may have significant impact on operating efficiency, a consequence which, even when recognized, is accepted as an appropriate cost for achieving affirmative action goals. When affirmative action is opposed, it is almost invariably condemned for its denial of merit as the paramount selection criterion, and for the consequent reduction of operating efficiencies.

Organizational Structure

One of the fundamental characteristics of an organization is the boundary within which it operates. When internal efficiency is the focus of attention, strong efforts are made to maintain a relatively closed boundary so as to minimize the impacts of a turbulent environment. The organizational boundary may be defended against intrusion by governmental agencies (*i.e.*, regulatory, taxing, or investigating bodies); against unions trying to organize the work force; against customers intruding their unreasonable demands for goods and services; and against the familial and community ties of organizational members that may distract from work performance (*i.e.*, to insure the commitment of the "organizational man"). Under some circumstances, the business organization may choose to provide all of its own needs by building an integrated production organization which is not economically dependent on suppliers of materials, parts, and sub-assemblies. It is very clear that, in the extreme, businesses and other kinds of organizations seek isolation from their environments by closing their boundaries as a means of minimizing outside influences that might dislocate internal productive efficiency.

Pressures for closing the boundaries of an organization, however, are not always derived from considerations of internal efficiency. Under circumstances of economic distress, there may be demands to satisfy social utility; for example, to eliminate foreign or illegal workers, to limit purchases of goods and services to those involving native labor, and even to discontinue some subcontracting in order to save jobs of present company employees.

Movements to open the boundaries of organizations are generally inspired by beliefs that greater social utility will be served. The modern movement to secure board of director appointments for public or minority group representatives presumes that this will induce a sense of greater social responsibility in the service of social goals. The demand that private construction be justified through impact studies opens private decisions to public scrutiny, thereby fostering the need to be congruent with social purposes.

The general point in this discussion is that the boundary of the organization is the very critical point at which the dilemma of efficiency versus social utility is highlighted around the issue of organizational effectiveness. Resolving the issue results in either maintaining or modifying the openness or closedness of the organizational boundary.

These several illustrations demonstrate the pervasive manner in which the fundamental dilemma appears in various aspects of business operations. This is by no means an exhaustive listing of circumstances under which the internal efficiency and external utility of output are in conflict. However, perhaps these examples will illustrate that the dilemma of two conflicting views of organizational effectiveness is encountered repeatedly, and in many areas of business activities.

SOME OPERATING STRATEGIES

What does one do about the dilemma? It has been a principal conclusion up to this point that the problem cannot be resolved without casting lots with one of the two views of organizational effectiveness. There is required, therefore, some sort of strategy for making the choice.

The first step in developing a strategy is to accept the fact that a choice must be made. A great deal of anger and anguish can be avoided if the inevitability of such a choice is recognized.

The second step is to recognize that within any given organization, and particularly a business organization, it is not always true that the preferred choice will be the one consistent with the view of an insider. There may be a number of occasions where social utility will be the preferred goal, and this choice can be made without any sense of inconsistency when other choices are based on internal efficiency. Consistency is not a virtue in a choice of this sort.

It is insightful and refreshing to realize that while a given situation may demand choosing between operating efficiency and social utility, over a given series of situations the decision base may vary between the two orientations. There is nothing wrong with a business firm satisfying the social utility criterion in a number of decision areas. Indeed, the rising popularity of the corporate social audit is one evidence that social utility may actually be coming into vogue as a basis for some business decisions. There is obviously also nothing wrong with the same organization satisfying the internal efficiency criterion in many other areas of business behavior. It is only when executives stubbornly insist that all business decisions meet the internal efficiency criterion that trouble ensues—witness reactions to the now famous dictum that "what's good for General Motors is good for the country."

The third element in the strategy of confronting the basic dilemma is to recognize that the measurement of organizational effectiveness is very different in the two opposing orientations. The benefits derived from output become the fundamental measurement of organizational effectiveness in terms of social utility. The efficiency with which resources are utilized is the corresponding means for measuring internal organizational effectiveness. Once a particular kind of organizational effectiveness is accepted as the goal in a particular situation, then it is imperative that that particular form of effectiveness be measured according to its appropriate criterion.

A fourth element in confronting the fundamental dilemma is to recognize that, under some circumstances, both views of organizational effectiveness will have to be taken into account simultaneously. Clearly, the whole area of industrial pollution is a case in point. In a situation involving pollution, there are evident trade-offs that must be made between operating efficiency and social utility. The important thing in working out the particular trade-offs is to be clear in measuring how much of what is being traded off for how much of what else. In this issue, for example, much of the argument between ecologists and industrialists is the result of both sides refusing to trade-off social utility for organizational efficiency.

If these four elements of a strategy for confronting the fundamental dilemma are utilized, there is a high probability that overall organizational effectiveness will be optimized. An appropriate amount of internal operating efficiency may be reached at the same time that social utility is also attained

ORGANIZATIONAL EFFECTIVENESS—A RIDDLE RESOLVED?

The linkage between private organizations and public welfare is achieved in the concept of organizational effectiveness. Private organizations are established, developed, and prosper as they achieve internal efficiency and produce goods or services that have some positive social utility. Both of these dimensions of organizations are features of organizational effectiveness. To argue for the dominance of one or the other point of view is to prolong the period in which the differing concepts will remain a dilemma. To recognize that the two points of view can be brought together in ways that guide organizational decision making is to conclude that the problem may be resolved. The fundamental dilemma cannot just be talked out of existence. The starting point for solving the problem is to rationally choose the point of view that will be applicable in a given operating situation; hence, the appropriate measure of organizational effectiveness may be applied to the chosen solution.

Organization Theory and Organizational Effectiveness: An Exploratory Analysis

WILLIAM M. EVAN
University of Pennsylvania

Notwithstanding the burgeoning literature in organization theory, it still suffers from a dearth of propositions with predictive and explanatory power. One of the underlying causes of this state of affairs is the striking neglect—almost systematic—of the problem of conceptualizing and measuring organizational performance or organizational effectiveness. This is indeed ironic, since a formal organization is by definition deliberately created to achieve one or more specified objectives. To compound this irony, one of the basic models in the field—Weber's (1947) rational-legal bureaucracy—postulates that it is the most "efficient" form of organization.

> Experience tends universally to show that *the purely* bureaucratic type of *administrative* organization—that is, the monocratic variety of bureaucracy—is, from a *purely technical point of view*, capable of attaining the *highest degree of efficiency* and is in this sense formally the most rational known means of carrying out imperative control over human beings. It is superior to any other form in precision, in stability, in the stringency of its discipline, and in its reliability. It thus makes possible a particularly high *degree of calculability* of results for the heads of the organization and for those acting in relation to it. It is finally superior both in intensive efficiency and in the scope of its operations, and is formally capable of application to all kinds of administrative tasks (Weber, 1947: 337).

And yet, virtually no effort has thus far been expended to test this proposition.

Nor has Barnard's (1938) distinction between organizational effectiveness and organizational efficiency been the basis for any new conceptual developments. In his concern with formulating a general theory of formal organizations, Barnard conceived of an organization as a "cooperative

For invaluable comments on an earlier version of this paper, I wish to express my gratitude to Jay R. Galbraith, Giorgio Inzerilli, Klaus Krippendorf, Bernard C. Reimann, Vladimir Sachs, Andrew H. Van de Ven, Eugene P. Wenninger, and Oliver E. Williamson.

system." His definition of organizational effectiveness is couched in terms
of the process of cooperation.

> What we mean by "effectiveness" of cooperation is the accomplishment
> of the recognized objectives of cooperative action. The degree of accom-
> plishment indicates the degree of effectiveness (Barnard, 1938:55).

Departing from common usage in industry, engineering, and economics,
Barnard defined organizational efficiency as follows:

> The efficiency of a cooperative system is the resultant of the efficiencies
> of the individuals furnishing the constituent efforts, that is, as viewed
> by them. If the individual finds his motives being satisified by what he
> does, he continues his cooperative effort; otherwise he does not . . . . The
> life of an organization depends upon its ability to secure and maintain
> the personal contributions of energy . . . necessary to effect its purposes
> (1938: 56–57, 92).

In the decades since the classic works of Weber and Barnard appeared,
there has been virtually no progress in refining the concept of organizational
effectiveness. With the exception of Price's (1972: 101–06, 1968) inventory
of propositions and Ghorpade's (1971) compilation of readings, the problem
of organizational effectiveness has not been the subject of systematic
analysis. Instead, it has been used as an omnibus concept with a multiplicity
of empirical referents, such as productivity, profitability, morale, etc.

The purpose of this paper is to analyze the concept of organizational
effectiveness in general terms applicable to all types of formal organizations.
Underlying this analysis are two propositions: (a) that current theoretical
frameworks in the field of organization theory have had the unintended
effect of diverting the attention of researchers from studying organizational
effectiveness; and (b) that sustained attention to this problem will redirect,
as well as stimulate, the further development of organization theory.

AN ASSESSMENT OF SELECTED RESEARCH

Short of undertaking an inventory of the extensive research literature
on organization theory, I shall select several outstanding and instructive
studies and consider them from the vantage point of the problem of organizational effectiveness. For the past decade, one of the most impressive programs
of research on organizations, from a structural perspective, has been that
of the Aston group (Hinings and Lee, 1971; Inkson, Pugh, and Hickson,
1970; Pheysey, Payne, and Pugh, 1971; Pugh, Hickson, *et al.*, 1969, 1968;
Pugh, Hickson, *et al.*, 1963). Starting with a structural concept of organizations, which is a variant of Weber's model, they have studied the interrelationships of structural dimensions in a sample of 52 organizations in Britain.
Among the structural variables studied are functional specialization, role
specialization, standardization, formalization, centralization, and configuration. Conspicuously omitted from the original inquiry is any concern with
differential organizational performance. Only recently have members of
the Aston group considered such facets of organizational performance
as reputation, productivity, profitability, adaptability, and morale (Pugh,

Hickson, *et al.*, 1969; Pugh and Pheysey, 1973). In their ongoing research, several members of the Aston group are seeking to come to grips with this obvious oversight (Child, 1972; Pugh and Pheysey, 1973).

Another outstanding structural study is that by Blau and Schoenherr (1971). In examining 53 employment security agencies, they analyze the interrelationships of various organizational variables, such as size, complexity, decentralization, and administrative overhead. They also include four measures of "service" or "agency output," though they admit that their:

> concern is with the structure of employment security agencies, not with
> how well they perform, but it is nevertheless of great interest to determine
> how various aspects of the structure affect operations and the ser-
> vices supplied to clients (Blau and Schoenherr, 1971:19).

As a consequence of their orientation, Blau and Schoenherr do not, in the course of their various regression analyses, emerge with any overall propositions as to the factors accounting for the differential effectiveness of the 53 employment security agencies. In fact, in formulating a theory of the formal structure of organizations which summarizes their empirical findings, the variable of "service," "agency output," or "organizational effectiveness" does not even appear in any of their propositions (Blau and Schoenherr, 1971: 297–339).

A quite different type of structural approach to organizations is based on the microeconomic theory of the firm and Chandler's (1962) comparative study of corporations, rather than on sociological theory. It is explicitly focused on explaining differences in organizational performance. Williamson (1970) in his analysis of corporations distinguishes between two types of organizational structure: the multidivisional of M-form and the unitary, functional structure of U-form. He argues in favor of the hypothesis that corporations with an M-form structure—primarily organizations that are large and complex—are economically more effective than those with a U-form structure.

A recent study by Negandhi and Reimann (1973) of 30 manufacturing firms in India inquired into the relationship between decentralization and organizational effectiveness. They found a positive relationship between decentralization and organizational effectiveness, based on behavioral as well as economic criteria. If we can assume that there is a strong relationship between "decentralization" and "divisionalization" of organization structure, this finding may be interpreted as supporting Williamson's hypothesis.

The "contingency theory" of Lawrence and Lorsch (1967) is explicitly concerned with differential organizational effectiveness. In their comparative study of a small number of firms in the plastics, foods, and containers industries, they found a relationship between organizational performance, organizational structure, and type of environment: Organizational effectiveness is a function of the "goodness of fit" between organizational structure and the type of environment. Negandhi and Reimann (1972) tested Lawrence and Lorsch's proposition in India by studying the "impact of decentralization on organizational effectiveness of the firm under differing market conditions" (p. 141). They concluded that:

the contingency theory appeared to be essentially valid in the environmental context of a developing country . . . we can not say that organization effectiveness requires decentralization under dynamic or competitive
market conditions and centralization under stable, non-competitive
conditions. Rather we would suggest that dynamic competitive market
conditions make decentralization more important to organizational
effectiveness than do stable non-competitive conditions (Negandhi
and Reimann, 1972:144).

Hirsch (1975), in a recent comparative study of the phonographic
records and pharmaceutical industries, accounts for the superior profitability
of the former in terms of market structure, as well as associated legal and
political institutional differences.

In contrast with research undertaken in a structural, microeconomic, or
contingency framework are numerous studies of a psychological and social-
psychological nature. Since the focus of inquiry is on individual, interpersonal,
or group variables, it is not surprising that studies such as those by Haire,
Ghiselli, and Porter (1966), Lawler and Porter (1967), and Vroom (1964)
are not concerned with *organizational* effectiveness, though they are
concerned with the differential effectiveness of *individual* managers.

In short, only a relatively modest number of organizational studies
have focused on performance or effectiveness as a principal dependent
variable. Some researchers omit this variable inadvertently and others
advertently (Stinchcombe, 1974: 3–4). It is a reflection on the state of the
art of this field that it has thus far failed to grapple with such a fundamental
variable as organizational effectiveness.

A SYSTEMS THEORY PERSPECTIVE

That theory and measurement are interrelated in science is a proposition
so often reiterated that it is virtually an aphorism. Blalock (1968) and Lazarsfeld (1959), to mention only two social scientists, have dealt with this
proposition on different occasions. In a sense, the foregoing discussion
provides some supporting evidence for the validity of this proposition.
The structural studies by Pugh, Hickson, *et al.* (1969, 1968), Pugh, Hickson,
et al. (1963), and Blau and Schoenherr (1971), and the psychological
and social-psychological studies by Haire, Ghiselli, and Porter (1966),
Lawler and Porter (1967), and Vroom (1964), all have in common an
intraorganizational orientation which tends to ignore questions of organizational effectiveness. By contrast, Hirsch (1975), Lawrence and Lorsch
(1967), and Negandhi and Reimann (1973, 1972) are all concerned with
interrelationships between organizational structure and environment, which
prompts them to measure organizational effectiveness. In other words,
as the focus of theoretical attention shifts from *internal* to *external* organizational variables, there is a greater likelihood that the researcher will include
organizational effectiveness as a major variable. In turn, we anticipate that
greater attention to organizational effectiveness will stimulate more theoretical concern with interorganizational relations.

A further impetus for attending to the variable of organizational
effectiveness is the ongoing effort to develop a systems theory of organiza-

tions (Evan, 1972, 1966; Katz and Kahn, 1966; Miller, 1972). From a systems theory perspective, an organization is a social system which, in its interaction with its environment, activates at least four systemic processes:

1. *inputs* (I) of various types of resources;

2. *transformations* (T) of resources with the aid of social and/or technical mechanisms;

3. *outputs* (O) which are transmitted to other systems; and

4. *feedback effects* (F), whether negative or positive.

To appraise the effectiveness of an organization with the aid of systems theory—one variant of which is the "organization-set model" (Evan, 1972, 1966)—one must measure its performance with respect to all four systemic processes as well as their interrelationships.

Organizational inputs consist of various types and quantities of resources, such as capital, people, information, energy, etc. To be sure, organizations differ greatly in their degree of success in mobilizing resources essential for their functioning. The factors accounting for differential success in obtaining organizational inputs may include such dimensions of the input organization-set as size, diversity, and structural configuration (Evan, 1972); and various dimensions of the culture (Evan, 1975a) and social structure (Evan, 1975b) of the organization's societal environment. In the case of business organizations, the market structure and associated legal and political institutions may significantly affect the flow of inputs to the focal organization (Hirsch, 1975).

The transformation process entails the application of social and physical technology to various organizational inputs. The effectiveness with which the focal organization processes inputs is partly a function of its organizational design which, apart from the task technology, includes the authority structure, the division of labor, and the system of rewards (Evan, 1963). Organizations evidently differ considerably in the extent of their efforts to minimize the costs involved in transforming inputs into outputs.

Organizational outputs, whether in the form of products, services, decisions, etc., are channeled to other organizations or to a population of individual consumers or clients. How effectively the outputs are channeled or marketed is partly a function of the various dimensions of the output organization-set, such as size, diversity, and structural configuration (Evan, 1972). In the case of the business firm, the product market in which the focal organization is operating transcends its output organization-set and may coincide with one or more industries. Clearly, the degree of concentration in the industry affects the success with which the focal organization can market its products.

With the disposition of organizational outputs, there are feedback effects to the organizational system which may be of a positive or a negative character. To the extent that an organizational system exhibits equilibrating properties, i.e., tendencies to counteract or reduce deviations from "initial conditions," negative feedback is operating; on the other hand, a system which tends to amplify or reinforce deviations from "initial conditions" is one in which positive feedback is operating (Maruyama, 1968).

The systems concept of feedback takes on many disciplinary forms. Developed initially by engineers, on the one hand, and by biologists, on the other, there is a strong preoccupation with the system's capacity to achieve an equilibrium condition or maintain homeostasis—static or dynamic—in relation to predetermined initial conditions as set by those designing technology or as developed through the process of evolution. By contrast, when we are dealing with various types of social systems that are subject to planned changes, or are deliberately designed (such as organizations), initial conditions (in the sense of one or more goals) are not static. An organizational system does not strive to maintain an initial state; instead, it may be conceived as seeking to maximize or minimize one or more values, whether they be profit, cost, influence, "adaptive capacity," or "adaptive upgrading" (Parsons, 1971: 11, 27; 1966: 22).

As a goal-setting, goal-seeking, and goal-changing type of social system, an organization is in the process of changing its initial conditions from one time period to the next. Therefore, it is not only concerned with *decreasing* deviations from a predetermined goal, namely, negative feedback effects, but also with amplifying deviations in a favorable direction, namely, with *positive* feedback effects of a beneficent and self-enhancing nature as distinguished from the self-destructive and vicious circle variety (Rapoport, 1968: 7–8). If one conceives of an organization as engaging periodically in the process of goal formation which, in principle, can yield quantitative standards of performance, then it is concerned with minimizing or decreasing the degree of underattainment of its objectives. In this sense, it may be conceived as being concerned with *negative* feedback effects. However, to the extent that it also strives for overattainment of its predetermined objectives, from one period to the next, we may also attribute to an organizational system a preoccupation with *positive* feedback effects.

To be sure, in the case of any ongoing organization which is divided into various subunits and pursues multiple objectives simultaneously—each of which may vary in time horizon as well as in degree to which it entails formulating measurable standards of performance—*mixed feedback loops* are likely to occur. Some of these feedback loops are likely to be beneficial and some detrimental to the organization's well-being. A related source of variation in the types of feedback loops occuring in organizations is the degree to which they are *visible*. Since organizations differ considerably both in the number of goals and in the extent to which they *quantify* their goals, as well as in the frequency with which they monitor their performance, they are also likely to differ in the time delay of their responses to observed feedback loops. Thus, in business organizations and political parties, feedback effects are, on the whole, more measurable, more visible, and more quickly responded to than they are in nonprofit organizations, such as government agencies, schools, colleges and universities, hospitals, courts, etc. A multinational corporation, with subsidiaries located in dozens of countries around the world, is concerned with collecting timely production and sales figures, on the basis of which it may make new decisions pertaining to staffing, production, marketing, investment, etc. Likewise, political parties generally assess their performance at the polls and—except for relatively small parties with social-movement orientations—make various adjustments in their programs and policies in order to enhance their chances of future electoral success.

Thus, in terms of the present formulation of organizational feedback, planned organizational changes in a desirable direction may be interpreted as involving negative feedback effects or positive feedback effects of a beneficial variety; organizational changes in an undesirable direction may be interpreted as involving positive feedback effects of a self-destructive nature. For example, a declining student enrollment in a college, an increasing wastage rate or absenteeism rate in a manufacturing firm, a declining bed-occupancy rate in a hospital, and an increasing backlog of cases in a court may all be viewed as indicators of positive feedback with negative organizational effects. On the other hand, an increasing volume of sales in a business organization, an increasing patient recovery rate in a hospital, a declining rate of recidivism among inmates discharged from a prison, an increasing student enrollment in a college, and a declining rate of administrative overhead in a government agency are all indicative of positive feedback with positive organizational effects.

From the perspective of a systems theory of organization, the four systemic processes outlined above suggest a new way of conceptualizing as well as operationalizing organizational effectiveness. As a multidimensional concept, organizational effectiveness may be defined as the capacity of an organization to cope with all four systemic processes relative to its goal-seeking behavior—however explicit or implicit this may be. Operationalizing these four processes in terms of systemic interrelations yields at least nine organizational effectiveness (OE) ratios:

$$1. \ \frac{O}{I} \qquad\qquad 4. \ \frac{\Delta I}{I} \qquad\qquad 7. \ \frac{\Delta T}{I}$$

$$2. \ \frac{T}{I} \qquad\qquad 5. \ \frac{\Delta T}{T} \qquad\qquad 8. \ \frac{\Delta T}{O}$$

$$3. \ \frac{T}{O} \qquad\qquad 6. \ \frac{\Delta O}{O} \qquad\qquad 9. \ \frac{\Delta O}{I}$$

All these OE ratios are, in principle, applicable to any type of organization. Ratios O/I, T/I, and T/O require only a single time slice in the systemic cycle of an organization; on the other hand, the feedback ratios $\Delta I/I$, $\Delta T/T$, $\Delta O/O$, $\Delta T/I$, $\Delta T/O$, and $\Delta O/I$ presuppose, by definition, at least two time slices.

It should be noted that not all nine OE ratios need be operationalized in any given study. It turns out that the most revered "black box" type of ratio, namely O/I, is mathematically deducible from T/I and T/O; similarly, $\Delta O/I$ can be deduced from $\Delta T/I$ and $\Delta T/O$.

William M. Evan

Table 1

ILLUSTRATIVE INDICATORS OF SYSTEMIC PROCESS VARIABLES OF ORGANIZATIONAL EFFECTIVENESS FOR DIFFERENT TYPES OF ORGANIZATIONS

Some Systemic Process Variables

Type of Organization	$\frac{O}{I}$	$\frac{T}{I}$	$\frac{T}{O}$	$\frac{\Delta I}{I}$	$\frac{\Delta T}{T}$	$\frac{\Delta O}{O}$	$\frac{\Delta T}{I}$	$\frac{\Delta T}{O}$	$\frac{\Delta O}{I}$
Business Organizations	Return on investment	Inventory turnover; Kilowatts of energy per direct employee	R and D: / Volume of sales	Change in working capital	Change in administrative personnel to total personnel (A/P); Change in labor unit cost; Change in automation	Change in volume of sales; Change in quality of products	Change in inventory turnover; Change in kilowatts of energy per direct employee	Change in R and D: / Volume or sales	Change in return on investment
Administrative Agencies (*e.g.*, FTC)	Total number of cases processed and decided / Annual budget	Cost of information system / Annual budget	Cost of information system / Total number of cases processed and decided	Change in workload; Change in annual budget	Change in A/P	Change in number of cases processed and decided	Change in cost of information system / Annual budget	Change in cost of information system / Total number of cases processed and decided	Change in rate of compliance with administrative regulations
Hospitals	Total number of patients treated / Annual budget	Capital investment in medical technology / Annual budget	Capital investment in medical technology / Total number of patients treated	Change in number of patients treated	Change in A/P	Change in patient recovery rate by type of cases	Change in capital investment in medical technology / Annual budget	Change in capital investment in medical technology / Total number of patients treated	Change in incidence of illness among discharged patients by type of case

Table 1 (*continued*)

Type of Organization	O/I	T/I	T/O	ΔI/I	ΔT/T	ΔO/O	ΔT/I	ΔT/O	ΔO/I
Courts	Total number of of cases disposed and adjudicated / Annual budget	Cost of information system / Annual budget	Cost of information system / Total number of cases disposed and adjudicated	Change in backlog of cases	Change in A/P	Change in number of cases decided	Change in cost of information system / Annual budget	Change in cost of information system / Total number of cases disposed and adjudicated	Change in number of cases decided / Number of cases on calendar, by type of case
Prisons	Number of inmates / Annual budget	Cost of information system / Annual budget	Cost of information system / Number of inmates	Change in number of new inmates	Change in A/P	Change in number of discharged inmates	Change in cost of information system / Annual budget	Change in cost of information system / Number of inmates	Change in rate of recidivism among inmates
Colleges and Universities	Number of students graduated / Annual budget	Cost of information system / Annual budget	Cost of information system / Number of students graduated	Change in student enrollment	Change in A/P	Change in number of students graduated; Change in number of publications of faculty	Change in cost of information system / Annual budget	Change in cost of information system / Number of students graduated	Change in rate of admission of students whose parents are alumni; Change in rate of alumni contributions

To explore the generality of our OE measures and the feasibility of operationalizing each of the four systemic processes for different types of organizations, Table 1 presents a set of *illustrative* indicators for six different types of organizations: business organizations, administrative agencies, hospitals, courts, prisons, and colleges and universities. Which indicator or set of indicators is selected to measure a particular OE ratio depends, of course, on the type of organization and on the purposes and resources of the investigator.

It is noteworthy that it is possible to develop OE measures for different organizations, as well as for suborganizations, without *directly* and explicitly identifying their goal or goals but *indirectly* by measuring dimensions of inputs, transformations, and outputs of an organization. In effect, Gross's (1965) "performance-structure" model setting forth seven organizational objectives suggests, for our purpose, the value of positing three *universal* organizational goals: input goals, transformation goals, and output goals. All organizations, though differing in degree of technical and administrative rationality, seek to minimize or maximize values associated with each of these three goals.

Unlike our systems-theoretic view of organizational effectiveness, the most common approach is in terms of goal achievement or the degree to which an organization attains its goals (Price, 1972: 101). This poses a problem of identifying or postulating the goals, manifest and latent, of an organization. Price, following Simon (1964: 21), resolves this problem by proposing to measure "the intentions and activities of the major decision-makers" (Price, 1972: 102). Others, however, may wish to measure the intentions and activities of other categories of organizational members, particularly rank-and-file members (or even in some instances, clients), whose conception of organizational goals and whose utility functions are likely to differ from those of "major decision-makers."

Yuchtman and Seashore (1967) seek to avoid the goal approach to organizational effectiveness and argue in favor of a "resource" approach. They define "the effectiveness of an organization in terms of its bargaining position, as reflected in the ability of the organization, in either absolute or relative terms, to exploit its environment in the acquisition of scarce and valued resources" (Yuchtman and Seashore, 1967: 898). While there is much merit in emphasizing the crucial importance of resources—or in our terms, of input processes and input goals—it ignores the other three systemic processes. On the other hand, the economist's bias of measuring outputs in relation to inputs overlooks the other systemic processes which eventually affect the organization's overall effectiveness. Clearly, the problems encountered in defining an organization's goals can be avoided by indirectly deriving the goals—by positing the three generic goals of input, transformation and output—with the aid of the foregoing OE ratios.

PROBLEMS OF MEASURING ORGANIZATIONAL EFFECTIVENESS

Theories of organization differ in their implications for the problem of measuring effectiveness. Thus, for example, a psychological or a social-psychological theory of organization, to the extent that it concerns itself with organizational effectiveness at all, tends to measure members' perceptions of the effectiveness of an organization. Georgopoulos and Mann (1962) and Mott (1972) use this type of measurement approach in their study .of hospitals and government agencies, respectively. Another factor which encourages researchers to rely on subjective measures of organizational effectiveness is the relative ease with which they can be constructed in contrast with the manifest difficulty of developing objective and unobtrusive measures (Webb, *et al.*, 1966) of organizational effectiveness. Subjective measures also have the advantage that they can be applied to all types of organizations, be it a business organization, a government agency, a hospital, a court, or a university. On the other hand, there are serious problems of both reliability and validity with such measures. Unless subjective ratings of organizational effectiveness are consistently and significantly associated with unobtrusive measures of an objective nature, there is little reason to accept them as either reliable or valid. Pennings' (1973) study interrelating objective and subjective measures of centralization and formalization dramatically highlights the absence of "convergent validity" of such measures of organizational structure. On the other hand, Lawrence and Lorsch (1967), in their study of organizations in the plastics industry, elicited from each chief executive a subjective evaluation of his organization's performance. They found that the subjective appraisals were highly correlated with their "total performance index," a composite score based on three measures: change in profits over the past five years; change in sales volume over the past five years; and new products introduced in the past five years as a percentage of current sales (Lawrence and Lorsch, 1967: 39–40).

Researchers skeptical of subjective measures.of organizational effectiveness tend to fall back on standard economic measures of business ratios, such as those Dun and Bradstreet (1973a, 1973b, 1972) and others (Robert Morris Associates, 1973; Troy, 1966). Such measures as earnings per share, return on investment, and profit as a percentage of sales emphasize output or relation between input and output; however, they ignore transformation processes and feedback effects. The recent spurt of interest in corporate audits (Bauer and Fenn, 1972), social accounting (Churchill, 1974), and human resource accounting (Flamholtz, 1974; Pyle, 1970) may, in effect, represent a groping effort in the direction of designing new measures of input and transformation effectiveness of the corporation.

In lieu of a set of reliable and valid objective measures of organizational effectiveness, based on a systems theory of organization, the strategy employed by Negandhi and Reimann (1973) is noteworthy: a combination of economic measures of effectiveness, such as growth in sales and net profits during the past five years, with behavioral science measures, such as turnover rates, absenteeism rates, employee morale, satisfaction in work, and utilization of high-level manpower. The principal drawback with this strategy is that it does not constitute a *general* measure of organizational effectiveness, nor is it theoretically grounded and applicable to the study of different types of organizations, particularly nonbusiness and nonprofit organizations. As Price (1972: 102) puts it, "general measures of effectiveness are urgently needed." The nine OE ratios based on the four systems-theoretic processes advanced in this paper and illustrated in Table 1 constitute a first approximation of a solution to the problem.

CONCLUSION

Much trial-and-error is needed in designing unobtrusive and non-reactive measures of organizational effectiveness based on alternative theories of organization. In addition, much exploratory research is needed to discover which organizational variables can predict which types of measures or dimensions of organizational effectiveness. Until such time as these kinds of problems are solved, comparative organizational research (Heydebrand, 1973), whether of a cross-organizational, cross-national, or cross-cultural variety (Evan, 1975c) will be seriously impeded. By undertaking comparative organizational studies, researchers can explore alternative measures of organizational effectiveness applicable to such diverse organizations as corporations, universities, churches, government agencies, and professional associations. Progress in developing *general* measures of organizational effectiveness will, in turn, contribute to the development of a *general* theory of organization applicable to all types of organizations. And general measures of organizational effectiveness, founded on a general theory of organization, will very likely generate a variety of ideas for organizational design and redesign.

REFERENCES

Barnard, C. I.   *The Functions of the Executive*. Cambridge, Mass: Harvard University
    1938   Press.
Bauer, R. A., and D. H. Fenn.   *The Corporate Social Audit*. New York: Russell
    1972   Sage Foundation.
Blalock, H. M., Jr.   "The Measurement Problem: A Gap Between the Language of
    1968   Theory and Research." In H. M. Blalock and A. Blalock (eds.), *Methodology
        in Social Research*: 5–27. New York: McGraw-Hill.
Blau, P. M., and R. A. Schoenherr.   *The Structure of Organizations*. New York:
    1971   Basic Books.
Chandler, A. D., Jr.   *Strategy and Structure*. Cambridge, Mass: MIT Press.
    1962
Child, J.   "Organizational Structure, Environment and Performance—The Role of
    1972   Strategic Choice." *Sociology*, 6:1–22.
Churchill, N. C.   "Toward a Theory for Social Accounting." *Sloan Management
    1974   Review*, 15:1–17.
Dun and Bradstreet.   "The Ratios of Manufacturing." *Dun's Review*, 100:122–123.
    1973a
————.   "The Ratios of Retailing." *Dun's Review*, 101:102–105.
    1973b
————.   "The Ratios of The Wholesalers." *Dun's Review*, 100:100–101.
    1972
Evan, W. M.   "Culture and Organizational Systems." *Organization and Administrative
    1975a   Sciences*, 5:1–16.
————.   "Social Structure and Organizational Systems." Mimeographed paper,
        Philadelphia Department of Sociology, The Wharton School, University of
        Pennsylvania.

———— (ed.) "Organizational Research: Cross-National and Cross-Cultural."
1975c   *International Studies of Management and Organization*, 5:3–113.

————. "An Organization-Set Model of Interorganizational Relations." In
1972   M. F. Tuite, M. Radnor, and R. K. Chisholm (eds.), *Interorganizational Decision Making*: 181–200. Chicago: Aldine Publishing Co.

———— "The Organization-Set: Toward a Theory of Inter-Organizational
1966   Relations." In J. D. Thompson (ed.), *Approaches to Organizational Design*: 75–190. Pittsburgh: University of Pittsburgh Press.

———— "Indices of the Hierarchical Structure of Industrial Organizations."
1963   *Management Science*, 9:468–77.

Flamholtz, E.   *Human Resource Accounting*. Encino, Calif.: Dickenson Publishing Co.
1974

Georgopoulos, B. S., and F. C. Mann.   *The Community General Hospital*. New York:
1962   Macmillan.

Ghorpade, J. (ed.)   *Assessment of Organizational Effectiveness*. Pacific Palisades,
1971   Calif.: Goodyear Publishing Co.

Gross, B. M.   "What Are Your Organization's Objectives?" *Human Relations*,
1965   18:195–215.

Haire, M., E. E. Ghiselli, and L. W. Porter.   *Management and Thinking*: An Inter-
1966   *national Study*. New York: John Wiley, Inc.

Heydebrand, W. V. (ed.)   *Comparative Organizations*. Englewood Cliffs, N. J.:
1973   Prentice-Hall.

Hickson, D. J., D. S. Pugh, and D. C. Pheysey.   "Operations Technology and
1969   Organization Structure: An Empirical Reappraisal." *Administrative Science Quarterly*, 14:378–397.

Hinings, C. R., and G. L. Lee.   "Dimensions of Organization Structure and Their
1971   Context: A Replication." *Sociology*, 5:83–93.

Hirsch, P. M.   "Organizational Effectiveness and the Institutional Environment."
1975   *Administrative Science Quarterly*, 20:327–344.

Inkson, J. H. K., D. S. Pugh, and D. J. Hickson.   "Organization Context and Structure:
1970   An Abbreviated Replication." *Administrative Science Quarterly*,15:318–329.

Katz, D., and R. L. Kahn.   *The Social Psychology of Organizations*. New York:
1966   John Wiley, Inc.

Lawler, E., III, and L. W. Porter.   "Antecedent Attitudes of Effective Management
1967   Performance." *Organization Behavior and Human Performance*, 2:122–142.

Lawrence, P. R., and J. W. Lorsch.   *Organization and Environment*. Cambridge,
1967   Mass.: Division of Research, Graduate School of Business Administration, Harvard University.

Lazarsfeld, P. F.   "Problems in Methodology." In R. K. Merton, L. Broom, and
1959   L. S. Cottrell, Jr. (eds.), *Sociology Today*: 39–78. New York: Basic Books.

Maruyama, M.   "The Second Cybernetics: Deviation-Amplifying Mutual Causal
1968   Processes." In W. Buckley (ed.), *Modern Systems Research for the Behavioral Scientist*: 304–313. Chicago: Aldine Publishing Co.

Miller, J. G.   "Living System: The Organization." *Behavioral Science*, 17:1–182.
1972

Mott, P. E.   *The Characteristics of Effective Organizations*. New York. Harper and
1972   Row.

Negandhi, A. R., and B. C. Reimann.   "Task Environment, Decentralization and
1973   Organizational Effectiveness." *Human Relations*, 26:203–14.

————. "A Contingency Theory of Organization Re-Examined in the Context
1972   of a Developing Country." *Academy of Management Journal*, 15:137–146.

Parsons, T.   *The System of Modern Societies*. Englewood Cliffs, N. J.: Prentice-
1971   Hall.

————. *Societies*: Evolutionary and Comparative Perspectives. Englewood
1966   Cliffs, N. J.: Prentice-Hall.

Pennings, J.   "Measure of Organizational Structure: A Methodological Note."
1973   *American Journal of Sociology*, 79:682–704.

Pheysey, D. C., R. L. Payne, and D. S. Pugh. "Influence of Structure at Organi-
1971   zational and Group Levels." *Administrative Science Quarterly*, 16:61–73.
Price, J. L.   *Handbook of Organizational Measurement*. Lexington, Mass.: D. C.
1972   Heath.
————.   *Organizational Effectiveness: An Inventory of Propositions*. Homewood,
1968   Ill.: Richard D. Irwin.
Pugh, D. S., D. J. Hickson, C. R. Hinings, K. M. MacDonald, C. Turner, and T. Lupton.
1963   "A Conceptual Scheme for Organizational Analysis." *Administrative
         Science Quarterly*, 8:289–315.
Pugh, D. S., D. J. Hickson, C. R. Hinings, and C. Turner.   "The Context of Organi-
1969   zation Structures." *Administrative Science Quarterly*, 14:91–114.
————.   "Dimensions of Organization Structure." *Administrative Science
1968   Quarterly*, 13:65–105.
Pugh, D. S., and D. Pheysey.   "A Comparative Administration Model." In A. R.
1973   Negandhi (ed.), *Modern Organization Theory*. Kent, Ohio: Kent State
         University Press.
Pyle, W. C.   "Monitoring Human Resources—'On Line.' " *Michigan Business
1970   Review*, 22:19–32.
Rapoport, A.   "A Philosophical View." In J. H. Milsum (ed.), *Positive Feedback:
1968   A General Systems Approach to Positive/Negative Feedback and Mutual
         Causality*. New York: Pergamon Press.
Robert Morris Associates.   *Annual Statement Studies*, 1973 ed. Philadelphia:
1973   Robert Morris Associates.
Simon, H. A.   "On the Concept of Organizational Goal." *Administrative Science
1964   Quarterly*, 9:1–22.
Stinchcombe, A. L.   *Creating Efficient Industrial Administrations*. New York:
1974   Academic Press.
Troy, L.   *Manual of Performances Ratios*. Englewood Cliffs, N. J.: Prentice-Hall
1966
Vroom, V.   *Work and Motivation*. New York: John Wiley, Inc.
1964
Webb, E. J., D. T. Campbell, R. D. Schwartz, and L. Sechrest. *Unobtrusive Measures*.
1966   Chicago: Rand McNally.
Weber, M.   *The Theory of Social and Economic Organizations*. Trans. by A. M.
1947   Henderson and T. Parsons. Glencoe, Ill.: The Free Press.
Williamson, O. E.   *Corporate Control and Business Behavior*. Englewood Cliffs.
1970   N. J.: Prentice-Hall.
Yuchtman, E., and S. E. Seashore.   "A Systems Resource Approach to Organi-
1967   zational Effectiveness." *American Sociological Review*, 32:891–903.

Contributions Research Can Make in Understanding Organizational Effectiveness

JOHN P. CAMPBELL
University of Minnesota

The following remarks are acknowledged to be largely from the perspective of a differential, measurement-oriented psychologist. There is much to be gained from this approach, parochial though it may be, since it is based on several attempts to determine the appropriate meaning for and measurement of organizational effectiveness. My colleagues and I have spent considerable time during the past few years studying the literature on this phenomenon and attempting to design research to study it (Borman and Dunnette, 1974; Campbell, *et al.*, 1974). In so doing, we were startled to discover how much of the ontogeny of the development of criteria of organizational effectiveness recapitulates the phylogeny of the individual performance "criterion problem." Thus, anyone attempting to develop or operationalize measures of organizational effectiveness is cautioned to first carefully examine the major milestones in the history of the search for criteria of individual performance.

The first milestone concerns the question, "Criterion for what decision?" The subsequent questions of what criterion variables to use and how to measure them cannot be answered without considering three main points: the decisions for which they are to be used; the identity of the decision makers; and the conditions under which the decisons must be made. Without having a precise answer to these questions, it is difficult to proceed. The history of performance measurement and personnel selection says that the situation becomes clearer and easier to interpret when it is cast into a decision-making context. Thus, a statement about the validity of a personnel selection tool means relatively little until the decisions for which it is to be used are defined precisely and the economic and political conditions in which it must operate are taken into account.

There are at least three kinds of decisions for which organizational criterion data could be used:

1. To decide whether some aspect of a system is in a "good" state or a "bad" state. Turnover rates would be an example of an indicator pointed toward such a decision. Profitability, or return on investment, would be another. Frequency of racial incidents would be yet another.
2. To "diagnose" or to decide why the system is in the state it is in. For example, what causes the high turnover rates, why is profitability high or low, why are there so many racial incidents?
3. The planning decisions concerning what actions should be taken to change the state of the system. That is, what should be done to lower turnover or lower the frequency of racial incidents?

In theory, at least, criterion measures could be derived that would contribute directly to all three kinds of decisions. For the most part, people in this field have been content to concentrate on the first kind of decision, leaving the rest to speculation and informal follow-up studies.

A second major consideration deals with who will use the criterion data to make the decisions. The identity of the decision makers will influence the strategy used to measure effectiveness, and, the traditional dichotomy between the technical quality of a criterion and its acceptance by the people who must use it operates here. If people cannot or will not use a particular kind of criterion data, it is useless to collect it.

The third consideration regards conditions under which a particular decision maker will use criterion data to make a particular decision. At the moment, the most salient example from individual performance measurement deals with equal employment opportunity. In this area, there are governmental guidelines which specify a number of constraints on the use of criterion data.

A second milestone in the history of the search for performance criteria concerns the difficult, mundane, but largely successful attempt to purge the notion of *the* criterion from industrial/organizational psychology. There is perhaps even less reason for entertaining any notion of *the* criterion with regard to organizational effectiveness than with regard to individual performance. Decisions about an organization rarely require the use of one overall effectiveness index.

ORGANIZATIONAL EFFECTIVENESS AS A CONSTRUCT

To move the area of inquiry forward, we must think of organizational effectiveness as a construct that has no direct operational definition, but which constitutes a model or theory of what organizational effectiveness is. The functions of such a model would be to identify the kinds of variables we should be measuring and to specify how these variables, or components of effectiveness, are interrelated—or should be interrelated.

Strictly speaking, it is not possible for anyone concerned with the effectiveness of organizations to avoid using it as a construct or to avoid operating via some kind of theory. Without a theory of some sort—even if it has never been made public—it is not possible to say that variable X is a measure of organizational effectiveness and variable Y is not, or to plan ways to change an organization. Thus, it is incumbent on all those concerned to make their theories of effectiveness as explicit as possible.

Two General Models of the Effectiveness Construct
The literature contains two general points of view, with variations, as to what constitutes organizational effectiveness. While they have been given various labels, the most popular are the *goal-centered view* and the *natural systems* view (*e.g.*, see Ghorpade, 1971; Price, 1972).

Briefly, the goal-centered view makes a reasonably explicit assumption that the organization is in the hands of a rational set of decision makers who have in mind a set of goals which they wish to pursue. Further, these goals are few enough in number to be manageable and can be defined well enough to be understood. Given that goals can be thus identified, it should be possible to plan the best management strategies for attaining them. Within this orientation, the way to assess organizational effectiveness would be to develop criterion measures to assess how well the goals are being achieved.

The natural systems view appears to make the assumption that if an organization is of any size at all, the demands placed upon it are so dynamic and so complex that it is not possible to define a small number of organizational goals in any way that is meaningful. Rather, the organization adopts the overall goal of maintaining its viability or existence without depleting its resources. Thus, to assess an organization's effectiveness, one should try to find out if an organization is internally consistent within itself, whether its resources are being distributed judiciously over a wide variety of coping mechanisms, whether it is using up its resources faster than it should, and so forth. However, the organization needs some theory or model that specifies the kinds of coping mechanisms it must have. It cannot prepare itself for literally everything. One example of such a natural systems model that incorporates specific a priori notions of which system variables should be assessed is the one developed by Likert (1967, 1961) and the Michigan group (Taylor and Bowers, 1973.)

The principal point here is that if a researcher were asked to develop criterion measures of the effectiveness of an organization, how he or she would begin depends in part on which of these two points of view had been internalized. The goal-oriented analyst would immediately seek out the principal power centres or decision makers and ask them to state their objectives. He might also employ techniques to reveal the actual operative goals of the organization, as well as the publicly stated ones. For better or worse, once the researcher had the goals defined, he would try to develop criterion variables that would measure how well the objectives (of either kind) were being met.

A natural systems oriented researcher would not immediately ask what the organization was trying to accomplish. Rather, he would explore and ask questions, perhaps about the degree of conflict among work groups, the nature of communications, the level of racial tension, the percentage of jobs that were filled by people with the appropriate level of training, the job satisfaction of the organization members, and the like. At the onset, he would not be concerned with the specific tasks the organization was trying to perform; his concern would be with the overall viability and strength of the system. He would have some a priori notions of what the characteristics of a strong system are, and he would center his questioning around those.

If both these analysts take their next logical steps, their efforts will tend to parallel each other—if not actually converge. If the goal-oriented analyst attempts to diagnose why an organization scores the way it does on the criteria, he soon will be led back to system-type variables. For example, perhaps an organization does not meet its goals because of racial tension. If the natural systems analyst wonders how various system characteristics affect task performance, he very soon will be trying to decide which tasks are the important ones on which to assess performance. Unfortunately, in real life these second steps often are not taken. The goal-oriented analyst tends not to look into the black box, and the natural systems oriented analyst does not like to worry about actual task performance unless he is pressed.

ALTERNATIVE VIEWS OF THE ORGANIZATIONAL EFFECTIVENESS CONSTRUCT

It is useful at this point to identify a number of alternative models of the effectiveness construct, both the natural systems and goal centered types. This will illustrate that a number of alternative theories are possible, relative to the meaning of organizational effectiveness, and that the theory one might adopt has some bearing on the kind of research one might do.

Cost/Benefit Analysis

Although its antecedents are in economics and its application to organizational behavioral science is rather recent, a cost/benefit model has sometimes been applied to the evaluation of effectiveness. It is most often used to measure the *relative* effectiveness of *alternative* courses of action toward some goal and thus is firmly rooted in the goal-oriented model. Inherent in the cost/benefit model is the notion that the components of both the numerator and the denominator can be reduced to a single composite score. A fairly large body of literature has developed around conceptual schemes and measurement methods for assessing both the cost side and the benefit side (Chase, 1965; Dorfman, 1965; Glennon, 1972; Mangum, 1971). Research under this model would be directed at defining both goals and alternative strategies for achieving those goals, and then developing ratio scale measures of the costs and benefits of each strategy.

A positive feature not so often recognized is the model's reminder that perhaps we can learn something about the relative effectiveness of different strategies or organizational subunits by comparing their *marginal* rather than the *average* cost/benefit ratio.

Management by Objectives

Management by Objectives (MBO) represents the ultimate in a goal-oriented model of effectiveness. Thus, rather than evaluating the organization on a single abstracted continuum, such as the cost/benefit ratio, or on several criterion continua that are in some sense abstractions from specific task behavior (*e.g.*, productivity or profit), MBO says that effectiveness is some aggregation of specific, concrete, observable, and *quantifiable* accomplishments and failures. Either an organization accomplishes a specific task that it is supposed to, or it does not.

Some relevant issues revolving around the MBO model are:

What group or individual sets the goals for a particular organization or unit? To what extent is it realistically possible to define quantifiable goals for an organization or organizational unit? How should the relative importance of each goal be judged? To what extent is it possible to know whether an objective has been accomplished? Is the organization willing to commit the necessary time and effort to the MBO procedure?

Assuming some resolution of the above questions can be found, the MBO model yields a definition of effectiveness that is unique to each organization. For a particular time period, each organization must specify in concrete detail the specific things it wishes to accomplish. The relevant measure of effectiveness is then an accounting of which objectives were accomplished and which were not.

The Organization Development Model

For present purposes, the term Organizational Development (OD) will be restricted to a class of behavioral science type intervention techniques which owe their historical antecedents to the work in T-group and sensitivity training at the National Training Laboratories.

It is reasonably apparent that OD adopts a systems view, not a goal model. Very seldom are goal outcomes mentioned by OD writers, researchers, or practitioners. If such things as profit, turnover, and the like are mentioned at all, it is in a fairly unsystematic way and only after much discussion about such factors as increased individual openness, better communications, greater individual self-actualization, etc., and other indicators of what is considered to be a healthy system.

However, Beckhard (1969) believes that most researchers and practitioners in the OD camp possess a strong consensus of what a healthy organization is, even though it may differ somewhat from one individual to another. He portrays this consensus by presenting a synthesized list of ten characteristics that define an effective or healthy organization (Beckhard, 1969: 10–11). This is shown in Table 1.

In other words, the OD model assumes that if an organization can achieve the state characterized by a list such as Beckhard's, it will be effective as an organization and will be optimally equipped to carry out its mission(s).

The Likert ISR Model

In somewhat of a class by itself is a systems model of organizational effectiveness that can be attributed to Likert (1967, 1961) and his colleagues at the University of Michigan (Taylor and Bowers, 1972). There is obviously a great deal of similarity between the Michigan characterization of an effective

Table 1

SYNTHESIZED LIST OF END STATES SPECIFIED BY OD THAT DEFINE A HEALTHY SYSTEM[1]

1. "The total organization, the significant subparts, and individuals manage their work against *goals* and *plans* for achievement of these goals.
2. "Form follows function (the problem, or task, or project determines how the human resources are organized).
3. "Decisions are made by and near the sources of information regardless of where these sources are located on the organizational chart.
4. "The reward system is such that managers and supervisors are rewarded (and punished) comparably for:
   —short-term profit or production performance,
   —growth and development of their subordinates,
   —creating a viable working group.
5. "Communication laterally and vertically is *relatively* undistorted. People are generally open and confronting. They share all the relevant facts including feelings.
6. "There is a minimum amount of inappropriate win/lose activities between individuals and groups. Constant effort exists at all levels to treat conflict and conflict situations as *problems* subject to problem solving methods.
7. "There is high 'conflict' (clash of ideas) about tasks and projects, and relatively little energy spent in clashing over interpersonal difficulties because they have been generally worked through."
8. "The organization and its parts see themselves as interacting with each other *and* with a *larger* environment. The organization is an 'open system.'
9. "There is a shared value, and management strategy to support it, of trying to help each person (or unit) in the organization maintain his (or its) integrity and uniqueness in an interdependent environment.
10. "The organization and its members operate in an 'action-research' way. General practice is to build in *feedback mechanisms* so that individuals and groups can learn from their own experience."

[1]This table originally appeared in R. Beckhard, *Organizational Development: Strategies and Models.* Reading, Mass.: Addison-Wesley (1969). Permission of the publishers is gratefully acknowledged.

organization, such as presented in the *Survey of Organizations* (Taylor and Bowers, 1972), and the OD characterization as portrayed by Beckhard's list. Many of the same summary statements apply; however, certain differences should also be noted. First, the Michigan group is much more research oriented and has devoted more effort to investigating the link between the variables defining the state of the system and criteria, such as profitability and turnover. Second, the Michigan list is not as heavily oriented toward interpersonal and self-actualization type variables.

The Industrial/Organizational Psychology Criterion Model

The criterion problem has a large and honorable niche in the literature of industrial and organizational psychology (Blum and Naylor, 1968: Chapter 6; Campbell, *et al.,* 1970; Dunnette, 1966; Schmidt and Kaplan, 1971; Wallace, 1965). At the base of the criterion issue, defined as this literature defines it, is the axiom that a criterion is a measure of the degree to which an individual contributes to the goals of the organization. Thus, if we were to transport this formulation of effectiveness from the domain of individual effectiveness to that of organizational effectiveness, it would be securely within the goal-centered view.

The criterion problem model seems to incorporate the following features:

1. Overall effectiveness is not one thing - but is made up of component criteria. *The* criterion was laid to rest some time ago. However, the model does say that each component criterion is defined *in the same way* for each individual being measured.

2. The specification of the individual component criteria flows from a detailed and systematic job or task description.

3. The empirical relationships among the component criteria should be determined; that is, a fairly large number of individuals should be assessed on each criterion component and multivariate analysis technique (*e.g.*, factor or cluster analysis) should be used to examine the pattern of relationships among the components.

4. The way in which individual criterion component scores are combined or otherwise used to make *specific* decisions (*e.g.*, promotions) is determined by expert judgment.

5. Criterion measures should be a reflection of what the individual actually does; that is, they should represent an assessment of accomplishments that are directly under the individual's control. Variability in criterion scores across individuals or across time should be the result of what the individual does, not the result of extraneous influences.

If we transport this model to a consideration of organizational effectiveness, it says several things. First, we need an organizational job analysis to tell us what the major tasks of the organization are. After some potential criterion measures are developed, we must try them out on a large number of organizations to examine the psychometric properties of the components. Finally, we need to assure ourselves that the component measures are indeed assessing variables over which the organization has some control.

In sum, the criterion problem model assumes that qualified experts can use one or more of several techniques to infer criterion measures from a description of tasks to be performed. It then demands a multivariate analysis of data collected on a large number of observations.

Summary of Alternative Models of Effectiveness Construct

It probably is not useful to make comparative statements about which of these various models is better or worse for a specific purpose. They simply provide a means for looking at different parts of the effectiveness construct. Rather than choose among them, a more viable objective should be to put them together and use the complimentary insights provided by each. Each suggests a somewhat different characterization of organizational effectiveness and thus a somewhat different set of research questions and research strategies.

EFFECTIVENESS CRITERIA PRODUCED BY PAST RESEARCH

Although not overwhelming in size or diversity, there is a certain amount of *empirical* literature dealing with criterion measures of organizational effectiveness. We have examined this literature and attempted to list the indices that have been used. They appear in Table 2.

Table 2

SYTHESIZED LIST OF POSSIBLE INDICATORS OF ORGANIZATIONAL EFFECTIVENESS

1. *Overall Effectiveness:* which is a general evaluation that takes in as many single criteria as possible and results in a single judgment about the effectiveness of the organization. It has been measured primarily by two methods: archival performance records, either singly or in some combined form, and overall ratings or judgements obtained from persons thought to be knowledgeable about the organization.
2. *Productivity:* which is usually defined as the quantity or volume of the major product or service that the organization provides and can be measured at three levels: individual, group, and total organization. Both archival records and ratings have been used, and in at least one case, independent observation of ongoing work was used to obtain a measure of production.
3. *Efficiency:* usually thought of in terms of a ratio that reflects a comparison of some aspect of unit performance to the costs incurred for that performance. There have been relatively few attempts to operationalize this concept, and all but one of these is a measure taken directly from organization records or a factor derived from such records.
4. *Profit:* the amount of revenue from sales left after all costs and obligations are met. Percent return on investment or percent return on total sales are sometimes used as alternative definitions.
5. *Quality:* the quality of the primary service or product provided by the organization may take many operational forms, which are largely determined by the kind of product or service provided by the organization. They are too numerous to mention here.
6. *Accidents:* or the frequency of on-the-job accidents resulting in lost time. We found only two examples of accident rates being used as a measure of organizational effectiveness.
7. *Growth:* or an increase in such variables as total manpower, plant capacity, assets, sales, profits, market share, and number of innovations. It implies a comparison of an organization's present state with its own past state. Only four studies attempted to use measures of growth.
8. *Absenteeism:* or the relative frequency with which people are absent from work. The usual definition stipulates unexcused absences but even within this constraint there are a number of alternative definitions.
9. *Turnover:* this is usually some measure of the frequency and amount of voluntary terminations and refers to a change in actual personnel within the organization, however that change occurs. All but one of the turnover measures we reviewed are archival, but even with this constraint there are a surprising number of variations and a few studies used directly comparable measures.
10. *Satisfaction:* Satisfaction has been defined many ways (e.g., see Wanous & Lawler, 1972) but perhaps the modal view references satisfaction to the achievement or possession of certain outcomes provided by the organization and defines it as an individual's perception of the degree to which he or she has received an equitable amount of the outcome. That is, satisfaction is the degree to which individuals perceive they are equitably rewarded by various aspects of their job situation and the organization to which they belong.

11. *Motivation:* In our present context this is the strength of the predisposition of an individual to engage in goal-directed action or activity on-the-job. It is not a feeling of relative contentment with various job outcomes as is satisfaction, but more akin to a feeling of readiness or willingness to work at accomplishing the job's goals. As an organizational index, it must be "summed" across people.

12. *Morale:* This is an often used variable that is difficult to define or even to understand how organizational theorists and researchers are using it. The modal definition seems to view morale as a predisposition in organization members to put forth extra effort in achieving organizational goals and objectives. It includes feelings of commitment and is a group phenomena involving extra effort, goal communality, and feelings of belonging. Groups have some degree of morale while individuals have some degree of motivation (and satisfaction). By implication, morale is inferred from group phenomena.

13. *Control:* refers to the degree of, and distribution of management control that exists within an organization for influencing and directing the behavior of organization members.

14. *Conflict/Cohesion:* a bipolar dimension defined at the cohesion end by an organization in which the members like one another, work well together, communicate fully and openly, and coordinate their work efforts. At the other end lies the organization with verbal and physical clashes, poor coordination, and ineffective communication.

15. *Flexibility/Adaptation* (Adaptation/Innovation): refers to the ability of an organization to change its standard operating procedures in response to environmental changes. Many people have written about this dimension (Benedict, Calder, Callahan, Hornstein, & Miles, 1967; Burns, 1961; Gomson, 1968; Hall, 1972; Henry, 1968; Humber 1960; Utterback, 1971; Indik, 1970; Bennis 1971; Price, 1968; Korman, 1971), but relatively few have made attempts to measure it.

16. *Planning and Goal Setting:* or the degree to which the organization systematically plans its future steps and engages in explicitly goal setting behavior.

17. *Goal Consensus:* refers to the degree to which all individuals perceive the same goals for the organization, which is distinct from actual commitment to those goals.

18. *Role and Norm Congruence:* the degree to which the members of an organization are in agreement on such things as what kinds of supervisory attitudes are best, performance expectations, morale, role requirements, etc.

19. *Managerial Interpersonal Skills:* or the level of skill and efficiency with which the management deals with superiors, subordinates, and peers and includes the extent to which managers give support, facilitate constructive interaction, and generate enthusiasm for meeting goals and achieving excellent performance. It is meant to include such things as consideration, employee centeredness, etc. We realize that this variable is often used as a "predictor" of other variables. However, within some models of organizational effectiveness it has the character of a systemic variable which is indicative of an organization's health.

20. *Managerial Task Skills:* or the overall level of skills the organization's managers, Commanding Officers, or group leaders possess for performing tasks centered on work to be done, and not the skills employed when interacting with other organizational members.

21. *Information Management and Communication:* refers to the collection, analysis, and distribution of information critical to organizational effectiveness.

22. *Readiness:* the usual definition of this variable is in terms of an overall judgment concerning the probability that the organization could successfully perform some specified task if asked to do so. Work on measuring this variable has been largely confined to military settings.

23. *Utilization of Environment:* The extent to which the organization successfully interacts with its environment and acquires scarce, valued resources necessary to its effective operation. For example, it includes the degree to which it acquires a steady supply of manpower and financial resources.

24. *Evaluations by External Entities:* such evaluations refer to evaluations of the organization or organizational unit by those individuals and organizations in its environment with which it interacts. Loyalty to, confidence in, and support given the organization by such groups as suppliers, customers, stockholders, enforcement agencies, and the general public would fall under this label.

25. *Stability:* as per Stogdill's (1971) definition, stability refers to the maintenance of structure, function, and resources through time, and more particularly through periods of stress (Stogdill, 1971).

26. *Internalization of Organizational Goals:* or the acceptance or internalization of organizational goals within that organization. It includes their belief that the organization's goals are right and proper. This is *not* the extent to which goals are clear or agreed upon by the organization members (goal consensus and goal clarity, respectively). Thus, it refers to the acceptance not the understanding of the organization's goals.

27. *Value of Human Resources:* which is a composite criterion, where the components refer to measures of individuals. It refers to the total value or total worth of the individual members of an organization, in an accounting or balance sheet sense, to the organization. It is another way of combining many of the variables discussed so far but it deals only with the role of human resources, not other kinds of assets, in organizational effectiveness.

28. *Participation and Shared Influence:* or the degree to which individuals in the organization participate in making the decisions which directly affect them.

29. *Training and Development Emphasis:* or the amount of effort the organization devotes to developing its human resources.

30. *Achievement Emphasis:* almost an analog to the individual need for achievement, this refers to the degree to which the organization appears to place a high *value* on achieving major new goals.

One can see that these potential indicators vary on a number of dimensions.

First, there are a multitude of them and only a few attempts have been made to weed out the overlap and get down to the core variables. This may be for good, if not sufficient, reasons. Within a particular model of the organizational effectiveness construct, for example, it is proper to demand such things as internal consistency, completeness, and parsimony for the dependent variables the model outlines. However, different people adhere to different models, and there is no correct way to choose among them. Thus, when putting together a list from different conceptual points of view, the composite list is almost preordained to look messy.

Second, the entries in the list vary considerably in terms of their generality/specificity, and some may be legitimately subsumed under others.

Third, they vary considerably in terms of the methods used to operationalize them. Archival records, direct on-line recording, retrospective ratings by independent observers, and aggregrated self-perceptions have all been used.

A fourth general characteristic of these variables is that they vary on a continuum which might be called "closeness to the final payoff." For example, is job satisfaction the continuum on which the real payoffs are made, or is it a means to an end? In other words, is satisfaction important because it is related to some more distal variable that is the organization's real concern? Which of these are means and which are ends is a value judgment on somebody's part. It is made implicitly or explicitly in organizations every day and cannot be avoided. Also, if the decision is that a particular variable is a means and not an end, is it necessary to demonstrate empirical relationships between that variable and the outcomes of real interest? Or should those relationships be assumed, since the outcomes of real interest are usually so difficult to specify and measure? It is precisely here that the goal model and the natural systems model diverge. Most theorists, researchers, and practitioners who adopt the natural systems point of view appear to accept the basic assumption that the systemic variables contained in their models are significantly related, in a causal fashion, to accomplishing a variety of organizational missions. In contrast, the goal model demands data, and if its adherents do not have such data, they feel an almost overwhelming sense of guilt.

In the best of all possible worlds, it would be nice to have some overall hierarchical map of how the criteria fit together in terms of their generality/specificity and means/ends relationships. Almost by definition, such a map would be impossible to construct, except perhaps within the confines of a particular theory of organizational effectiveness.

OBJECT LESSONS FROM PREVIOUS RESEARCH

Based on these consideration of organizational effectiveness as a construct, and based on previous empirical research, a series of generalizations are set forth about the positive and negative features of previous attempts to measure effectiveness.

First, it probably is counterproductive to follow the multivariate approach in the development of effectiveness measures. While it sounds like a good idea to assemble a large sample of organizations, measure each of them on a set of potential criteria, and then examine the patterning of relationships among the measures, it simply is not physically or economically possible to conduct such a study in ways that will yield useful information. To date, there have been only three or four such attempts, and all of them have fallen short of the mark. Remember, each organization is only one degree of freedom and we need lots of degrees of freedom. Also, archival or objective measures never seem to be defined the same way across organizations, and this sometimes leads to rather strange looking correlations between variables.

Second, searching for so-called objective measures of organizational effectiveness is a thankless task and virtually preordained to fail in the end. The conventional wisdom says objectivity is good, but perhaps a more accurate wisdom says an objective criterion is a subjective criterion once removed. For example, one might think that the number of units produced is an objective measure of an automobile assembly plant's effectiveness. However, a specific number of units means nothing until some metric or standard is applied that informs us which numbers are good and which numbers are bad. Many subjective judgments go into the development of such standards (*e.g.*, where should production be three weeks after the model year starts), and also into the quality control judgment as to whether a unit is fit to sell. Similar kinds of subjective judgments can be found in any so-called objective measure of effectiveness, making it very risky to use available objective measures (where the subjectivity is unknown) as criteria in a research study.

Third, at this stage, it probably is a mistake to concentrate scarce research resources on attempts to develop results-oriented measures, that is, measures of the more terminal outcomes of organizational functioning, such as return on investment, productivity, and the like. These measures often are a function of many things other than what the organization does (*e.g.*, economy), and teasing out those parts which are under the control of the organization itself is a difficult task.

Lastly, a large number of the variables in Table 2 are aggregated perceptions of individuals (*e.g.*, job satisfaction, morale, and climate). Most organizations are so complex that averaging over everybody in the class covers up so many individual differences that it renders the indicator useless.

RESEARCH THAT SHOULD BE DONE

We cannot conduct massive studies on huge samples of organizations over long periods of time; hence, we should recognize our limitations as researchers and devote our resources to investigating problems upon which we can have some impact. Also, there is no algorithm of science that will specify which variables should be labeled as criteria of organizational effectiveness. That begins as a value judgment and ends as a political decision. Rather, it seems fairly obvious that scientists might achieve more by studying the *process* by which people in organizations resolve the question of effectiveness. Thus, our research resources could best be spent on research activities such as those listed below.

Recovery of Operative Goals and Criteria

While there has long been a distinction between formal goals and operative goals, very little research actually has been devoted to studying the specific goals or effectiveness criteria that control decision-making behavior in organizations. We propose that a variety of methods be used in an attempt to recover the operative criterion variables that seem to govern the behavior of various relevant parties. The objectives of such research would be to:

1. Determine whether operative goals have anything at all to do with formal goals;
2. Determine how much communality there is in operative goals across different groups in the organization and across organizations;
3. Determine how much communality there is across time.

In other times and places, this kind of research goes under such labels as "process" research or "policy capturing." It assumes that while people might not be able to state their goals or criteria accurately, operative goals and criteria can be inferred from the way they behave.

There are perhaps three general approaches to this kind of research, although few of them have ever been used in the organizational context.

These can be labeled the direct judgment; indirect judgment; and critical incident methods. All three methods require panels of knowledgeable judges, and the question of who judges is paramount. There is no straight-forward answer—except to say that in any situation there are probably several groups of individuals who might offer differing perspectives or expertise. Systematic comparisons between groups of judges would reveal important differences regarding the value systems that operate in an organization and should add a great deal to the meaning of the effectiveness construct.

In addition to the question of who judges, two other parameters are important to consider at the outset. One deals with whether the potential components of effectiveness are specified on some a priori grounds before we start, or whether they are generated as part of the research study. For example, the variables in Table 2 comprise one a priori starting point. The second parameter involves the target decisions for which criterion information is to be used. In certain kinds of studies, systematic variation in this "decision set" would be important.

Direct Judgment. Given these three parameters, we could ask a panel of judges to do things like the following:

1. Ask them to rate the importance of each potential criterion in terms of its contribution to the making of each specific target decision. For example, how important is voluntary turnover for deciding whether the organization is effective or ineffective? To make the rating feasible, the context of the judgment would have to be specified in a systematic way, either by specifying the conditions under which the organization must operate or by letting the judges specify the relevant conditions that would make a difference in their judgments.

2. Ask the judges to rate the similarity among measures. For example, for every pair of variables, to what extent would the judges expect them to covary (*e.g.*, if an organization scores this way on X, how will it score on Y)? Such judgments could then be subjected to multivariate analysis like any other covariation matrix. This is not a particularly powerful procedure, but it could offer a few clues.

3. Ask the judges to rate the extent to which each variable is a consequence of each other variable. A number of interesting scaling problems emerge from such a question. Thus, something analogous to paired comparisons could be used to rate the extent to which A (*e.g.*, quality of production) is a consequence of B (morale), and the extent to which B (morale) is a consequence of A (quality of production). The anguish and the inconsistencies that are revealed in this process should reveal a great deal about how the relevant parties conceptualize effectiveness.

Indirect Judgment. There are a number of indirect ways to obtain the above kinds of judgments. Some of them depend on the researcher's ability to construct a large sample of hypothetical organizations for which the "scores" on the various indicators are systematically varied. This is a difficult task, but it has been done in other contexts. Why not here?

For example, one task for the judges would be to have them judge the "similarity" of each pair of organizations, using some form of paired comparisons procedure. Multidimensional scaling procedures (*e.g.*, Shepard, Romney, and Nerlove, 1972) could then be imposed on the similarity judgments to determine the number of recognizable clusters of organizations that emerged. The characterstics of the organizations in each cluster could then be examined to determine the criteria most salient for each cluster.

Varying the instructions for the similarity judgment would be a valuable source of information. For example, insights could be gained by asking for judgments in terms of which of two organizations is more *effective* (vis-a-vis some very general or more specific mission statement) and which is more *ineffective*. The two judgments probably are not symmetrical, and it would be valuable to know which criterion variables characterize the asymmetry.

A similar procedure could be used if we could assemble a sample of real organizations with which a set of judges would be reasonably familiar. Notice that in this case the investigator would not be limited to an a priori list of variables to characterize the organizations in each cluster. The characteristics identifying each cluster would be searched for "after the fact." Such a procedure has some obvious advantages and disadvantages. Variables not in the original model, but which are important determinants of the similarity judgments, can possibly be identified. However, the investigator also runs the risk of attributing certain variables to be more highly characteristic of a cluster than they really are. In other words, the investigator may see more distinctions than actually exist.

Critical Incident Methodology.   Another judgmental procedure that could be applied is the critical incident methodology developed in the context of individual performance (Campbell, *et al.*, 1973; Smith and Kendall, 1963). The investigation of individual job performance really did not begin to make progress until behavioral scientists attempted to facilitate organizations processes as a means of defining good and bad performance.

For example, groups of judges could be asked to generate specific examples of events that occurred in their organizations which caused them to think that the organization was in a good state or a bad state. This is analogous to asking for descriptions of examples of effective and ineffective job performance on the part of individuals. The usual questions about which set of observers should generate critical incidents and whether the incidents should be recorded as they happen or described in retrospect, apply here as well. Using different sets of observers (e.g., top management, middle management, the union hierarchy) and different methodologies would be a source of valuable comparative data.

The critical incident method is, in fact, one approach that could be used to systematically sample the entire domain of potential effectiveness criteria. By varying the instructions to the judges, the potential population of criteria could be stratified along a number of parameters.

The second step would be to use another set of judges to carry out a qualitative "cluster analysis" of the incidents (as in Campbell, *et al.*, 1973) in an effort to identify the major system components represented by the incidents. These tentative dimensions could then be discussed at length by the relevant parties to thoroughly refine and complete their definitions. To further check on the understandability of the factors, Smith and Kendall's (1963) retranslation step could be carried out as a third step. This procedure would represent a logical analysis of the specific "bits" of the total domain of organizational health or organizational effectiveness which were sampled by the critical incident technique. Moreover, the analysis would be checked out by members of the organization itself.

Why all this emphasis on scaling technology? Because in the end, organizational effectiveness is what the relevant parties decide that it should be. There is no higher authority (in a secular society) to which we can appeal. On the applied level, the task of behavioral science is to assist the people in the organization in articulating what they really mean by organizational effectiveness, to show where there are gaps and inconsistencies, reveal conflicts, and help resolve those conflicts. This does not preclude the behavioral scientist's imposing his own value system as to what constitutes effectiveness; but it should be recognized for what it is.

Do-It-Yourself Theory Capturing

One practical implication contained in the above discussion is that managers and administrators should be assisted in learning how to conduct a systematic recovery of their own operating goals and criteria. Such recovery procedures should be taught, just as accounting methods or supervisory techniques are taught. It follows that we need some research and development on how best to teach people the techniques they can use to discover the theories under which they operate.

Non-Judgmental Research

At this point, one might legitimately ask, "Isn't there any type of research that investigates which independent variables actually distinguish between organizations that are effective and organizations that are ineffective in the real world?" The answer is yes, but certain qualifications must be attached. First, the definition of effectiveness must be explicated and that requires research of the nature just specified. Second, it is clear that the cause and effect relationships, or even the patterns of covariation among different variables, cannot be determined by massive studies that cover many organizations and rely on multivariate analysis. A few people with good hearts and superhuman effort have tried such strategies, most notably those at Michigan (*e.g.*, Franklin, 1974); but the payoff has been depressingly small and difficult to interpret.

What then can one do? There are really only two choices: (1) carefully conducted simulation studies, and (2) very intensive and very thorough case studies. Using the organization as the unit of analysis simply leaves no reasonable alternative. There is already a large body of literature on laboratory simulations and experimentation in organizations (Fromkin and Streufert, in press; Weick, 1965). It offers many possibilities that have not been fully exploited, perhaps because there are so few people nurtured in the experimental tradition who also are interested in these messy, molar organizational phenomena. By case study, I refer to a very intensive longitudinal monitoring of each relevant variable in a specific organization, using a variety of observational and data collection techniques. For example, behavior observation, interviews, questionnaires, and archival records all could be used to monitor changes in supervisory practices and changes in productivity. Enough questions could be asked and enough data collected to enable the researcher to trace the effect, if any, of one on the other. All of this is no small undertaking, and I know of no good example from the organizational literature. The approach that comes the closest is from ecological psychology, most notably the studies by Barker (1968) and his colleagues. In fact, the developing methodology in ecological psychology (Graik, 1973) would not be a bad literature for organizational theorists to examine. Also, it should be noted that while case studies have their own set of problems, the potential for learning something fundamental about how different facts of organizational effectiveness go together is considerable.

SUMMARY COMMENTS

In summary, the study of organizational effectiveness needs an increased emphasis on what this paper has called criterion-capturing research, followed by a much greater use of simulations and case studies. Large-scale field studies across many organizations, in the manner of Pugh, Hickson, and Hinings (1969), Seashore and Yuchtman (1967), and Woodward (1965), were prodigious efforts to be admired. However, they will not advance our understanding of organizational effectiveness. We must be content with less.

REFERENCES

Barker, R. G. *Ecological Psychology: Concepts and Methods for Studying the*
    1968   *Environment of Human Behavior.* Stanford, Calif.: Stanford University
            Press.
Beckhard, R. *Organizational Development: Strategies and Models.* Reading, Mass.:
    1969   Addison-Wesley.
Blum, M. L., and J. C. Naylor. *Industrial Psychology: Its Theoretical and Social*
    1968   *Foundations.* New York: Harper and Row.
Borman, W. C., and M. D. Dunnette.   "Selection of Components to Comprise a
    1974   Naval Personnel Status Index (NPSI) and a Strategy for Investigating
            Their Relative Importance." Final Technical Report, 1974, ONR Contract
            NO0014–73–C–0210, NR156–020. Minneapolis: Personnel Decisions,
            Inc.
Campbell, J. P., D. A. Bownas, N. G. Peterson, and M. D. Dunnette. "The Measure-
    1974   ment of Organizational Effectiveness: A Review of Relevant Research and
            Opinion." Final Report, 1974, Navy Personnel Research and Development
            Center Contract N00022–73–C–0023. Minneapolis: Personnel Decisions,
            Inc.
Campbell, J. P., M. D. Dunnette, R. D. Arvey, and L. V. Hellervik.   "The Development
    1973   and Evaluation of Behaviorally Based Rating Scales." *Journal of Applied*
            Psychology, 57:15–22.

Campbell, J. P., M. D. Dunnette, E. E. Lawler, and K. E. Weick. *Managerial Behavior,*
1970   *Performance, and Effectiveness.* New York: McGraw-Hill.
Chase, S B., Jr. (ed.) *Problems in Public Expenditure Analysis.* Washington,
1965   D. C.: Brookings Institution.
Craik, K. H. "Environmental Psychology." In P. H. Mussen and R. M. Rosenzweig
1973   (eds.), *Annual Review of Psychology.* Palo Alto, Calif.: Annual Reviews,
        Inc.
Dorfman, R. (ed.) *Measuring Benefits of Government Investments.* Washington,
1965   D. C.: Brookings Institution.
Dunnette, M. D. *Personnel Selection and Placement.* Belmont, Calif.: Wadsworth.
1966
Franklin, J. L. "A Path Analytic Approach to Describing Causal Relationships
1973   Among Social Psychological Variables in Multi-Level Organizations."
        Office of Naval Research Technical Report. Ann Arbor, Mich: Institute for
        Social Research, University of Michigan.
Fromkin, H., and S. Streufert. "Laboratory Experimentation." In M. D. Dunnette
in   (ed.), *Handbook of Industrial and Organizational Psychology.* Chicago
press   Rand McNally, in press.
Ghorpade, J. *Assessment of Organizational Effectiveness.* Pacific Palisades,
1971   Calif.: Goodyear.
Glennon, R. "Issues in the Evaluation of Manpower Programs." In P. Rossi and
1972   W. William (eds.), *Evaluating Social Programs: Theory, Practice, and
        Politics.* New York: Seminar Press.
Likert, R   *The Human Organization.* New York: McGraw Hill.
1967
—————. *New Patterns of Management.* New York: McGraw-Hill.
1961
Mangum, G. L. "Manpower Research and Manpower Policy." In Industrial Relations
1971   Research Association, *A Review of Industrial Relations Research,* vol. 2
        Madison, Wisc.: Industrial Relations Research Association.
Price, J. L. "The Study of Organizational Effectiveness." *Sociological Quarterly,*
1972   13:3–15.
Pugh, D. S., D. J. Hickson, and C. R. Hinings. "An Empirical Taxonomy of Structures
1969   of Work Organizations." *Administrative Science Quarterly,* 14:115–126.
Seashore, S., and E. Yuchtman. "Factoral Analysis of Organizational Performance."
1967   *Administrative Science Quarterly,* 12:377–395.
Schmidt, F. L., and L. B. Kaplan. "Composite vs. Multiple Criteria: A Review and
1971   Resolution of the Controversy." *Personnel Psychology,* 24:419–434.
Shepard, R., A. K. Romney, and S. Nerlove (eds.) *Multidimensional Scaling: Theory
1972   and Applications in the Behavioral Sciences.* New York: Seminar Press.
Smith, P. C., and L. M. Kendall. "Retranslation of Expectations: An Approach to
1963   the Constitution of Unambiguous Anchors for Rating Scales." *Journal
        of Applied Psychology,* 47:149–155.
Taylor, J. C., and D. G. Bowers. *Survey of Organizations.* Ann Arbor, Mich.: Institute
1972   for Social Research, University of Michigan.
Wallace, S. R. "Criteria for What?" *American Psychologist,* 20:411–417.
1965
Weick, K. "Laboratory Experimentation with Organizations." In J. G. March (ed.),
1965   *Handbook of Organizations.* Chicago: Rand McNally.
Woodward, J. *Industrial Organization: Theory and Practice.* New York: Oxford
1965   University Press.

Section II

ORGANIZATIONAL EFFECTIVENESS —RESEARCH—

This section contains reports on four outstanding studies concerned with the determinates of organizational effectiveness. First, Srivastva and Salipante present a summary and critique of the existing literature on the relationship between autonomy and organizational effectiveness. Next, Price provides a systematic codification of extant literature dealing with the relationship between personnel turnover and organizational effectiveness. The third paper, authored by Marsh and Mannari, reports empirical findings on the determinates of employee performance in Japanese firms. In the final paper in this section, Stewart empirically assesses the range of factors accounting for organizational effectiveness within different time frames.

Autonomy in Work

SURESH SRIVASTVA
PAUL F. SALIPANTE, JR.
Case Western Reserve University

Autonomy in work and at the workplace is both conceptually and empirically a major variable. As such, it is related to job satisfaction, productivity, and organizational effectiveness.

This paper is divided into four components: an analysis of the concept of autonomy as it relates to work and workers; a related review of research on autonomy and its relationship to variables like performance and job satisfaction; some suggestions on developing strategies to implement research findings related to autonomy, job satisfaction and productivity; and some thoughts on developing social policy regarding quality of work life and organizational effectiveness.

THE CONCEPT OF AUTONOMY

People need autonomy at work because it enhances satisfaction and increases productivity. Organizations benefit from employee autonomy because organizational effectiveness depends in part on employee productivity. Autonomy, however, is not independence or freedom; rather, it is based on the assumption that all work is performed under conditions of independence among the several components of the workplace. In this sense, autonomy means either absence of constraints or presence of facilitators for the interdependent functioning of an organization. In one sense, autonomy could mean absence of supervision as a control or as a major source of feedback, absence of piece-rate reward structure, or absence of technological constraints on human performance, such as time clocks. In another sense, it could mean organization of autonomous work groups, self-developed feedback mechanisms, peer relationships which foster understanding and open dialogue, or placing value on internal rewards as a major source of satisfaction.

In our study, autonomy is examined both as a subjective feeling state or an environmental ethos, and as an objective, structural intervention in the organized workplace. In both instances, specific statements are needed regarding the concept of autonomy and its implications for understanding organizational effectiveness. Operationally, autonomy has been defined in one or more of the following ways:

1. Autonomy from the supervisor with regard to responsibility for the primary task, such as determining the quality of performance and the means or procedure for accomplishing the task.

2. Increased span of activity and time span of discretion in the area of decision making and experiences of collective responsibility with the work group.

3. Autonomy in regard to effort required for the performance of a task.

4. Autonomy in regard to feedback for accomplishment or non-accomplishment of a task.

An effort is made here to develop a framework which will explain the major finding of our search and research in the field of job satisfaction and productivity. Autonomy was found to be the one single and major variable which could explain the variance in empirical studies dealing with this subject matter. But why? Basically, there are three views.

First, the notion of increased effort for productivity is antithetical to the concept of autonomy; therefore, strategies toward this end are often counterproductive. The struggle between management and organized labor is an appropriate example. If, for instance, management sees the problem as maximizing performance, given fixed technology and work methods (optimized by scientific management procedures), then the problem becomes one of maximizing effort. The result is pressure on employees to work closest to their maximum physical and mental levels. The protective response of workers and their unions is to resist efforts to increase pressure. Some prominent labor leaders resist quality of work-life programs because they see them, perhaps accurately, as effort-increasing programs. From the workers' perspective, it might well be possible to increase performance if the problem were not unidimensional (*i.e.*, if methods of production, scheduling, and production rates were not fixed). Since effort is well below the maximum physical level in any long-term work situation, effort can only be self-generated through autonomous initiative. In other words, autonomy over inputs and outputs is requisite to expanding outputs. In light of this argument, the issue is one of autonomy rather than effort or the work ethic.

Second, the importance of autonomy comes from the psychological literature on self-esteem. It has been argued that development of self is grounded in the struggle for autonomy that begins at birth. In this sense, autonomy at the workplace is an expression of self-esteem and affirmation of a developed self. The need to be self-determining and self-directing might be a part of this adult phenomenon.

Third, autonomy at the workplace is intertwined with the concept of interdependence among the components. In this sense, autonomy is an expression of the interdependence of others on self and vice versa. It is also related to the experience of feeling significant and indispensable in the organization. If others see self as necessary, then the interdependence is operative. Autonomy, therefore, is not independence. It is, however, a demand on others to accept each other as interdependent and not dependent.

RESEARCH ON AUTONOMY

At best, people distort their motivations and intentions when questioned by researchers. Empirical studies on job satisfaction are invariably questionnaire or interview studies. But if motivation is being studied as a conscious psychodynamic, then people tend to respond in socially desirable ways. If it is studied as an unconscious psychodynamic, people are pressurized to bring their repressed experiences to the conscious level—making it impossible to study the phenomenon in its true form. Repressed experiences become part of the unconscious and they should not be expressed during such studies. Thus, autonomy becomes a phenomenon which could be verifiable both at subjective as well as objective levels. At subjective levels, one could express a need for autonomy without having a socially undersirable consequence. At an objective level, one could observe the phenomenon in operation by studying structural changes and ordering organizational structures in ways which guarantee autonomy. Correlational (cross-sectional) studies have investigated autonomy at the subjective level, while field experiments have covered the objective level. By drawing on both sets of studies, we can gain a more valid view of the efficacy of autonomy.

Over the past few years, we and several of our colleagues have reviewed the contemporary empirical literature investigating the relationship of organizational and individual variables to job satisfaction and productivity. Our basic strategy in assessing the validity of these findings was to look for convergence (*i.e.*, agreement) across studies investigating the same variables. This strategy was especially important for the correlational studies, since the internal validity of any one of these studies taken singly was inevitably quite low. Therefore, correlational studies were reviewed separately from field experimental studies. The field experiments had quasi-experimental designs offering higher internal validity, and validity assessments of each individual experiment were made. (For a more detailed description of the review's methodology and findings, see Srivastva, *et al.*, 1975).

Several findings from both the correlational and field experimental sections of the review are pertinent to the issues of autonomy presented above. First, autonomy itself received the most consistent support of any variable in the review. A large number of correlational studies converged in relating autonomy to satisfaction, and autonomy was one of the few variables unambiguously related to performance in a positive direction. Several other variables relevant to dimensions of autonomy also were found to be important to but the most convincing evidence came from the field experiments. Autonomy was a theme which permeated almost all of the experiments.

Let us now consider the review's findings on autonomy in more detail, first, with regard to job satisfaction, and then, to performance.

Findings on Job Satisfaction

In addition to the correlational studies explicitly dealing with autonomy, several other groups of correlational studies investigated autonomy-relevant dimensions (see Figure 1). Freedom from supervisory control is, as we argued above, one aspect of subordinates' autonomy. A large number of correlational studies found democratic supervisory style to be positively related to satisfaction. Similarly, a large number of studies found organizational climate to be related to satisfaction; in most of these studies, climate appeared to be primarily a measure of autonomy. Finally, there was a smaller group of alienation studies investigating low control and variety on the job; such low control and variety was related to increased alienation. All of these findings support the general view that autonomy as a subjective-feeling state is positively related to job satisfaction. In addition, the finding on democratic supervisory style, a behavioral dimension, suggests that objective changes in autonomy may also be related to satisfaction.

The methodology in the field experiments permitted a stronger assessment of the causal impacts that objective changes in organizational variables, including those related to autonomy, would have on satisfaction. Table 1 presents a summary of results on the 57 field experiments reviewed. These quasi experiments were grouped into four categories according to their underlying organizing principle: socio-technical work groups job restructuring; participative management; and organization-wide change. The percentages in the first ten columns of Table 1 give the proportion of experiments in a particular category which manipulated the variable listed at the top of these columns. Column 2 is most relevant for our present purposes; it shows the percentage of experiments in each category which involved changes in employees' autonomy. For example, 88 percent of the socio-technical experiments changed the amount of autonomy which workers possessed. The right-hand columns of the table show the percentage of experiments claiming beneficial impacts on various outcome variables. Only the final columns represent attitudes or satisfaction. These columns show the percentage of studies reporting totally positive results; for example, the last column shows the percentage of studies which reported no negative or null effects on any set of attitudinal measures.

Most all of the studies grouped into the organizing principle categories had positive effects on attitudes. Participative management and job restructuring studies had the highest percentage of totally positive attitudinal results, while the organization change studies showed the lowest percentage of such results. This order of attitudinal results is exactly the same as the order of the organizing principles on the basis of the percentage of studies manipulating autonomy. Another important finding is that the participative management studies (with the exception of only one study out of seven) manipulated only autonomy, yet produced the highest percentage of totally

Figure 1

SUMMARY OF CONVERGENT RELATIONS

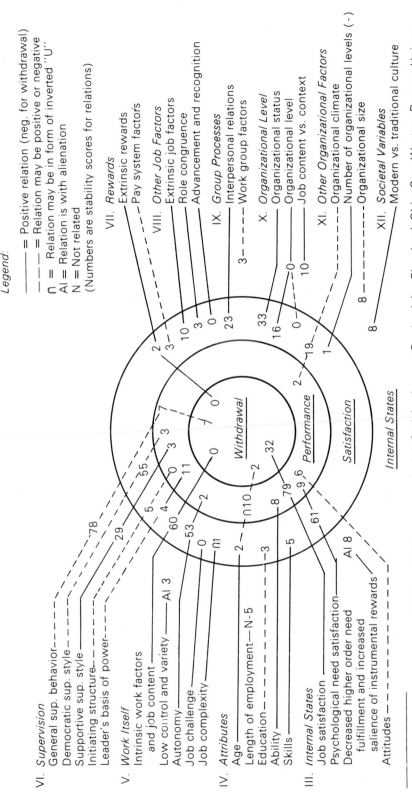

Figure 1 originally appeared in, Suresh Srivastva, *et al.*, *Job Satisfaction and Productivity*. Cleveland, Ohio: Case Western Reserve University (1975). Permission of the publishers is gratefully acknowledged.

Table 1

INDEPENDENT VARIABLES: A SUMMARY OF THE PERCENTAGE OF FIELD EXPERIMENTAL STUDIES THAT MANIPULATED A PARTICULAR VARIABLE

DEPENDENT VARIABLES: A SUMMARY OF THE PERCENTAGE OF FIELD EXPERIMENTAL STUDIES THAT PRODUCED TOTALLY POSITIVE RESULTS

	Pay/ Reward Systems	Autonomy/ Discretion	Support	Training	Organization Structure	Technical/ Physical	Task Variety	Information/ Feedback	Interpersonal/ Group Process	Costs	Productivity	Quality	Withdrawal	Attitudes
Socio-Technical/ Autonomous Groups (n=16)	56% (16)	88% (16)	31% (16)	44% (16)	19% (16)	63% (16)	63% (16)	63% (16)	75% (16)	88% (8)	93% (15)	86% (7)	73% (7)	70% (10)
Job Restructuring (n=27)	14% (27)	92% (27)	22% (27)	33% (27)	14% (27)	22% (27)	79% (27)	45% (27)	4% (27)	90% (10)	75% (20)	100% (17)	86% (7)	76% (21)
Participative Management (n=7)		100% (7)		14% (7)	14% (7)					100% (1)	57% (7)	100% (1)	80% (5)	80% (5)
Organization Change (n=7)	29% (7)	43% (7)	43% (7)	43% (7)	100% (7)	29% (7)	14% (7)	71% (7)	43% (7)	50% (2)	100% (4)	100% (2)	67% (3)	50% (6)

Note: Numbers in parentheses indicate the base number of studies on which the percentage is based—i.e., the denominator.

Note: The percentages represent those studies which reported no negative, mixed, or zero-change findings for the dependent variable in that column.

positive attitudinal results. This is in sharp contrast with the large number of factors manipulated by the other groups of field experiments. Combining the above two findings, the most parsimonious conclusion is that autonomy alone is sufficient to account for positive attitudinal results. This is an extremely important finding, since it implies that if attitudes are the primary target, increasing the population's autonomy is likely to be sufficient. In fact, the manipulation of certain other factors in addition to autonomy may detract from this satisfaction increase, as is consistent with experimental findings on the negative impact of extrinsic rewards on intrinsic motivation (Notz, 1975).

However, there is an exception to the generalization that increased autonomy leads to increased job satisfaction. It is clear that individuals with low need for autonomy are not likely to have their job satisfaction increased by being granted greater autonomy. The reports of field experiments categorized as participative management suggested that one of the contingencies for success is that workers possess higher-order needs. In a similar vein, there are a few correlational studies in the areas of autonomy, democratic supervisory style, and organizational climate that did not find autonomy to be positively related to attitudes. More telling, a couple of the correlational studies specifically reported that positive relationships between job satisfaction and autonomy or autonomy-related variables held only for workers with independence needs or low authoritarianism. It is possible that given increased autonomy in their work situation, even workers with initially low autonomy needs would develop such needs, or at least learn to cope satisfactorily with their new situation. However, it will be proposed below that such workers' low needs for autonomy be explicitly recognized, and that autonomy be operationalized as the establishment of a contract—a contract with the individual workers specifying the degree of autonomy and discretion to be held by the worker vis-a-vis that held by his superior.

Findings on Performance

Narrowly defined, autonomy alone cannot account for the performance differences among field experimental studies grouped by organizing principles. In fact, participative management studies showed the lowest percentage of totally positive performance results. In the correlational studies, autonomy was found to be an important variable in its possible effects on performance; however, several correlational studies found a negative relationship between democratic supervisory style—clearly an autonomy-relevant variable—and performance, the critical intervening variable again being the degree of authoritarianism of workers.

Autonomy covaries closely with beneficial impacts on costs in the field experiments, indicating autonomy does have payoffs on that dimension of performance. Also in the field experiments, there was a variable essential to autonomy (as we have defined it) which did covary with the productivity results: feedback. Feedback was highest in the organization change and socio-technical experiments (Table 1, column 8), as was the percentage of totally positive performance results. Feedback was next highest in the job restructuring studies, which similarly had the next highest performance results. Finally, feedback was not manipulated in any of the participative management studies, and it was these studies which had the lowest percentage of totally positive productivity results. Feedback alone cannot account for the performance results because it was manipulated in a lower percentage of the studies (in each organizing principle category) than showed totally positive results on performance. Other independent variables relevant to autonomy which seemed to covary in the experimental studies with performance percentages, and thus can be considered to have positive impacts on performance, are interpersonal and group process (column 9), task variety (column 7), and technical and physical (column 6).

As with attitudes, almost all the studies which tested for an effect on work quality found a positive one. Again as with attitudes, the most parsimonious explanation is that autonomy accounted for these quality improvements. Yet, if this was so, why did autonomy not account for the productivity results? If a worker granted increased autonomy improves his work quality, why does he not also improve his productivity? The answer may be that his productivity is not largely under his control and may be constrained by the technology or by the worker's dependence on the work of others. In this regard, the comparatively low performance results of the participative management and job restructuring studies can be explained by the failure of these studies to extend autonomy to dimensions removing some technical and social constraints on worker performance. In contrast, the socio-technical and organization change studies did change several such dimensions. Feedback is one such factor. By providing workers with feedback on their performance, workers are facilitated in making changes in their procedures and then observing the effects on performance. As argued in the opening discussion, feedback is a central element of autonomy. Without feedback, self-regulation and, hence, autonomy are not possible.

Another change which can serve to remove performance constraints is the facilitation of interpersonal and group processes, processes manipulated by many of the organization change and socio-technical studies. A substantial portion of the social-psychological literature argues that groups are more effective than individuals in solving some problems. This would certainly be the case for many technical problems among interdependent workers. As discussed above, interdependence is an important element of autonomy; thus, it is not surprising that field experiments indicate facilitation of group processes to be important for productivity.

Another possible reason for autonomy alone not accounting for the performance results relates to our previous argument on the constraints imposed on workers. If autonomy in production methods were established but production goals were constrained, then satisfaction would be increased within that constraint. Performance, however, would not. If autonomy also extended to goal setting, then performance would be more likely to increase. Some field experiments did not extend autonomy to the setting of performance goals.

Reviewing the empirical research, then, leads to several results consistent with our conceptual treatment of autonomy. Autonomy has a generally positive effect on job satisfaction; since both the correlational and the field experimental studies indicated this effect, we can have increased confidence that as both a feeling state and as a manipulable variable, autonomy has favorable impacts on satisfaction. Autonomy also has impact on job performance, if it is accompanied by several factors which facilitate the maintenance of autonomy. Primary among these is feedback of information on performance. Also important is the acquisition of interpersonal skills.

ORGANIZATIONAL STRATEGIES FOR INCREASING AUTONOMY

The field experiments provide models which can be used to develop strategies for increasing autonomy. Literature on the individual field experiments, plus conceptual literature on their underlying organizing principles, can be cited. The choice of a particular approach depends on several criteria: (a) the goal of the intervention (*e.g.*, if job satisfaction, participative management appears adequate); (b) congruence between the approach and the organization's philosphy; and (c) the contingencies of the particular organizational context (Cummings and Salipante, 1974). All of the existing approaches, however, fail to take into explicit account the individual differences in response to autonomy which are suggested by the correlational studies. For the truly experimental innovator (Campbell, 1969), we present here an approach more consistent with the observed individual differences.

We propose that the degree of autonomy held by a subordinate and the degree held by his superior should be determined by mutual worker-superior agreement. Thinking of work as a psychological contract, an essential part of the contract is the amount of discretion the subordinate has over his various activities. The amount of control possessed by the worker may vary from one activity to the next. A possible basis for determining how much discretion over a particular activity should be held by each party is the relative task expertise of the subordinate and the superior. Where the subordinate possesses much expertise related to a specific activity, the worker can be allowed much discretion over performance of that activity. For activities in which the subordinate does not possess much expertise, or over which the worker does not desire discretion, the contract would be one of the superior prescribing and the subordinate performing. However, we do feel that some discretion over work output rates should be explicitly given to the subordinate.

With regard to such a contract, clarity is primary. Without clarity, exercises of discretion are not likely to be sanctioned or, in other cases, workers may not realize they are being held responsible for self-controlled performance of some activities.

As has already been discussed, feedback is necessary if autonomy is to result in higher performance. Such feedback must not only be available, it must also be as immediate as possible. It is important that the feedback be descriptive rather than evaluative, facilitative rather than controlling. Otherwise, the feedback itself becomes a control mechanism by which the superior imposes performance constraints, reducing worker autonomy. The source of the feedback is, therefore, critical. If the superior determines which information is fed back, it probably will be perceived as controlling. If the information to be gathered is either specified by the subordinate or actually gathered by him, autonomy is maintained. Thus, the supervisor-subordinate relationship, in terms of who has control over and access to information, is crucial in determining autonomy.

To the degree that workers or work groups are interdependent, increasing workers' discretion will increase their need to effectively interact with others. For this reason, acquisition of interpersonal and group skills is necessary to facilitate performance improvement through autonomy.

An essential characteristic of the autonomy/discretion contracted to subordinates is that it must encompass innovation opportunities. One of the chief differences between the socio-technical and the job restructuring field experiments is that the former studies engaged workers in the innovation itself, whereas the latter type of studies had "experts" determine at least the initial technical and autonomy-granting innovations. That is, socio-technical approaches do not treat technology as a constraint. This may be one reason why the socio-technical studies as a group had better performance results than the job restructuring studies. The opportunity to have some control over innovations can affect performance in two ways. First, the subordinates may possess good ideas for technical or procedural innovation, being connected first-hand with the production or service process. Second, as we argued earlier, having control over technology rather than having it totally imposed enlarges the issue from the unidimensional one of effort to a multidimensional one allowing performance expansion. In addition, subordinate-initiated innovation is one way in which the autonomy contract can be operationalized and modified.

The result of the above—a clear contract of discretion over specified activities; immediate, non-evaluative feedback controlled by those possessing autonomy; increased interpersonal or group skills to facilitate autonomous actions; and subordinate-controlled innovation opportunity—should be increased satisfaction and performance.

SOCIETAL CONSIDERATIONS ON INCREASING ORGANIZATIONAL EFFECTIVENESS THROUGH AUTONOMY

The above discussion makes clear that it is our view, supported by empirical research, that increasing and facilitating autonomy in an organization will lead to increased job satisfaction and increased job performance. Aggregation problems notwithstanding, it is very likely that in most organizations such increases would lead to increased organizational effectiveness overall. This view on the benefits of autonomy runs head on into the realities of current practices in industrial organizations. If autonomy is so functional, why do so few organizations employ it at lower and middle levels?

One could argue that work innovations encompassing autonomy increases are unproven, at least to the satisfaction of organizational decision makers. However, our review provides substantial evidence that the prospect for improved performance is quite high. Further, a number of authorities on organizational innovations are saying that it is time to stop treating these innovations as experiments and to see them instead as practical alternatives for widespread adoption (Bjork, 1975). Arguing even more convincingly that it is not their validity which prevents adoption are the indications that where field experiments have been successful in a particular organization, they have not spread to other parts of the organization or even continued where they were shown to be successful. The Tavistock Institute's coal mine experiments in England are one example (Jenkins, 1973). We believe that the forces impeding widespread adoption of autonomy-increasing innovations are at the societal level and inherently tied to inconsistencies between autonomy and prevailing views of what "managing" is.

To the degree that managing is seen as maintaining control, as regulating various organizational processes, and as defining tasks and the constraints within which others operate, allowing employees to be self-regulating is an abdication of management. At the very least, subordinate autonomy raises the thorny issue of what the superior is left to do (Clark and Krone, 1972). A fear that is likely to be even greater is that employees will use autonomy for their personal benefit, to the detriment of the organization. While academicians may be content with the notion of control as an expandable entity, most managers (at least those we have encountered in graduate classes, special workshops, and when consulting) are not. Further, research shows that managers attribute control over subordinates to themselves even when subordinates' performance is, in fact, independent of them (Strickland, 1958); that is, managers might not recognize subordinates' self-regulation

At the base of all this, we believe, is management's view of the subordinate performance problem as unidimensional, in the sense described at the beginning of this paper. If management constrains all performance-relevant dimensions over which it can possibly exert control, that leaves only one degree of freedom to the employee, his effort. Management's attempts to increase effort by imposing overt behavior control, or by extending incentives and inducements lead to employees' attempts to regain control by restricting effort. Effort, in the guise of work rates, standards, and hours, then becomes a conflict or bargaining issue to be traded off against remuneration. Existing work institutions, such as unions, management associations, and mediation services, are committed to this issue. If management proposes an autonomy-based work innovation, workers and unions are likely to suspect it as an attempt to increase their effort. At best, this unidimensional view results in suboptimization of labor and technology. At worst, it results in long-term performance at a consciously restricted level.

However, it is naive to expect changes soon in the prevailing and institutionalized views of the meaning of managing. If change does occur toward a multidimensional view, one allowing explicit discretion over goals and technology, it will be long-term and, very probably, politicized. Two scenarios occur to us. The first has a referent—the Industrial Democracy Movement in Norway. If it were decided on a national level that improved organizational productivity would result from autonomy improvements, large-scale change could be pursued in a political manner—e.g., laws providing tax incentives or laws requiring mechanisms for employee autonomy or compliance requirements for government contracts. Alternatively, the government could support adoption of autonomy-increasing innovations on a permanent basis in highly visible and respected firms. If large productivity gains resulted, competitive forces would hasten adoption elsewhere.

Another scenario recognizes the identity between employees and citizens. If employees as a mass form a movement demanding work autonomy in its own right, then the same political process as above might result. The difference from the first scenario is that autonomy itself, rather than productivity, would be the goal. The likelihood of this occurring might be increased by adoption of national indicators of life quality, as opposed to the strictly economic indicators now used. A variation on this scenario would be employees making demands for work autonomy on their union representatives, as some splinter groups in the UAW seem to have done. However, this seems to us less likely to result in change because of the institutionalized views of which issues are relevant for bargaining.

While these scenarios are highly speculative, our point is that demonstrating the organizational efficacy of autonomy is not likely to lead to its large-scale adoption. We feel that its efficacy has already been established but that societal-level forces will have to materialize before worker autonomy will have any substantial or broad-scale effect on organizational effectiveness.

REFERENCES

Bjork, L. E. "An Experiment in Work Satisfaction." *Scientific American*, 232:17—23.
1975

Campbell, D. T. "Reforms as Experiments." *American Psychologist*, 24:409—29.
1969

Clark, J. V., and C. G. Krone. "Towards an Overall View of Organizational Develop-
1972 ment in the Early Seventies." In J. M. Thomas and W. G. Bennis (eds.),
Management of Change and Conflict. Baltimore: Penguin Books.

Cummings, T. G., and P. F. Salipante. "The Development of Research-Based
1974 Strategies for Improving the Quality of Work Life." Paper delivered at the
NATO Conference on Personal Goals and Work Design. York, England.
To be published in P. Warr, *Personal Goals in Work Design*. London:
Wiley and Sons (1976).

Jenkins, D. *Job Power: Blue and White Collar Democracy*. Garden City, N. Y.:
1973 Doubleday and Company.

Notz, W. W. "Work Motivation and the Negative Effects of Extrinsic Rewards:
1975 A Review of Some Research Findings and Their Implications for Theory
and Practice." *American Psychologist*, 30: 884—891.

Srivastva, S., et al. *Productivity, Industrial Organization and Job Satisfaction:
1975 Policy Development and Implementation*. NSF Award Number GI-39455
(RANN). Cleveland, Ohio: Department of Organizational Behavior, Case
Western Reserve University.

Strickland, L. H. "Surveillance and Trust." *Journal of Personality*, 26:200—215.
1958

The Effects of Turnover on the Organization

JAMES L. PRICE
University of Iowa

INTRODUCTION

This paper presents a codification (Merton, 1957: 12–16), a systematic ordering of the literature on the effects of turnover on the organization (Harechmak, 1974; Woodhouse, 1973).[1] Turnover is the degree of movement across the membership boundary of an organization (Price, 1972: 185–92).[2] Included within this movement are individuals either coming into or leaving the organization; excluded from this movement are promotions and transfers within the organization. The literature concerned with "mobility," "migration," and "succession," to cite but a few of the more prominent labels, contains information relevant to the effects of turnover on the organization. Literature about the effects of *managerial* succession on the organization is especially relevant.

The literature dealing with the effects of turnover seems to have two major concerns. First, there is documentation of the costs of turnover, usually monetary, to the organization. Different types of costs are identified and various procedures are described to calculate these costs. Second, there is concern with the effects of these costs on effectiveness, or on the organization's capacity to achieve its goal(s) (Price, 1972: 101–106). It is usually implied that the costs of turnover reduce effectiveness. If the organization is a business firm, for example, the implication is that the costs reduce profits, however profits are measured.

This paper reconceptualizes the literature dealing with the costs of turnover and critically examines the asumption that turnover, by increasing costs, reduces effectiveness. The major focus of this paper, however, is to examine the effects of turnover on variables other than costs and effective-

---

[1]Two of my students, John R. Harechmak (1974) and Robert H. Woodhouse (1973), have done helpful work on the effects of turnover on the organization. This paper, however, departs significantly from their work.

[2]Nearly all of the definitions cited in this paper are discussed in Price (1972). The handbook and the paper, however, use different units of analysis in defining the concepts. The handbook refers to social systems, whereas the paper refers to organizations.

ness. The preoccupation with costs and effectiveness has resulted in a relative neglect of the effects of turnover on other organizational variables. These relatively neglected effects will be carefully examined here. Strange as it may seem for such an important problem, there is no existing codification of the literature concerning the effects of turnover on the organization. Most of the codification efforts to date have dealt with determinants and correlates of turnover (Price, in press; Price, 1975).

This paper is concerned only with the effects of turnover on the organization. And, as previously implied, "on the organization" refers to organizational variables, such as effectiveness. No attempt is made to examine the effects of turnover on the society, community, family, or individual. Literature exists about the effects of turnover on these other systems, and these effects are topics worthy of concern. This paper, however, is limited to codification of the effects of turnover on the organization.

THE EFFECTS OF TURNOVER

Three preliminary comments are required before presenting the effects of turnover. First, the effects are stated in the form of propositions. The following propositional format is used: successively higher amounts of X probably produce successively lower (or higher) amounts of Y. The X's are always turnover, whereas the Y's change throughout the paper. Second, the propositions are ranked, albeit crudely, by the amount of supporting evidence. Two rankings are used, medium and low. A high ranking was avoided because none of the evidence compiled for the different propositions is methodologically very rigorous. Third, the qualification, "other things being equal," should be attached to each proposition.

Propositions Supported by a Medium Amount of Data

Proposition No. 1: Successively higher amounts of turnover probably produce successively higher proportions of adminstrative staff members relative to production staff members.

This is the first of three propositions supported by a medium amount of data.

Organizational members may be classified into those who directly or indirectly contribute to the system's primary output (Price, 1972:19–26). In an autombile plant, for example, the blue-collar workers who man the assembly line are directly involved in producing the plant's primary output, automobiles. The white-collar workers in the plant's office indirectly contribute toward the production of automobiles through their organization of work.[3] The production staff constitutes the organizational members who directly produce the system's primary output, whereas the administrative

---

[3]Blau's (1973:267) definition of administration is used throughout this paper. Blau includes material about the effects of turnover in this publication; however, it came to the attention of this author too late for its findings to be included systematically in this codification.

staff constitutes the system's indirect contributors. The size of the production staff is commonly used as the numerical base for computing the proportionate size of the administrative staff. The administrative staff on an organization is often referred to as its "bureaucracy."

The first proposition is supported by data from empirical studies by Carlson (1962, 1961) and Kasarda (1973). A statement on this proposition is also found in McNeil and Thompson (1971: 634). Kasarda's study is particularly impressive. He sought to explain variations in administrative intensity (the proportion of administrative personnel) and administrative overhead (the relative costs of administrative activities) by collecting data about 130 school systems. Kasarda's results indicate that high turnover increases administrative intensity and administrative overhead. From the perspective of this paper, administrative intensity and administrative overhead are two different measures of the relative size of the administrative staff. The proportion of administrative personnel and the relative costs of administrative activities are two indicators of the proportion of the organization's resources allocated to administrative staff activities. Kasarda's findings, therefore, may be cited as support for the idea that successively higher amounts of turnover probably produce proportionately larger administrative staffs.

Carlson's research is concerned with the effects of executive succession on the organization. Since executive succession refers to the process of "making replacements" in executive offices (1962: 2), and since some of these replacements are recruited from outside the organization, Carlson's research about executive succession is relevant to turnover. Turnover is one type of executive succession. To investigate the effects of executive succession on the organization is to investigate, at least partially, the effects of turnover on the organization.

Carlson studied the effects of the superintendents' succession on 130 school systems. New superindendents were classified into two categories, those from within the school system (inside successors) and those from outside the system (outside successors). Carlson's (1962: 46–47) results indicate "that during the early stages of the succession cycle the number of outside successors who add to their central office staff will be greater than the number of inside successors who add to their central office staff . . ." Since outside successors are examples of turnover, and since an increase in the central office staff is another way to indicate an increase in the relative size of the administrative staff, Carlson's data thus support the idea that successively higher amounts of turnover probably produce proportionately larger administrative staffs.

The question arises as to *how* turnover produces an increase in the relative size of the administrative staff. Kasarda and Carlson have different answers to this question. Kasarda (1973) notes that:

> When personnel turnover is high, *more training and supervision* of newcomers are required, which raises administrative intensity. In addition to raising administrative intensity, high personnel turnover has a direct effect on administrative expenses. It is suggested that with increasing personnel turnover, greater administrative expenditures are incurred to

meet the *costs of employee separation, recruitment, and placement*
(p. 357, emphasis added).

Kasarda thus emphasizes the increased work load (more training and
supervision, and greater costs incurred in employee separation, recruitment,
and placement) produced by turnover. The increased work load is handled
by increasing the relative size of the administrative staff. Carlson (1962: 44)
states that " [the] need for *loyalty* seems to be the connecting link between
new leadership and expansion of the administrative hierarchy . . . ."
(emphasis added). A new superintendent who comes from outside the
school system encounters the problem of obtaining loyal subordinates,
and one way to manage this problem is to recruit loyal subordinates to the
school system's central office.

Because of his more general focus, Kasarda's discussion of how
turnover increases the relative size of the administrative staff is probably
more important for explanatory purposes than Carlson's comments. Kasarda
(1973: 353) examined the turnover of all "personnel whose primary function
is classroom teaching,"[4] whereas Carlson restricted himself to the turnover
of a single person, the school superintendent. Most organizational turnover
is at the classroom teaching level rather than at the school superintendent
level. Therefore, in most instances, turnover is likely to increase the administrative staff, not because of the problem of loyalty it produces, but because
of the increased work load it entails for the organization.

Three additional comments are required about the first proposition.
First, the introductory section of this paper indicates that the costs of
turnover are reconceptualized. The concept of administrative staff can be
used to examine some of the literature describing the costs of turnover.
The costs of employee separtion, recruitment, and placement, referring
again to Kasarda's study, means that an organization has a proportionately
larger administrative staff because separation, recruitment, and placement
are part of the organizing work of the administrative staff. In short, some of
the references to turnover costs indicate an increase in the relative size of
the administrative staff. The costs of turnover will be examined more inten-
sively in a later discussion of the relationship between turnover and
effectiveness. Second, all of the supporting data for the first proposition
come from school systems, including the data used by McNeil and Thompson
(1971). The proposition would be strengthened with data from other types
or organizations. Third, no negative data were located, and this lack of
negative data slightly increases one's confidence in the proposition.

Proposition No. 2: Successively higher amounts of turnover pro-
bably produce successively higher amounts of formalization.

Formalization is the degree to which the norms of an organization are explicit
(Price, 1972: 107–117). An organization which compiles its norms in written
form, for example, generally will have a higher degree of formalization than

---

[4]It would have been better had Kasarda examined the turnover of *all* school
personnel, not just that of the teachers.

an organization which does not compile its norms in this manner. Material relevant to formalization is found in discussions of rules, regulations, procedures, and policies, to mention but a few of the rubrics used to discuss the explicitness of organizational norms.

The suggested relationship between turnover and formalization is supported by four studies (Carlson, 1962; Gouldner, 1954; Grusky, 1959; McCleery, 1957). The seminal study in this area is Gouldner's gypsum-plant research. Gouldner's (1954: 17 and 27) problem is the determinants of bureaucratization. The dimension of bureaucratization which is relevant at this point is an increased emphasis on rules. One way that an organization makes its norms more explicit, or one way that formalization is increased, is by an increased emphasis on rules. This emphasis may come through enforcement of hitherto unenforced rules, or through the establishment of new rules.

Goulder (1954: 94) notes that "there is a close connection between *succession* and a surge of bureaucratic development, particularly in the direction of formal rules . . ."[5] (emphasis added). Succession to Gouldner means essentially what it means to Carlson: the process of making replacements in executive offices. When the successor comes from outside the organization, as was the case of the new manager in the gypsum plant, turnover is involved. The development of formal rules, as previously indicated, is one way that an organization makes its norms more explicit. Gouldner's (1954) classic study may therefore be cited as support for the idea that turnover produces increased formalization.

Carlson's research on the effects of school superintendents' succession was discussed in connection with the suggested relationship between turnover and the relative increase of the administrative staff. New school superintendents not only add to the central office staffs, but "tend to become preoccupied with rules and rule-making early in their stay in office . . . ." (Carlson, 1962: 23). When the new superintendents come from outside the school system, they are even more preoccupied with rules and rule making (p. 29). Outside school superintendents, as previously indicated, are examples of turnover. Their preoccupation with rules and rule making seems to be indicative of formalization, or making organizational norms more explicit.

Grusky has long been concerned—perhaps longer than any major scholar—with what this paper refers to as the effects of turnover. His study of role conflict among prison camp officials (Grusky, 1959) may be examined in the context of formalization. Like Carlson and Gouldner, he is interested in the effects of administrative succession on the organization (Grusky, 1959: 463). All three researchers use essentially the same definition of administrative succession. Grusky is concerned with the effects that the arrival of a new chief administrative official has on the prison. The new official, mostly referred to as the new supervisor, comes from outside the prison. The following comment is pertinent:

---

[5]Critical material about this proposition is found in Gouldner (1954:45–104).

> The new supervisor, confronted with a role in which he had no previous experience and being relatively uncommitted to the quasi-milieu treatment goal, responded by *formalizing* relationships in the organization. The most important changes which he instituted involved *the substitution of formal rules for informal ones.* After being in charge of the camp for about a month, he inaugurated a list of fifty-two *rules* that the inmates were instructed to abide by rigorously . . . (Grusky, 1959:464, emphasis added).

The new supervisor of the prison is an example of turnover, and the substitution of formal rules for informal ones is an instance of formalization. Grusky's research thereby supports the suggested relationship between turnover and formalization.

McCleery's (1957: 7) problem was the determinants of authority and power, and his site of investigation was a prison. During the ten-year period described by McCleery, a new warden entered the prison from outside its ranks. Two results of the new warden's arrival were the publication of "a Policy and Philosophy manual" (McCleery, 1957: 23–24), and the issuance of "new regulations" (pp. 25–26). The manual consisted of a reformulation of policy, whereas the new regulations constituted a procedural revolution. The arrival of the outside warden is an instance of turnover; publication of the policy manual and the issuance of new regulations are examples of formalization. McCleery's research also supports the relationship between turnover and formalization.

The linkage between turnover and formalization is treated most extensively by Gouldner (1954). Grusky's (1959) comments on the matter are brief, but his description of the process is compatible with Gouldner's. Carlson (1962: 24–27) provides only a very brief discussion of the matter, while McCleery (1957) offers almost no data on the process.

The sequence of events in the gypsum plant was not crystal clear, but they seem to have occurred as follows: The new manager from outside the plant was oriented to rational norms, whereas the old manager and the workers were oriented to traditional norms. Gouldner refers to the traditional norms, and their embodiment in practice, as the "indulgency pattern." The arrival of the new manager reduced the consensus which formerly existed between the manager and the workers. Because they did not share the new manager's rational norms, the workers reduced their informal interaction with him and were not motivated to conform to his norms. The new manager was thereby denied information about the plant's operation and viewed the workers as unwilling to fulfill their obligations, that is, comply with his rational norms. From the new manager's perspective, the plant's control of its members (the workers) was threatened. To maintain control, the new manager began to enforce existing rules which hitherto had been unenforced, and to establish new rules. In brief, formalization was increased. Therefore, the key variables which link turnover and formalization seem to be reduced consensus and the decreased likelihood of control.

Two final comments about the suggested relationship between turnover and formalization. First, two of the four studies which contain data supporting the proposition are studies of prisons. The data base for the second proposition needs to be broadened. Second, no negative data could be located. The lack of negative data provides a weak form of support for the proposition.

Proposition No. 3: Successively higher amounts of turnover probably produce successively lower amounts of participation in primary groups.

This is the last of the propositions supported by a medium amount of data.

Primary and secondary relationships are commonly contrasted (Price, 1968: 146). A relationship is primary to the degree that it is diffuse, emotionally involved, biased, and governed by ascribed criteria. A good example of a primary relationship is a family in a rural area, especially in a society little touched by industrialization and urbanization. A relationship is secondary to the degree that it is specific, emotionally neutral, impartial, and focuses on achieved criteria. The physician-patient relationship in a large, urban, university-affiliated hospital in a highly industrial society is a good approximation of a secondary relationship. Primary groups in organizations clearly are not like rural families. Rather, they appear to be located approximately midway between the extreme primary relationships and the extreme secondary relationships. The following discussion, to avoid complexity, does not distinguish between organizational primary groups and familial primary groups. It should be remembered, however, that primary group in the proposition does not describe a familial group.

Three empirical studies have data which support the suggested relationship between turnover and participation in primary groups (Burling, Lentz, and Wilson, 1956; Moskos, 1970; and Uyeki, 1960). Blau (1957: 68), and van der Merwe and Miller (1973: 425–426) also have made statements relevant to this proposition.

Moskos (1970), in discussing the behavior of combat soldiers in Vietnam, notes that soldiers were rotated home after a one-year tour of duty. The rotation system which operated in Vietnam, according to Moskos, constituted, "rapid *turnover* of personnel . . . [which] hinder [ed] the development of *primary-group* ties" (p. 142, emphasis added). (Moskos also pointed out that rotation increased satisfaction among combat soldiers.) Rotation out of Vietnam did not constitute turnover from the army's perspective, since the soldiers rotated were still in the army; however, from the perspective of the combat units in Vietnam, rotation did constitute turnover and is relevant to the problem of this paper.

Uyeki's (1960) research deals with draftee behavior in the cold-war army. He notes that a number of studies of military organizations during World War II emphasized the role of the primary group in giving support to the individual. However, this "type of primary group support is *weakened* in the cold-war army" (Uyeki, 1960: 156, emphasis not added). One variable which weakened the primary group support was the army's policy of frequent transfers between units. "Except for basic training," according to Uyeki, "the draftee is not participating in common tasks with a group of individuals having the same fate as he does over any length of time . . . ." (p. 156). From the army's perspective, frequent transfers between units were not instances of turnover because the draftees never left the army. However, from the perspective of the units to which the draftees were assigned, frequent transfers were instances of turnover and are relevant to the topic of this paper. Uyeki's research supports the suggested relationship between turnover and participation in primary groups.

The third and final study supporting the third proposition is Burling, Lentz, and Wilson's (1956) research on six medical hospitals. The following comment with respect to nurses is relevant:

> It was our observation that where *nurses had worked together for a long period of time,* they came to feel that they "*belonged*" to that floor and had a vested interest in maintaining its reputation. Along with the individual's desire to live up to her own standards was a reluctance to let her *team* down. Where *turnover* was acute, on the other hand, this second impetus to moral conduct was missing. Each individual felt *isolated* and perhaps discouraged in her fight to maintain standards . . . . (p. 106, emphasis added).

Nurses who had worked together for a long period of time had a low rate of turnover. Nurses who belonged to a team, and who were not isolated on the floor where they worked, would seem to have participated in primary groups. Burling, Lentz, and Wilson's study thereby provides additional support for the idea that reduced turnover increases the amount of participation in primary groups.

There does not seem to be an intervening variable linking turnover to participation in primary groups. A low amount of turnover in an organization usually means that a sizeable proportion of the membership has been with the organization for an extended period of time. Primary ties among the members are likely to form with the passage of time, and low turnover provides the time necessary for primary group relationships to form.

Two final comments about the third proposition are needed. First, two of the three supporting studies are of military organizations. Confidence in the proposition will be increased when this narrow data base is broadened. Second, no negative data were located. Confidence in the proposition is somewhat increased by the absence of negative data.

Summary.   Figure 1 provides a diagram of the three effects of turnover which are supported by a medium amount of data.

Excluded from the diagram are mutual effects between administrative

Figure 1

THE EFFECTS OF TURNOVER ON ADMINISTRATIVE STAFF, FORMALIZATION, AND PRIMARY GROUPS

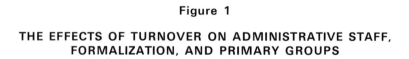
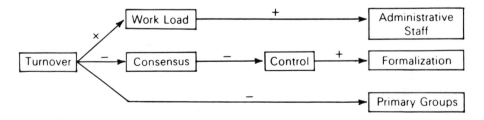

staff, formalization, and primary groups. For example, an increased administrative staff, to increase its organizing efficiency, may increase further the formalization of the organization. Also excluded from the diagram are the effects of these three variables on turnover. There is, for example, research which indicates that low participation in primary groups, by decreasing satisfaction, produces increased turnover (Price, 1975). Turnover reduces participation in primary groups, which subsequently results in more turnover. Turnover thus feeds upon itself. These excluded effects are topics for further research.

It is noteworthy that the three propositions in Figure 1 seldom enter into most of the literature dealing with the effects of turnover. As was noted earlier, the literature dealing with the effects of turnover seems to focus on the increased monetary costs incurred as a result of turnover and, mostly by implication, the fact that these increased monetary costs reduce organizational effectiveness. Only the first proposition briefly alludes to the monetary costs of turnover. One virtue of a codification is that it gently forces the examiner to view the full range of literature pertaining to a topic. The result, as in the present case, is the location of relatively obscured propositions.

The question of organizational effectiveness receives extensive treatment in a later section of this paper. However, the question must be briefly treated at this point because of the relationship which is assumed to exist between administrative staff and primary groups, on the one hand, and effectiveness, on the other hand. To a number of researchers, a relative increase in the size of the administrative staff and reduced participation in primary groups are harbingers of reduced effectiveness. These researchers believe that a discussion of these two effects of turnover clearly involves, at least tacitly, a discussion of effectiveness.

Three comments about effectiveness are appropriate concerning the three propositions. First, it may be plausibly argued—and it is probably true—that the increased administrative staff resulting from high turnover decreases effectiveness (Price, 1968: 152–62). However, this relationship, *which is mostly assumed*, must be empirically verified. One might also plausibly argue that the increased administrative staff resulting from high turnover also improves, to some extent, the organizing capacity of the system, thereby increasing effectiveness. The question then becomes one of evaluating the *net* effects of turnover on effectiveness. The point is that the assumed relationship between administrative staff and effectiveness, and this includes the net effects, must be empirically verified.

Second, there are data which indicate that participation in primary groups produces increased organizational effectiveness (Price, 1968: 138–139, esp. fn. 4). However, even this proposition urgently requires systematic verification, despite its rather wide acceptance among organizational scholars.

Third, the increased formalization resulting from turnover, by reducing uncertainty, may actually increase effectiveness. Such an impact on effectiveness is especially likely to occur when the environment of the organization is relatively unchanging (Burns and Stalker, 1961). If formalization increases effectiveness, at least in some instances, then the negative effects of

administrative staff and primary groups—if such negative effects do exist—
must be balanced against the positive effects of formalization. Again, an
evaluation is required to determine the net effects of turnover on effectiveness.
This author believes that further research will probably demonstrate that
turnover decreases effectiveness by the increased administrative staff and
weakened primary group participation which it produces, despite the positive
effects which may result from increased formalization.

Propositions Supported by a Low Amount of Data

> *Proposition No. 4: Successively higher amounts of turnover*
> *probably produce successively lower amounts of satisfaction.*

This is the first of three propositions supported by a low amount of data.

Satisfaction is the degree of affect that the members of an organization
have on membership in the system (Price, 1972: 156–173). Members who
have a positive affective orientation are satisfied, whereas members who
have a negative affective orientation are dissatisfied. Literature pertaining
to satisfaction is commonly found in discussions of morale.

The suggested relationship between turnover and satisfaction runs
through the much-cited work by Grusky. In an early review of research
dealing with administrative succession in formal organization, Grusky
(1960:105–106) notes that *"succession* can ... promote conflict among
the staff and lower employee *morale..."* (emphasis added). In a later
empirical study[6] dealing with the effects of succession in a military and a
business organization, Grusky's (1964a: 85) introductory review of the
literature states that a "number of studies of small organizations have
indicated that *succession* is disruptive, typically producing low *morale*
and conflict among the staff . . . ." (emphasis added). Previous parts of
this paper have indicated that turnover is one type of succession. The literature dealing with succession is therefore relevant to turnover, especially
when so much of it deals with the effects produced on the organization
by the arrival of a new chief executive recruited from *outside* the organization.
Morale, like satisfaction, designates the affect that organizational members
have toward the system. Grusky's reviews of the literature thus support the
idea that turnover reduces satisfaction.

Grusky (1964a, 1960) also indicates how turnover lowers satisfaction.
The key variable seems to be conflict, which is referred to in both of the
previously cited quotations. Turnover produces conflict which, in turn,
lowers satisfaction. This interpretation is consistent with the empirical
literature which Grusky reviews. Consider again, for example, Gouldner's
(1954) study of the gypsum plant. It was previously noted in the discussion
of formalization that the arrival of the new manager decreased the amount of
consensus in the plant. The new manager was oriented toward rational
norms, whereas the old manager and the workers were oriented toward

[6]The sources cited by Grusky (1964a and 1960) are mostly the same. Two
different sets of data are not being used.

traditional norms. Gouldner refers to the embodiment of the traditional norms in the plant as the "indulgency pattern." The reduced consensus resulted in conflict between the new manager and the workers,[7] and the workers' reluctance to conform to the new manager's rational norms was an expression of their reduced satisfaction. The workers derived satisfaction from the indulgency pattern and became dissatisfied when the new manager modified the pattern in the interest of promoting efficiency. Turnover lowers satisfaction because it lowers consensus and thereby increases conflict.

The question arises as to the generality of the intervening variables cited by Grusky and implied in the literature he reviews. Most of it focuses on the arrival of a new chief executive, usually from outside the organization, who shares few norms with existing members. Certainly these are extreme cases. Most turnover does not involve the chief executive officer, and it is definitely not characterized by the deep normative cleavages described in the studies cited by Grusky. The extent to which the intervening variables can be generalized to most organizational turnover is an empirical question. However, what may be seen in bold relief in Grusky's reviews may also be apparent, though in a much less observable form, in the turnover of lower level supervisors and nonsupervisors. Research on chief executive turnover thus may have been a strategic site from which to investigate the organizational effects of turnover—precisely because of its extreme nature.

Instances exist where turnover *increases* satisfaction. Guest's (1962a, 1962b) study of an automobile plant is one such instance. Like Gouldner, Guest was interested in the effects of managerial succession on the organization. The gypsum and automobile plants both experienced the arrival of new managers from outside the plant. However, unlike the effects produced in the gypsum plant, the arrival of the new manager in the automobile plant *increased* the workers' satisfaction. Guest's (1962a) study describes how the new plant manager was able to increase worker satisfaction and improve plant performance.

The fourth proposition is compatible with *instances* where turnover increases satisfaction. The probabilistic format of the proposition allows for exceptions. Basically, what is being asserted by the fourth proposition is that *most of the time* turnover decreases satisfaction. Instances where turnover does not decrease satisfaction must be compiled, a pattern of deviation must be established, and a general exception to the proposition must be conceptualized.[8] Meanwhile, this paper abides by the probabilistic assertion that turnover *generally* decreases satisfaction.

Proposition No. 5: Successively higher amounts of turnover probably produce successively higher amounts of innovation.

Innovation is the degree to which an organization is a first or early user of

---

[7]Not all conflict is produced by the lack of consensus. Most conflict probably arises from different interests. For an excellent discussion of conflict, see Dahrendorf (1959).

[8]Examples of this process are found in Price (1968). A good example is the frequently cited condition of a "very high degree of professionalization."

an idea among its set of similar organizations (Price, 1972: 118–28). A business firm that is the first to produce a new product, a university that is the first to establish a new type of curriculum; a hospital that is the first to implement a new treatment program—these are examples of innovation. Material relevant to innovation is contained in discussions of social change, generally defined as any modification of the social structure and/or culture of an organization. Innovation, however, is a less general term than social change. All innovation is social change, but not all social change is innovation.

Statements asserting a relationship between turnover and innovation are not too difficult to locate. The work of Grusky (1960) is again relevant. In his review of research dealing with administrative succession in organizations, Grusky notes that "by bringing in *'new blood'* and *new ideas, succession* can vitalize the organization so as to enable it to adapt more adequately to its everchanging internal demands and environmental pressures . . . ." (p. 105, emphasis added). Succession, as previously indicated, encompasses turnover, and new blood and new ideas would seem to be examples of innovation. Dubin (1970), in giving his impressions of management in Great Britain, makes the following comments:

> one of the important consequences of *immobility* in the work careers of British management is what Thorstein Veblen once labelled "trained incapacity." For *non-mobile* British executives "trained incapacity" is the inability to conceive of, or utilize, *new ideas*. This is obviously dysfunctional to *innovation* . . . (p. 193, emphasis added).

Mobility, like succession, is a general term that often includes turnover.[9] Dubin (1970: 192–193), however, seems to use mobility as the equivalent of turnover as defined in this paper. New ideas and innovation are clearly linked in Dubin's mind. Grusky and Dubin, therefore, suggest a relationship between turnover and innovation, as do Canfield (1959: 414), Downs (1974: 134–135), McNeil and Thompson (1971: 633), and Scheer (1962).

Empirical support for the turnover-innovation proposition comes from Carlson's (1961) previously cited research on school superintendents. Referring to the new superintendent from inside the system as "the insider," Carlson notes that the "limited evidence available demonstrates that the *insider* conforms to the expectation that *he will not make great changes*" (p. 216, emphasis added). Success for the new superintendent from outside the system, however, "tends to be defined in terms of change . . . ." (p. 217). School boards who want little or no change hire new superintendents from within the system, whereas school boards who want more change hire superintendents from outside the system. As previously indicated, outside school superintendents are examples of turnover, and some of the changes they introduce certainly would be examples of innovation.

Statements and empirical data which link turnover and innovation can be located. The next question is, how does turnover produce innovation? Two intervening processes may be suggested. The first means is suggested by Carlson (1962), when he states that the "conditions of employment

---

[9]A good discussion of mobility is found in Parnes (1954:13–35).

indicate that school boards will be satisfied if the insider keeps things as they are, but they *expect* and are satisfied with an outsider only when some changes are made . . . ." (p. 18, Emphasis added). Carlson also notes that the school boards *supported* the efforts of the outside superintendents to effect change (pp. 20–22). Turnover produced change, some of which was probably innovation, because change was expected and supported by the power holders within the system, the school boards.

The second intervening process is found in Gouldner's (1954) study of the gypsum plant. Like the outside school superintendents, the new manager was expected to change the plant and was supported in his efforts to do so by higher executives within the organization. Also, the new manager was not constrained by prior obligations within the plant. Had a new manager been appointed from within, his ability to effect change would have been limited by prior obligations to the existing membership. The new manager could end the indulgency pattern because he was outside of any network of obligations to the workers. Turnover produces innovation, especially when a new manager is involved, because the main power-holders within the system expect and support innovation, and because innovation is not constrained by a set of obligations.

No negative data could be located. The lack of negative data thus slightly strengthens the fifth proposition.

> *Proposition No. 6: Successively higher amounts of turnover among superordinates probably produce successively lower amounts of conformity.*

This is the last of three propositions for which there is a low amount of supporting data.

The sixth proposition is the first in which reference is made to the turnover of a specific category of organizational members, superordinates. It is likely that all of the effects of turnover are more pronounced when super-ordinates rather than subordinates are involved, as observed by Grusky (1960: 113). The effects of superordinate turnover on conformity, however, seem to be especially pronounced, and the proposition is given greater specificity to describe the situation.

Conformity is the degree to which performance corresponds with the norms of an organization (Price, 1972: 195). (In this paper, norm always refers to a desired course of action, never, as in psychological testing, to a statistical average. Conformity is viewed from the perspective of the *official* norms of the organization, and organizational norms are often referred to as rules.) For example, if an organization has a "no absenteeism rule" and high proportion of the membership comply with the organization's definition of the rule, then conformity is high as concerns that particular rule or norm. Deviant behavior is, of course, the opposite of conformity.

Two empirical studies contain data which may be cited to support the suggested relationship between turnover and conformity. Scheff (1961) studied a state mental hospital in which the administration had made an unsuccessful attempt to change the hospital from a custodial to a therapeutic organization. The most effective resistance to the new policy came from the attendants, the largest staff group within the hospital. Since the new policy was intended to bring about a more therapeutic hospital, and since the staff, especially the attendants, successfully resisted the implementation of this policy, what Scheff describes is an instance of deviant behavior. Control over hospital policy was exercised by attendants rather than the administration, and this is deviant behavior from the perspective of the hospital's official norms.

One reason the attendants were able to successfully resist implementation was the vulnerability of the ward physicians, key officials in the administration's attempt to bring about a more therapeutic treatment program. It was the ward physician, for example, who was responsible for treating the ward patients and insuring staff conformity to hospital policy. The ward physician, however, was vulnerable because of his short stay on the ward. "During this study," according to Scheff (1961: 94), "the *modal length of stay* of a physician on a ward was approximately *two and one-half months* . . . ." (emphasis added). This very brief "length of stay" was the result of: (a) a high turnover rate of ward physicians, and (b) the administrative practice of rotating physicians through the different wards of the hospital. From the perspective of the ward, a stay of two and one-half months' duration constituted a high amount of turnover, regardless of the reason. The ward physicians were, of course, superordinates in the hospital. Hence, one reason the hospital could not implement its new policy was the high rate of turnover among some of its key superordinates. Scheff's study, therefore, illustrates how turnover among superordinates produces reduced conformity to official organization norms.

The second study supporting the sixth proposition is Grusky's (1964a) research on the effects of succession in a military and a business organization. Grusky first posits a relationship between succession and executive control. He notes that:

> *Rapid succession is associated with limitations on executive control.* It is frequently argued that in an organization where few executives can anticipate long periods of service and most can look forward to relatively short tenures in that particular organization, the ability of the executive to implement major policy changes is greatly weakened . . . (p. 36, emphasis not added).

The amount of executive control was measured by asking military officers and business executives to indicate "the amount of authority the person believes he has." When officers who had been stationed at a military base for more than two years were compared with officers at the base for less than two years, a greater proportion of the former felt that they had a "great deal of authority" (p. 97). Essentially the same relationship was found in the business organization. Grusky concludes that "frequent *succession* conditions personal *executive* authority . . . ." (p. 97, emphasis added). An executive who has a high amount of executive control can obtain a high degree of conformity to organizational norms; he can implement major policy changes. Military officers and business executives are, of course, superordinates in their respective organizations.

Scheff and Grusky also indicate how turnover among superordinates reduces conformity to organizational norms. In the mental hospital, Scheff notes that complaints about the turnover of ward physicians were raised in several ward meetings. He quotes the following complaint of a supervisory attendant about the ward physicians: "Just about the time we have them broken in to our ward, off they go to somewhere else" (Scheff, 1961: 94). Grusky is even more specific in his discussion of the executive control of military officers. He says, in summarizing his findings, that *"knowledge* of the military base . . . served to strengthen perceived authority . . . ." (1964a: 97, emphasis added).[10] A superordinate will not be able to enforce conformity to organizational norms unless he has knowledge of those norms and of the standard operating procedures of the area where the conformity is to be secured. Or again, a superordinate is not likely to achieve conformity unless he has feedback on the extent to which the norms are being followed. In Scheff's study, the attendant who complained about "breaking in" the physicians on the ward was actually complaining about the amount of attendants' time required to socialize the ward physicians and provide them with the knowledge required to operate the ward. Grusky's summary specifically refers to "knowledge of the military base." Superordinate turnover reduces conformity to organizational norms because it decreases the amount of knowledge superordinates have about the organization.

Summary. The diagram in Figure 2 depicts the three effects of turnover which are supported by a low amount of data.

The arrows in Figure 2 run only in one direction, from turnover to satisfaction, innovation, and conformity. Organization reality, of course, is hardly this simple. Links must be specified between the three effects.

Figure 2
THE EFFECTS OF TURNOVER ON
SATISFACTION, INNOVATION, AND CONFORMITY

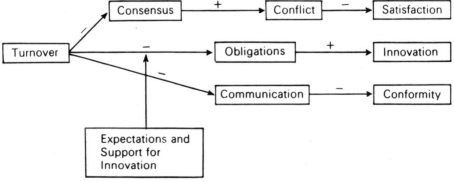

[10]In addition to knowledge, this quotation by Grusky also refers to the "integration of the officer" into the "organizational structure" of the base. The quotation about integration was excluded because one way to obtain knowledge is to be integrated into the structure of an organization. In short, nothing new would have been added, and some confusion would have been introduced, by adding the integration quotation.

Satisfaction, for example, probably produces increased conformity. Or again, innovation is commonly a source of dissatisfaction in organizations. Further research will have to specify and verify the multiple relationships among satisfaction, innovation, and conformity. The relationships between turnover and the three effects are also reciprocal. Turnover, for example, probably reduces satisfaction; this, in turn, probably serves to increase turnover (Price, 1975). Further research will also have to specify and verify these mutual exchanges.

The propositions summarized in Figure 2 probably are also related to the propositions summarized in Figure 1. If, for example, turnover weakens the primary groups of an organization (Figure 1), then it probably will also reduce satisfaction (Figure 2) because primary groups are often an important source of satisfaction for organization members. Or again, a relatively large administrative staff (Figure 1) probably will be able to secure greater conformity (Figure 2) to organizational norms. Further research will also have to specify and verify the relationships which exist between the two sets of propositions.

The bulk of the literature dealing with the effects of turnover, focusing as it does on costs (mostly monetary) and effectiveness, devotes relatively little time to the effects on satisfaction, innovation, and conformity. The virtue of a codification is again demonstrated. To systematically order the findings on the effects of turnover requires an examination of all the literature dealing with these effects. Such an examination, as it does in this instance, often yields relatively unemphasized relationships.

Literature dealing with satisfaction and conformity commonly assumes that these variables are positively related to effectiveness, with high degrees of both variables producing high degrees of effectiveness. Such an assumption appears plausible, as demonstrated by various citations in Price (1968). Satisfied employees, for example, should work harder and thereby increase effectiveness. Or again, organizational norms are primarily formed to increase effectiveness; therefore, conformity to these norms should bring about the intended effect.

Two comments may be made about these assumptions. First, the links between satisfaction and conformity, on the one hand, and effectiveness, on the other hand must be empirically demonstrated. The link between satisfaction and effectiveness is especially tenuous (Price, 1968: 5–6). Deviant behavior, in a great many instances, may increase effectiveness by promoting the ability to respond to situations unanticipated by organizational norms. These positive effects of deviance must be subtracted from the negative effects to arrive at a *net* balance of effects for effectiveness. Second, the increased innovation resulting from turnover may assist the organization in adapting to a changing environment and/or result in increased productivity, thereby enhancing effectiveness. Turnover's negative effects on satisfaction and conformity, if such effects are empirically demonstrated, must be subtracted from turnover's positive effects on innovation to arrive at a net assessment of turnover's impact on effectiveness. The point is that the relationship between turnover, satisfaction, and conformity is problematic rather than axiomatic.

TURNOVER AND ORGANIZATIONAL EFFECTIVENESS

The effect of turnover on effectiveness has been treated in the introductory comments and in the discussion of each of the two sets of propositions. This section examines the full range of data bearing on this phenomenon.

As indicated earlier, effectiveness is the degree to which an organization achieves its goal (s) (Price, 1972: 101–106). If a prison has a custodial goal, for example, and if it maintains a low escape rate among its inmates, it is an effective prison. A mental hospital which has a therapeutic goal is effective if it successfully releases a high proportion of its inmates into the community. Effectiveness is often equated with "performance" in much of the organizational literature.

Effectiveness must be distinguished from productivity, that is, the ratio of output to input (Fabricant, 1969: 3–11). A business firm whose goal is profits, as measured, for example, by the rate of return on investment, may attain a high degree of productivity, but, due to a declining market for its output, for example, suffer from a low rate of return on its investment, that is, low profitability. The business firm, in brief, is characterized by high productivity but low effectiveness. Effectiveness and productivity are probably positively related; however, the two concepts are different and can vary independently.

Positive Data

Two types of data support the idea that successively higher amounts of turnover probably produce successively lower amounts of effectiveness. The first type is certainly the most extensive, that describing the costs (usually monetary) of turnover for the organization.[11]

Various types of costs are described. Gaudet's (1960a: 39–57) widely cited discussion, for example, indicates four general types of costs: recruitment, selection and placement, on-the-job, and separation. Each general cost category includes a number of specific types of costs, and various procedures for calculating these costs are indicated. Gaudet, for example, refers to the replacement cost "method" and the "survey method" (1960a: 39–59). Since the costs of turnover vary by occupation, some studies attempt to arrive at cost estimates for different types of occupations (*i.e.*, Tuchi and Carr, 1971). Still another list of costs is presented by Canfield (1959).[12]

The cost literature can be conceptualized as reduced productivity. Most of the costs associated with turnover are input costs; they refer to resources used to produce the organization's output. Gaudet's costs of recruitment, selection-placement, and separation are examples of input

---

[11]Several reviews of the literature describe the costs of turnover for the organization, including Gaudet (1960a), Katzell, Korman, and Levine (1971), Moffatt and Hill (1970), and Pearce (1954). The best reviews are by Gaudet and Pearce.

[12]Grant W. Canfield, whose work is widely cited in discussions of the costs of turnover, is the manager, Orange Country Office, Merchants and Manufacturers Association, Garden Grove, California.

costs. Most of Gaudet's on-the-job costs are also input costs; however, some of the on-the-job costs are output costs because they refer to the amount of output produced (1960a: 51). Newer employees, for example, do not produce as much as older employees; hence, the output of the new employees is lower. Turnover may also reduce output by its "interruption of continuous and effective production time . . . ." (Moffatt and Hill, 1970: 147). Since productivity refers to the ratio of output to input, what the cost literature is asserting is that reduced productivity results from a high rate of turnover. The assumption, sometimes quite explicit, is that reduced productivity negatively influences effectiveness (Melbin and Taub, 1966; Pearce, 1954: 80–81; Scheer, 1962). The cost literature thus implicitly argues that turnover decreases productivity which, in turn, decreases effectiveness.

The second type of data supporting the idea that turnover reduces effectiveness are empirical studies which make no mention of costs. These studies support linear and curvilinear relationships between turnover and effectiveness. Consider the following five studies which seem to argue for a linear relationship between turnover and effectiveness.

1. The work of Grusky is again relevant. In a much-cited study of 16 professional baseball teams, he found a negative relationship between managerial succession and organizational effectiveness (Grusky, 1963).

2. Kahne's (1968) important but neglected study of a mental hospital indicates that turnover rates of hospital personnel are related to the times at which patients commit suicide. It is, according to Kahne, the *acquisition* of personnel rather than their *separation* which is related to patient suicide. As previously indicated, turnover includes both acquisitions and separations. The suicides of mental patients can be viewed as instances of ineffectiveness.

3. Revans (1964), in a study of 15 hospitals in Great Britain, notes that there "is some evidence to suggest that hospitals able to *retain their staffs* are also able to *discharge their patients more rapidly* . . . ." (p. 83, emphasis added). The staff in Revans' study refers to qualified nurses. Hospitals which can retain their staffs are characterized by low turnover. Revans implies that more rapid treatment indicates better patient care, or improved effectiveness.

4. Burling, Lentz, and Wilson's (1956) study of six medical hospitals states that a "force which influenced *standards of nursing care* was the rapid *turnover* of personnel . . . ." (pp. 105–106, emphasis added). Standards of nursing care refer to the quality of patient care and thus deals with effectiveness.

5. Finally, Christensen's (1953) study of over 100 small manufacturing firms describes the problems that top management succession, some of which was turnover, created in maintaining profitability. Some of the problems could have been mitigated by proper planning, but it is clear that change in the chief executives threatened profitability in the small manufacturing firms studied by Christensen. Trow's (1961) analysis of Christensen's study is also useful in understanding this phenomenon.

Kahne (1968) dealt with the problem of how the acquisition of new hospital personnel was linked to patient suicide. The following statement is relevant:

> If personnel values are to be *transmitted* effectively to the patients, the patients' perspectives *communicated* to their caretakers, and an accurate *evaluation* of these made by all who are involved, the participants must be present in appropriate proportions to each other long enough to develop *reliable techniques for effective interchange* and a sense of personal relatedness . . . (p. 259, emphasis added).

According to Kahne, the acquisition of new personnel reduced the amount of accurate information communicated; thus, reliable techniques for effective interchange were not developed between the new personnel and the patients. The result was "increased suicide among the most vulnerable participants—the patients" (p. 259). Turnover (acquisitions, in this case) had a negative impact on communication which, in turn, reduced effectiveness.

Three empirical studies provide data which support a curvilinear relationship between turnover and effectiveness.

1. Eitzen and Yetman (1972), in a study of college basketball teams, attempted to replicate Grusky's research on baseball teams. They note that "the longer the coaching *tenure*, the greater the likelihood that a coach will be *successful*, but . . . there is a certain length of time (thirteen years or more) beyond which effectiveness begins to decline" (p. 110, emphasis added). If turnover (tenure) increases effectiveness (a successful coach) for a limited period of time, after which effectiveness begins to decline, then turnover and effectiveness are related in a curvilinear manner.

2. Wells and Pelz (1966), in a study of 83 research and development work groups (49 in business and 34 in government), found "a curvilinear effect for *usefulness*, peaking at 4 to 5 years of *group age* . . . ." (p. 241, emphasis added). Group age is relevant to turnover (a low age indicates high turnover), and usefulness, though undefined in the research, seems to be pertinent to effectiveness.

3. The school superintendents studied by Carlson (1962) "see long *tenure* as detrimental to the *development* of the school system . . . ." (p. 67, emphasis added). Development in the context of Carlson's study clearly refers to effectiveness (pp. 61–67). If short tenure by a superintendent promotes the development of a school system, whereas long tenure retards its development, then turnover and effectiveness are related in a curvilinear manner.

Summary. There is certainly an impressive amount of data supporting the idea that successively higher amounts of turnover probably produce successively lower amounts of effectiveness. First, there is a massive amount of data documenting the costs of turnover for the organization. These costs are conceptualized in this paper as reduced productivity. The clear assumption of the literature is that decreased productivity decreases effectiveness. Second, there is a sizable body of literature which, although it does not describe costs as such, supports a relationship between turnover and effectiveness. Five studies support a linear relationship, and three studies support a curvilinear relationship between turnover and effectiveness.

Ordinarily, such a volume of data supporting a proposition would guarantee its inclusion in the codification. There is more data supporting this proposition than there is for any of the first three propositions in this paper. There is, however, an impressive amount of negative data which must be examined.

Negative Data

There are five different types of data which, in one way or another, contradict the idea that turnover reduces effectiveness.

The first set of data is an argument which asserts that the cost data assumes, but does not empirically demonstrate, a relationship between turnover, productivity (to use the conceptualization of this paper), and effectiveness. It is not sufficient to assert, so runs this argument, that turnover, by reducing productivity, decreases effectiveness; the relationship must be empirically demonstrated, rather than merely asserted.

The second set of data is a critique (Gamson and Scotch, 1964) of Grusky's (1963) study of 16 professional baseball teams, a study which is widely cited in support of the idea that turnover reduces effectiveness. Gamson and Scotch, in a reanalysis of Grusky's data, argue that managerial change has little effect on team performance.[13] Like Gamson and Scotch, Eitzen and Yetman's (1972) study of college basketball teams argues that coaching shifts do not affect team performance. The second set of data neutralizes some of the support for the idea that turnover reduces effectiveness.

The third set of negative data consists of two studies which found no support for the idea that turnover depresses effectiveness. Pomeroy and Yahr (1967), in a study of the effects of caseworker turnover on welfare clients, state that their "initial research hypothesis, *that high turnover is associated with low performance levels*, has not been borne out . . . " (p. 45, emphasis added). Turnover in Pomeroy and Yahr's research refers to the number of different caseworkers per client (p. 9). A caseworker who changed clients did not necessarily leave the public welfare agency; the caseworker may, for example, have been assigned to other clients within the agency. However, from the client's perspective, both turnover and a changed assignment had the same effect—a different caseworker. Pomeroy and Yahr's data are thus relevant to the effects of turnover. "Performance," as is often the case, is very close in meaning to effectiveness (p. 12).

Mueller (1969), in studying the effects of teacher turnover on student achievement, found no significant differences between turnover and achievement in nine out of twelve tests of the proposition.[14] Achievement in

---

[13]Grusky's (1964b) "Reply" to Gamson and Scotch is also relevant. The reply immediately follows the Gamson and Scotch critique.

[14]This author's conclusion differs from Mueller's. Mueller is apparently of the opinion that, "teacher turnover was a statistically significant source of variance in student achievement" (1969:154). This opinion is reflected in the abstract of the dissertation where reference is made to three "statistically significant" findings. However, an analysis of the dissertation itself reveals that Mueller could not disprove nine out of twelve of his null hypotheses. The three null hypotheses that he could disprove are apparently the basis for his three "statistically significant" findings cited in the abstract. One cannot properly conclude that teacher turnover produces varia-

Mueller's research refers to, "the scores that students obtain on the Science Research Associates Achievement tests for grades 4 and 6" (p. 9). Achievement in reading and arithmetic were two of the three areas measured by the tests. Since schools are oriented to accomplishing this type of achievement goal, Mueller's data are relevant to effectiveness.

The fourth set of negative data consist of four studies, the results of which can be interpreted as supporting the idea that turnover *increases* rather than decreases effectiveness.

1. The previously cited work by Wells and Pelz (1966) (studying 83 research and development work groups) examined scientific contribution as well as usefulness. They found "a general decline in *scientific contribution* as *group age* increased . . . ." (p. 241, emphasis added). Increased group age means decreased turnover; and a decline in scientific contribution, though undefined, certainly would seem to be relevant to the effectiveness of groups in research and development work. Low turnover in these work groups appears to decrease effectiveness.

2. Guest's (1962b) study of the automobile plant found that by "every measure of performance . . . [the automobile plant] . . . improved following the succession of the new manager . . ." (p.54). Most of Guest's measures of performance are relevant to effectiveness (1962a:97–107).[15]

3. Torrence (1965), in a laboratory study of three-man bomber crews, found that temporary crews produced a higher percentage of correct solutions to an arithmetical problem than did permanent crews.[16] Permanent crews had been together for several months, whereas temporary crews had not previously served together. The permanent and temporary crews, respectively, approximate low and high turnover situations. The correct solutions to an arithmetical problem may be an indication of ability to work together to solve combat problems. If such be the case, it is relevant to effectiveness. Torrence, therefore, found that laboratory groups with high turnover (temporary crews) have higher effectiveness (correct solutions to an arithmetic problem) than laboratory groups with low turnover (permanent crews).

4. Ziller, Behringer, and Goodchilds (1962), in a laboratory study of creativity, state that "groups which experienced membership changes (*open groups*) were more *creative* than the stable groups (*closed groups*)" (p. 43, emphasis added). Open and closed groups, respectively, approximate high and low turnover situations. In this study, creativity was measured by the ability to write clever or amusing captions for a *Saturday Evening Post* cartoon within a time limit of five minutes (p. 45). This type of creativity

---

tion in student achievement when the null hypothesis could not be disproved nine out of twelve times! This author, therefore, concludes that Mueller finds no relationship between teacher turnover and student achievement.

[15]Most of Guest's (1962a:97–107) measures of performance are indications of productivity. Productivity is probably positively related to effectiveness. See Price (1968) for some supporting data.

[16]Torrence (1965:601–603) gave each three-man crew four decision-making problems. The arithmetical problem referred to here is the one he calls the "Maier Horse-Trading Problem."

may be related to certain types of problem-solving tasks in organizations, such as advertising agencies, and, if such be the case, is relevant to effective-ness. Ziller and his colleagues found that laboratory groups with high turnover (open groups) had higher effectiveness (were more creative) than laboratory groups with low turnover (closed groups).

The fifth and final set of negative data consists primarily of two very provocative laboratory studies by Trow (1964, 1960).[17] The two main findings are as follows:

> It was found that team *performance* did not vary with the *mean rate of replacement*, but did vary with the *variability of the rate*, the perfor-mance of a team tending to decrease when the number of positions in which replacements occurred was greater than usual for the team. The impact of replacement was also conditioned by the *ability* of the successors, the teams' performance tending to decrease if the successors were below average in general intelligence and to remain relatively constant if they were above average . . . (1960:268, emphasis added).

Up to this point, this paper has stressed only the amount of turnover, whether it was high or low. This is what Trow refers to as the "mean rate of replace-ment." What is most significant about Trow's experiments are his findings with respect to the variability of the rate, rather than the mean rate, as the variable that produces a decline in effectiveness (performance, in Trow's experiments). McNeil and Thompson (1971) also provide support for this idea.

In short, it is not the *absolute* amount of turnover which is significant for effectiveness, but whether or not there is *variability* in the amount of turnover. None of the propositions to this point has specified conditions, such as Trow's "ability."[18]

Summary and Conclusions

An impressive amount of data thus contradict, in various ways, the idea that successively higher amounts of turnover probably produce succes-sively lower amounts of effectiveness. The criticism exists that the massive literature about the costs of turnover asserts—but does empirically demons-trate—the relationships between turnover, productivity, and effectiveness. There is also the criticism, buttressed by one study, of Grusky's widely cited research supporting the idea that turnover reduces effectiveness. There are the results of two studies which find no support for the idea that turnover depresses effectiveness. There are the results of four studies whose data seem to indicate that turnover increases, rather than decreases, effectiveness.

---

[17]Trow's 1964 study is basically a replication of the 1960 study. The 1964 study also considers succession when a "control position" is involved and finds that this condition is important. Also relevant is Trow's (1961) article on executive succession.

[18]Trow (1964, 1960) refers to "ability" and "intelligence" in the laboratory studies. The correct reference should be to intelligence, since this is what he clearly measures. Trow's (1961) article, the analysis of Christensen's (1953) study of management succession, refers to "ability." Ability is an accurate reference in the 1961 work.

Finally, there are data from two studies which support the idea that it is the rate of change in turnover, rather than the absolute amount of turnover, which produces the impact on effectiveness.

Three concluding comments can be made about turnover and effectiveness. First, it would not be appropriate, given the contradictory nature of the data, to include in the codification a proposition indicating that turnover reduces effectiveness. More work is obviously needed, both in the area of better-designed research and in the formation of theory, to resolve the contradictions in the data.

Second, although the relationship may be weaker in some situations than in others, four of the six propositions in the codification support, in varying degrees, the idea that successively higher amounts of turnover will produce successively lower amounts of effectiveness. The positive data presented in this section also support this relationship. There are also situations where turnover certainly promotes the achievement of organizational goals. When the positive effects are subtracted from the negative effects, this author predicts that the net balance of effects will show that successively higher amounts of turnover, more often than not, produce successively lower amounts of effectiveness.

Third, the value of a codification is again demonstrated. This author, like most researchers in the field, initially believed that the data strongly supported the idea that turnover reduces effectiveness. This belief persisted even *after* the literature had been reviewed! The first proposition of the codification would indicate that turnover reduces effectiveness and, unlike the other propositions, would be supported by a large amount of data. *It was not until an effort had been made to codify the impact of turnover on effectiveness that the author became aware of the amount and variety of negative data which he had read and duly recorded.* Entrenched ideas stubbornly resist disturbance, and it took the exacting requirements of a codification to clearly reveal the problematic nature of the relationship between turnover and decreased effectiveness.

OVERALL SUMMARY AND CONCLUSIONS

Summary

The effects of turnover on effectiveness are summarized in the following six propositions:

Medium Amount of Support

1. Successively higher amounts of turnover probably produce successively higher porportions of administrative staff members relative to production staff members.

2. Successively higher amounts of turnover probably produce successively higher amounts of formalization.

3. Successively higher amounts of turnover probably produce

successively lower amounts of participation in primary groups.

Low Amount of Support

4. Successively higher amounts of turnover probably produce successively lower amounts of satisfaction.

5. Successively higher amounts of turnover probably produce successively higher amounts of innovation.

6. Successively higher amounts of turnover among superordinates probably produce successively lower amounts of conformity.

Intervening processes are also indicated. Turnover, by increasing the work load of an organization, increases the relative size of its administrative staff. Turnover, by its negative impact on consensus and control, increases formalization. Turnover appears to reduce the amount of participation in primary groups without an intervening process. Turnover, by its negative impact on consensus and conflict, decreases satisfaction. Turnover, because it is accompanied by the expectation of and support for innovation by the powerholders in the organization, and because it results in a reduced number of obligations, increases innovation. Finally, superordinate turnover, because of its disruption of the communication process, reduces the amount of conformity.

This paper also summarizes a large and impressive body of literature which supports the idea that successively higher amounts of turnover probably produce successively lower amounts of effectiveness. Equally large and impressive, however, is another set of summarized literature which in various ways contradicts the idea that turnover decreases effectiveness. The two sets of literature neutralize each other, and the paper concludes that no proposition can be advanced at this time concerning the effects of turnover on effectiveness. *The relationship between turnover and effectiveness is problematic rather than axiomatic.* It is the belief of this author, however, that, more often than not, the negative impact of turnover on effectiveness will be greater than the positive impact. In short, this author believes that, in its net effect, turnover generally reduces effectiveness.

Conclusions

Six suggestions for further research on the effects of turnover on the organization emerge from this codification.

1. Systematic verification of the propositions is urgently required. The literature on turnover is truly massive. Three bibliographies in particular, Gaudet (1960b), Institute of Manpower Studies (1973), and Pettman (1973), provide a rough approximation of the wealth of data available on this topic. Turnover research, of a fairly rigorous nature, goes back to approximately 1900; it includes data from many countries (though its focus is mostly Western); it encompasses the work of specialists from a variety of disciplines and applied areas; it examines the operation of many types of organizations (though its emphasis is mostly on manufacturing

organizations); and it contains data about all types of occupations (though its special concern has been with manual occupations). And most of this massive literature has been prompted by the presumed effects of turnover, especially the widespread belief that turnover reduces effectiveness. Not only has this literature remained uncodified, but there is only amazingly weak support for its propositions. This is especially true of the most significant proposition, the presumed impact on effectiveness.

2. Verification of the propositions should focus on *rates* of turnover. Much of the research relevant to the effects of turnover investigates the problem by studying turnover among the chief executives of organizations. This is certainly a defensible strategy, since the effects of turnover probably are magnified several times (and are thus much more visible) when the chief executive is replaced by an outsider. It might be very difficult to observe comparable effects, though the effects may be present, if the turnover of lesser executives and nonexecutives were studied. However, initial explorations have been conducted; the problem has been opened. It is now appropriate to study the effects of turnover for all organizational members, and one way to do this is to study variations in the rates of turnover. The work of Kasarda (1973) indicates the direction. There is, however, no reason to restrict research to nonexperimental designs, such as those used by Kasarda. Various types of experimental designs are certainly appropriate, as has been demonstrated by Trow (1964, 1960).

3. The *strength* of the different effects must be assessed in the verification research. Though this paper may classify the six propositions into medium- and low-support categories, the classificaton is impressionistic, rather than systematic. The extent to which turnover effects the different variables must be specified empirically. Ultimately, the variables should be ranked by the degree to which they are influenced by turnover.

4. Additional relationships must be specified and, utlimately, verified. This paper, given its purpose, has focused almost totally on the effects of turnover on seven dependent variables; however, it is noted that organizational reality is considerably more complicated. The effects mutually influence each other, and some of the effects have an impact on turnover. In short, the results must be progressively complicated.

5. It may be advisable to lower the level of abstraction in the propositions. The sixth proposition, for example, refers not only to turnover, but to turnover among superordinates. It is turnover among superordinates which particularly seems to promote reduced conformity. This type of reduced abstraction may characterize the other propositions and should be investigated.

6. Finally, interaction effects should be investigated. Turnover, for example, may have markedly different effects on effectiveness when different degrees of routinization are involved (Price, 1972: 150–155). Situations of very low and very high routinization (the established professional and the unskilled blue-collar worker, respectively) may not experience drastic reductions in effectiveness with high turnover because little communication of knowledge is involved. The established professional is already trained when employed by the organization, and the unskilled

blue collar worker requires little training. The work of the established professional—and here the work of Torrence (1965), Wells and Pelz (1966), and Ziller, Behringer, and Goodchilds (1962) comes to mind—may also benefit from the stimulation provided by the arrival of new colleagues. Turnover may be most dysfunctional for effectiveness where medium amounts of routinization are involved. Turnover may also have a considerably different impact on effectiveness when different degrees of formalization are involved.[19] A highly formalized organization may not experience the reduction in effectiveness that is produced by high turnover in a less formalized organization. Formalization may provide an organization with one means to manage the adverse effects produced by turnover. (A relatively large administrative staff is another means to contain the negative effects produced by turnover.) The investigation of interaction effects, such as routinization and formalization, would appear to be a fruitful topic for further research.

REFERENCES

Blau, P. M. *The Organization of Academic Work*. New York: John Wiley and Sons.
1973

————. "Formal Organizations: Dimensions of Analysis." *American Journal*
1957 *of Sociology*, 63:58–69.

Burling, T., E. Lentz, and R. N. Wilson. *The Give and Take in Hospitals*. New York:
1956 G. P. Putnam's Sons.

Burns, T., and G. M. Stalker. *The Management of Innovation*. Chicago: Quadrangle
1961 Books.

Canfield, G. W. "How to Compute Your Labor Turnover Costs." *Personnel Journal*,
1959 37:413–417.

Carlson, R. O. *Executive Succession and Organizational Change*. Chicago: Midwest
1962 Administration Center, University of Chicago.

————. "Succession and Performance Among School Superintendents."
1961 *Administrative Science Quarterly*, 6:210–227.

Christensen, C. R. *Management Succession in Small and Growing Enterprises*.
1953 Boston: Division of Research, Graduate School of Business Administration,
Harvard University.

Dahrendorf, R. *Class and Class Conflict in Industrial Society*. Stanford, Calif.:
1959 Stanford University Press.

Downs, A. "The Successes and Failures of Federal Housing Policy." *The Public*
1974 *Interest*, 34: 124–145.

Dubin, R. "Management in Britain—Impressions of a Visiting Professor." *Journal*
1970 *of Management Studies*, 7:183–198.

Eitzen, D. S., and N. R. Yetman. "Managerial Change, Longevity, and Organizational
1972 Effectiveness." *Administrative Science Quarterly*, 17:110–116.

Fabricant, S. *A Primer on Productivity*. New York: Random House.
1969

Gamson, W. A., and N. A. Scotch. "Scapegoating in Baseball." *American Journal*
1964 *of Sociology*, 70:69–72.

Gaudet, F. J. *Labor Turnover*. New York: American Management Association.
1960a Research Study 39.

————. *The Literature on Labor Turnover*. New York: Industrial Relations
1960b Newsletter, Inc.

---

[19]This idea, though in a different form, is suggested by Grusky (1959:463). He refers not to formalization, but to bureaucratization.

Gouldner, A. W.   *Patterns of Industrial Bureaucracy.* Glencoe, Ill.: The Free Press.
1954

————————.   "The Problem of Succession in Bureaucracy." In R. K. Merton, A. P.
1952   Gray, B. Hockey, and H. C. Selvin (eds.), *Reader in Bureaucracy:* 339–351.
          Glencoe, Ill.: The Free Press.

Grusky, O.   "The Effects of Succession: A Comparative Study of Military and
1964a   Business Organizations." In M. Janowitz (ed.), *The New Military.* New
          York: Russell Sage Foundation.

————————.   "Reply to Gamson and Scotch's Critique." *American Journal of Socio-
1964b   logy,* 70:72–76.

————————.   "Managerial Succession and Organizational Effectiveness." *American
1963   Journal of Sociology,* 69:21–31.

————————.   "Administrative Succession in Formal Organizations." *Social Forces,*
1960   39:105–115.

————————.   "Role Conflict in Organization: A Study of Prison Camp Officials."
1959   *Administrative Science Quarterly,* 3:452–472.

Guest, R. H.   *Organizational Change.* Homewood, Ill.: Richard D. Irwin, Inc.
1962a

————————.   "Managerial Succession in Complex Organizations." *American Journal
1962b   of Sociology,* 68:47–56.

Harechmak, J. R.   "The Relationship Between Hospital Staff Turnover and Noso-
1974   comial Infections." Unpublished Ph.D. dissertation. Iowa City: University
          of Iowa.

Institute of Manpower Studies.   *Labor Wastage Bibliography.* Brighton, England:
1973   Institute of Manpower Studies, University of Sussex.

Kahne, M. J.   "Suicides in Mental Hospitals: A Study of the Effects of Personnel
1968   and Patient Turnover." *Journal of Health and Social Behavior,* 9:255–266.

Kasarda, J. D.   "Effects of Personnel Turnover, Employee Qualifications, and
1973   Professional Staff Ratios on Administrative Intensity and Overhead."
          The Sociological Quarterly, 14:350–358.

Katzell, R. A., A. K. Korman, and E. L. Levine.   *Overview Study of the Dynamics
1971   of Worker Job Mobility.* Washington, D. C.: Social and Rehabilitation
          Service, Department of Health, Education and Welfare.

McCleery, R. H.   *Policy Change in Prison Management.* East Lansing, Mich.:
1957   Bureau of Social and Political Research, College of Business and Public
          Service, Michigan State University.

McNeil, K., and J. D. Thompson.   "The Regeneration of Social Organizations."
1971   *American Sociological Review,* 36:624–637.

Melbin, M., and D. L. Taub.   "The High Cost of Replacing a Nurse." *Hospitals,*
1966   40:112–122.

Merchants and Manufacturers Association.   *Labor Turnover.* Los Angles: Merchants
1959   and Manufacturers Association.

Merton, R. K.   *Social Theory and Social Structure.* Glencoe, Ill.: The Free Press.
1957

Merwe, R. van der, and S. Miller.   "Near-Terminal Labor Turnover: An Analysis
1973   of a Crisis Situation." *Human Relations,* 26:415–432.

Moffatt, G. W. B., and K. Hill.   "Labor Turnover in Australia—A Review of Research,
1970   Part 1." *Personnel Practice Bulletin,* 26:142–149.

Moskos, C. C., Jr.   *The American Enlisted Man.* New York: Russell Sage Foundation.
1970

Mueller, E. H.   "The Relationship Between Teacher Turnover and Student Achieve-
1969   ment." Unpublished Ph.D. dissertation. Charlotsville, Va.: University
          of Virginia.

Parnes, H. S.   *Research on Labor Mobility.* New York: Social Science Research
1954   Council.

Pearce, F. T.   *Financial Effects of Labor Turnover.* Birmingham, England: Research
1954   Board, Faculty of Commerce and Social Science, University of Birmingham.

Pettman, B. O.   *Wastage Analysis: A Selected International and Temporal Biblio-*

1973   *graphy*. Hull, England: Emmasglen, Ltd.

Pomeroy, R., and H. Yahr.   *Studies in Public Welfare*. New York: The Center for the
1967   Study of Urban Problems, Graduate Division, Bernard M. Baruch College,
          The City University of New York.

Price, J. L.   "The Correlates of Turnover." *International Journal of Manpower*,
in   in press.
press

——————   "Toward a Theory of Turnover." In B. O. Pettman (ed.), *Labor Turnover*
1975   *and Retention*. Epping, Essex, England: Gower Press.

——————   *Handbook of Organizational Measurement*. Lexington, Mass.: D. C.
1972   Heath and Co.

——————   *Organizational Effectiveness*. Homewood, Ill.: Richard D. Irwin, Inc.
1968

Revans, R. W.   *Standards for Morale*. London: Oxford University Press.
1964

Scheer, W. E.   "Reduce Turnover—Increase Profits." *Personnel Journal*, 41:559–561.
1962

Scheff, T. J.   "Control Over Policy by Attendants in a Mental Hospital." *Journal*
1961   *of Health and Human Behavior*, 2:93–105.

Torrence, E. P.   "Some Consequences of Power Differences on Decision Making
1965   in Permanent and Temporary Three-Man Groups." In A. P. Hare, E. F.
          Borgatta, and R. F. Bales (eds.), *Small Groups*: 600–609. New York:
          Alfred Knopf.

Trow, D. B.   "Teamwork Under Turnover and Succession." Technical Report No. 2
1964   Springfield, Va.: National Technical Information Service.

——————.   "Executive Succession in Small Companies." *Administrative Science*
1961   *Quarterly*, 6:228–239.

——————.   "Membership Succession and Team Performance." *Human Relations*,
1960   13:259–269.

Tuchi, B. J., and B. E. Carr.   "Labor Turnover." *Hospitals*,   45:88–92.
1971

Uyeki, E. S.   "Draftee Behavior in the Cold-War Army." *Social Problems*, 8:151–158.
1960

Wells, W. P., and D. C. Pelz.   "Groups." In D. C. Pelz and F. Andrews (eds.),
1966   *Scientists in Organizations*: 240–260. New York: John Wiley and Sons.

Woodhouse, R. H.   "An Essay on the Effects of Turnover: A Study of Effectiveness."
1973   Unpublished paper. Iowa City: University of Iowa.

Ziller, R. C., R. D. Behringer, and J. D. Goodchilds.   "Group Creativity Under
1962   Conditions of Success or Failure and Variations in Group Stability."
          Journal of Applied Psychology, 46:43–49.

Employee Performance in Japanese Firms: An Explanation

ROBERT M. MARSH
Brown University

HIROSHI MANNARI
Kwansei Gakuin University
Nishinomiya, Japan

INTRODUCTION

The effectiveness of organizations and the performance of their members have been central theoretical issues at least since Weber. This is no accident, of course, since organizations typically have been defined as seeking to achieve goals. Thus, Price (1972: 101, 1968) defines an organization's effectiveness as the degree to which it achieves its goals. An organization's goal is defined, following Etzioni (1964: 6), as "a desired state of affairs which the organization attempts to realize."

Attempts to measure effectiveness or performance have met with certain difficulties. One problem is posed by the fact that different members of an organization may, even within the context of the organization, pursue different goals. We shall handle this problem by defining organizational goals as those goals which the major decision makers pursue. A second measurement problem is the difficulty of developing a general measure of effectiveness that is applicable to profit-making and nonprofit organizations, to manufacturing as well as to "people-processing" service organizations, etc. We do not resolve this problem; but by focusing on only one type of organization—manufacturing firms—we are able to use comparable measures of effectiveness.

Relatively little has been done in the cross-national study of organizational effectiveness. By analyzing two Japanese firms, we hope to contribute to this area.

Another objective of this paper is to attempt to test *alternative theories* of organizational performance. Three theories are considered: cultural-relativist theory, structural theory, and human relations theory. All too often in the social sciences, the analysis deploys only one theory or explanation of a given phenomenon. Although this may be confirmed and may appear to account for the observed relationships, there usually are one or more alternative explanations which could equally well account for the facts. Stinchcombe (1968) has urged the deliberate attempt to deploy theories which make *different* predictions concerning a given phenomenon, a strategy which would enable us to *reject* some theories. Our attempt in this area is twofold: when the propositions of two or more of these theories make the *same* predictions concerning performance, we shall explore the extent to which this "unified theory" can explain performance. When the theories make *different* predictions concerning performance, our interest will be in rejecting a theory which appears to be less capable than another theory in accounting for the facts.

DATA AND METHODS

Electric Company and Shipbuilding Company, the names given to the two firms studied, are each among the five leading firms (in terms of sales) in Japan in their respective industries—household electrical appliances, and shipbuilding and heavy machinery. Each company has plants located in various parts of Japan; we studied one in each company. The one we call the Electric Factory is located in a small city with a rural hinterland northwest of Kobe; the one we call the Shipbuilding Factory is in metropolitan Osaka. The authors collaborated in field work of three months' duration in each factory, conducted between July, 1969, and February, 1970. Data were collected from four sources: (a) observation of work and nonwork activities of factory personnel; (b) company personnel and production records; (c) interviewing individual personnel at various hierarchical levels; and (d) a questionnaire distributed to all production, staff, and managerial personnel. Completion rates for the questionnaire were 86 percent in the Electric Factory and 79 percent in the Shipbuilding Factory.

The Shipbuilding Company dates from the latter part of the nineteenth century. In 1969, its 18,000 employees were engaged in the construction of a variety of types of ships (supertankers, naval craft, etc.) and heavy land machinery for industrial use, such as cement mills, sugar plants, and steel structures. The plant studied has 756 employees and specializes in building diesel and turbine engines for ships, as well as industrial machinery. The technology is nonautomated and the work force consists primarily of highly skilled machinists and less-skilled assemblers.

The Electric Company was established at the end of World War II; as a result of the postwar Japanese "household electrical appliance boom," it has already attained a commanding sales position among Japanese firms in any industrial category. The Electric Company has developed extensive product diversification within the category of household appliances; the plant studied specializes in the production of electric fans, vacuum cleaners, and other small appliances. The company had 13,500 employees in 1969, 1,200 of whom worked in the plant studied. Though moving in the direction of greater automation, the factory studied in 1969 was still based mainly upon classical assembly line batch production technology. The majority of workers perform highly fractionated, repetitive tasks, although there are some complex lathes and other machines (run by men).

MEASUREMENT OF PERFORMANCE

Conceptually, the dependent variable called organizational effectiveness has two components. The goals of economic organizations are productivity and sales and, if they are part of a capitalist economy, profits. This component of effectiveness is measured in terms of *labor productivity*. To achieve these goals, organizations must also meet ancillary or subsidiary goals: a low rate of absenteeism, suggestions from employees which improve efficiency, and eliciting a desire among employees to fulfill production goals. These form the second component of organizational effectiveness, which we call *employee performance* and investigate in this paper.

The first of five variables with which we measure performance is attendance. Table 1, column 1 shows that only a small minority of employees in either factory were absent one or more days in excess of the number of their legitimate vacation days during the previous year. (In both factories, employees are entitled to more days' paid vacation as their seniority increases.) In other words, levels of attendance are so relatively high that the real variations are in terms of how many of one's *vacation* days one reports for work. (On each of those days one receives vacation pay and an extra day's pay for working.) On this variable, the Electric Factory employees work significantly more of their paid vacation days than do the Shipbuilding Factory employees ($C/C_{max} = .21$).[1]

Variables 2 through 4 in Table 1 concern the suggestion system. Although the Electric Factory employees claim they "think about making suggestions" somewhat *less* often than those in Shipbuilding ($C/C_{max} = .17$), they are much *more* likely than those in Shipbuilding to have made five or more suggestions during the preceding year ($C/C_{max} = .47$). Yet, the amount of award money for suggestions is significantly higher in the Shipbuilding Factory ($C/C_{max} = .56$).

These differences in award money are probably related to the technological and economic scale and complexity of the two factories. A suggestion is more likely to involve larger and more complex tools, machinery, and products in shipbuilding than in the manufacture of such products as fans and vacuum clearners. Although employees give more suggestions in the Electric Factory, the typical suggestion involves relatively minor and small-scale adjustments and thus brings a smaller money award than in the Shipbuilding Factory.

The fifth performance variable in Table 1 shows no significant differences between Electric and Shipbuilding factory personnel concerning the extent to which they are "anxious to fulfill each day's production goal." The modal

---

[1]C/C_{max} is a measure of the strength of relationship between variables which corrects for C, the coefficient of contingency. $C\sqrt{\dfrac{X^2}{X^2 + N}}$ C equals O when the variables are independent, but its upper limit depends on the number of rows and columns and is always less than 1.00. C/C_{max} corrects for this by dividing the value of C by the maximum value of C, $\dfrac{k-1}{k}$ where k is the number of rows or columns, whichever is smaller.

Table 1

MEASURES OF PERFORMANCE OF ELECTRIC AND SHIPBUILDING FACTORY EMPLOYEES (IN PERCENTAGES)

	Electric Factory	Shipbuilding Factory
1. Attendance (number of days absent in relation to the number of legitimate vacation days during the previous year).		
worked 8 or more days of vacation	41.8	43.1
worked 4–7 days of vacation	30.3	18.7
worked 1–3 days of vacation	21.6	26.0
absent one day or more than number of legitimate vacation days	6.3	12.2
N (= 100%)	1,033	566
$P < .01$ C/C $_{max} = .21$		
2. How often do you think about making suggestions?		
always	18.5	17.9
sometimes	60.0	67.6
rarely	19.3	11.0
not at all	2.1	3.5
N (= 100%)	1,030	593
$P < .01$ C/C $_{max} = .17$		
3. How many times have you submitted suggestions during the past 12 months?		
0–2 times	31.8	66.8
3–4 times	31.8	22.2
5–11 times	31.2	8.9
12 or more times	5.2	2.1
N (= 100%)	1,033	585
$P < .01$ C/C $_{max} = .47$		
4. During the past year, how much award money did you receive for suggestions (total amt.)?		
¥ 0	65.3	31.6
¥ 499 or less	20.9	14.2
¥ 500 or more	13.8	54.2
N (= 100%)	1,033	572
$P < .01$ C/C $_{max} = .56$		
5. Are you anxious to fulfill each day's production goal?		
very anxious	22.9	21.6
fairly anxious	42.3	48.1
not very anxious	31.4	26.4
not anxious at all	3.4	3.9
N.S. N (= 100%)	1,027	594

response in both factories is "fairly anxious," and approximately two-thirds of the employees in each factory say they are either "very anxious" or "fairly anxious" to fulfill production goals.[2]

Table 2 presents a matrix of relationships between all pairs of these performance variables in each factory. All relationships are positive; all but two are statistically significant, and in strength they range from weak (C/C_{max} = .12) to strong (.78).

Since variables 1, 3, and 4 measure *actual* or objective performance, in contrast to variables 2 and 5, which are more subjective aspects of performance, we computed the mean association: (a) between all pairs of objective performance variables; (b) between the subjective performance variables; and (c) between all objective and all subjective performance variables. These were:

	$\overline{X}$ Electric Factory	C/C_{max} Shipbuilding Factory
1. Objective performance variables (awards for suggestions, number of suggestions, attendance);	.31	.40
2. Subjective performance variables (production goal, thinks of suggestions);	.57	.43
3. Relationship between objective performance variables and each subjective performance variable.	.25	.30

When objective performance variables are correlated with each other, or when subjective performance variables are correlated with each other, there are somewhat stronger relationships than when objective variables are correlated with subjective variables. Thus, we may tentatively conclude that performance contains two somewhat distinct subclusters of variables, an objective and a subjective performance cluster. There is considerable independent variation between employees' *claims* to being concerned about suggestions and production goals, on the one hand, and their objective performance, on the other.

The five performance variables were subjected to item analysis by means of a computer program, ITEMA. Taken together, they form our performance index. The index's alpha coefficient of reliability is 0.57 in

---

[2]To our mild surprise, we even encountered the phenomenon of the rate-breaker and the attendant social interaction between the rate-breaker and his fellow workers in the Shipbuilding Factory. A 55-year old worker, about to retire after 22 years' service, said: "I'm seen by my fellow workers as a rate-breaker because I try to finish a blueprint job in eight hours, then go home. My fellow workers want to stretch out the same amount of work into the evening and get overtime pay, so I have a low evaluation among them."

Table 2

**RELATIONSHIPS AMONG PERFORMANCE VARIABLES IN
ELECTRIC AND SHIPBUILDING FACTORIES** [a]

Variable	2	3	4	5
1. Attendance	.34**	.30**	.19**	.34**
	.21*	.20	.21**	.23**
2. Thinks of suggestions		.30**	.16**	.57**
		.50**	.42**	.43**
3. Number of suggestions			.44**	.21**
			.78**	.21
4. Awards for suggestions				.12*
				.25**
5. Production goal				

[a] Upper number in each cell is C/C_{max} for Electric Factory employees; lower number is the C/C_{max} for Shipbuilding Factory employees.
  *Significant at the .05 level.
  **Significant at the .01 level.

the Electric Factory and 0.57 in the Shipbuilding Factory. Performance index scores range from a low of 5 to a high of 20. The mean score in the Electric Factory is 12.5, with a standard deviation of 2.5; the comparable figures for the Shipbuilding Factory are 12.9 and 2.8.

Before attempting to explain performance, we should note some evidence for the *validity* of our index of performance. That the index does in fact measure effectiveness is indicated when we compare the labor productivity of the five production sections in the Electric Factory. Labor productivity is a company measure, constructed entirely independently of our measure of performance. Described more fully elsewhere (Marsh and Mannari, 1976), labor productivity measures basically the number of units produced per worker per month. Our data show that employees in the sections with higher labor productivity have significantly higher performance index scores (C/C_{max} = .40) than those in sections with lower labor productivity.

TWO THEORIES OF PERFORMANCE

The first two theories of organizational performance to be considered are cultural-relativism and structural theory. On the most general level, a cultural-relativist theory of performance asserts that performance varies most importantly with the *cultural setting* in which an organization is found, and with the deposit of cultural characteristics observable in the behavior and attitudes of members of the organization. Structural theory, on the other hand, holds that performance varies more with the *structural properties* of organizations and the position of individuals in the organizational structure, rather than with whether the individual has certain, say, "Japanese" or "American" cultural characteristics.

For students of Japanese organizations, the best-known example of a cultural-relativist theory of performance is that of James Abegglen (1974, 1969, 1958). It is Abegglen's position that Japanese firms have a typical social organization which differs in important respects from that found in firms in the West, especially the United States. This social organization, in turn, derives from a cultural tradition which also contrasts with that of the West. However, though different, this Japanese factory social organization is not inferior to the Western type with regard to effectiveness in general, or to performance and labor productivity in particular. "Japanese methods of organization, when different from those in the United States, are not necessarily less effective or less rational . . . . There is little indication that these [25 Japanese] companies are moving toward the American, or Western, model in the ways in which they recruit, reward, and punish personnel . . ." (Abegglen, 1969: 118). "Indeed, it seems likely that it is a consequence of having developed a different, Japanese approach to organization that Japan has accomplished the industrial success that it has" (1969: 100).

Hypotheses To Be Tested

First, we list the hypotheses concerning the determinants of performance (as measured by the performance index) in which the cultural-relativist theory (as interpreted in the present context, though it may make other predictions in different socio-cultural contexts) and the structural theory make the *same* predictions. We then list those in which the two theories make *different* predictions.

1. *Organizational Status.* This index measures the individual's status in the company in terms of six components. High-status employees have higher educations, higher job classifications, work in sections with higher informational levels, have more seniority, and have higher rank and higher pay. Low-status employees have the opposite characteristics. The reliability (alpha) of the index is 0.78 in the Electric Factory and 0.47 in the Shipbuilding Factory. Scores on the status index range from a low of 6 to a high of 18; the mean status score is 9.2 in the Electric Factory and 10.7 in the Shipbuilding Factory; the standard deviations are 2.9 and 2.0, respectively. On theoretical grounds, because higher status employees are expected to perform better and are rewarded better, we hypothesize a positive relationship between status and performance.

2. *Sex.* Because males have higher organizational status and are more satisfied with their jobs than are female employees, we hypothesize that males have higher performance than females. Sex is not used as an independent variable in the Shipbuilding Factory, since 96 percent of its personnel are men.

3. *Age.* On the one hand, given rapid changes in technology and

information, younger employees should be higher in performance than older ones. On the other hand, there is "the experience of age" that has some positive consequences for performance; moreover, older workers are more likely to have responsibilities and a "Work" rather than a "Pleasure" value orientation (see Hypothesis No. 8, below). Given these cross-pressures, the best hypothesis is that there is a weak relationship between age and performance. Age and status are highly positively correlated (.86) in the Electric Factory, but only moderately positively correlated in the Ship-building Factory (.47). To avoid multicollinearity among the hypothesized independent variables, age is dropped in the Electric Factory. Since this is not a problem in the Shipbuilding Factory, performance is regressed on both status and age.

4. *Size of Community of Origin.*   It is often said that employees from rural areas have been more socialized into a hard work ethic than those from urban and metropolitan areas. Therefore, we hypothesize that performance varies inversely with size of community of origin.

5. *Job Satisfaction.*   This index measures the individual's satisfaction with six aspects of his or her job. A high score indicates that the individual thinks the job: (a) is interesting rather than dull; (b) is identical to his or her interests and desires; (c) has enough variety; (d) requires more ability than one has; (e) is generally good and satisfying; and (f) does not want to be moved to another job in the factory. A low job satisfaction score indicates the opposite. The reliability (alpha) of the index is 0.82 in the Electric Factory and 0.76 in the Shipbuilding Factory. On a range from 6 (low score) to 23 (high), the mean job satisfaction score is 13.4 in the Electric Factory and 15.5 in the Shipbuilding Factory; the standard deviations are 3.1 and 3.8, respectively. We hypothesize that performance varies positively with job satisfaction.

6. *Knowledge of Procedures.*   One condition of high performance is that the employee know the company's procedures concerning work. This was measured by responses to the question, "In your shop, when there is an accident, do you know how to deal with it?—always/sometimes/hardly ever know how." Shipbuilding Factory employees claimed to know procedures significantly more often than Electric Factory personnel ($C/C_{max} = .14$). We predict a positive relationship between knowledge of procedures and performance.

7. *Perceived Promotion Chances.*   The better one thinks his chances are for promotion, the more incentive one would have for high performance; therefore, we predict a positive relationship between perceived promotion chances and performance.

8. *Values.*   We hypothesize that employees who give primacy to "Work" values ("work is my whole life") will have higher performance than those who give primacy to "Family" values ("happy family life is more important than a job in a company"), or "Pleasure" values ("work is only a means to get pay to spend on the pleasures of life").

Alternative predictions concerning performance would be made by cultural-relativist theory and structural theory with regard to another set of independent variables. These can be conceptualized as several aspects of the degree of *the employee's social integration into the firm:*

9. Employee cohesiveness;
10. Paternalism;
11. Residence (company versus private housing);
12. Participation in company recreational activities;
13. Previous interfirm mobility;
14. Lifetime commitment to the firm;
15. Recruitment channel.

Abegglen's version of the cultural-relativist theory is that, in Japan, there is a positive relationship between the degree of the employee's social integration into the firm (on variables 9 through 15) and employee performance. Thus, he predicts that performance is maximized when employees: (a) are highly cohesive with their fellow employees;[3] (b) prefer paternalistic, functionally diffuse relationships with their superiors and with the company, rather than nonpaternalistic, functionally specific relationships;[4] (c) live in company housing; (d) participate frequently in company-sponsored recreational activities;[5] (e) have always worked for the same firm,

---

[3]Our index of employee cohesiveness is based on six questionnaire items which measured: (a) how troubled one would be if moved to another job in the factory, away from the people they now work with; (b) whether one's best friends are inside or outside the company; (c) how many of the people who work near one are their friends; (d) how much interaction one has outside of work with workmate friends; (e) whether the atmosphere of social relationships in the factory is warm or cold; and (f) perceived teamwork in the shop. Cohesiveness scores summed over these six items ranged from 6 (low cohesiveness) to 18 (high). The mean cohesiveness score is 12.5 in the Electric Factory and 12.2 in the Shipbuilding Factory; the standard deviations are 1.8 and 2.2, respectively. The reliability (alpha) of the index is 0.30 in the Electric Factory and 0.47 in the Shipbuilding Factory.

[4]Our paternalism index is based on questionnaire responses to two items: (1) Suppose in this company there are two types of superiors. Which would you prefer to work under? (a) A man who always sticks to the work rules and never demands any unreasonable work, but on the other hand never does anything for you personally in matters not connected with work; or (b) A man who sometimes demands extra work in spite of rules against it, but on the other hand looks after you personally in matters not connected with work. (2) There are two companies. From your experience, which would you choose? (a) Management thinks their relationship to the worker is simply work, therefore management doesn't find it necessary to take care of workers' personal matters; or (b) Management thinks they are like parents to workers; therefore they regard it as better to take care of the personal affairs of workers.

Paternalistic preferences are indicated by the choice of alternative (b) in each question. One's paternalism score falls between a low of 2 and a high of 4. The Electric Factory's mean score is 3.4, with a standard deviation of 0.7; the comparable figures are 3.5 and 0.7 in the Shipbuilding Factory. The alpha reliability coefficient of the index is 0.41 in the Electric Factory and 0.38 in the Shipbuilding Factory.

[5]Our index of participation in company-sponsored recreational activities is based on three items in the questionnaire: (a) belonging to cultural or atheletic clubs sponsored by the company; (b) number of times one participated in company recreational activities during the previous year, and (c) proportion of times one participated in those activities during the previous year. The distinction between the latter two is that one may, for example, have participated a total of three times in all activities, but missed two other occasions sponsored by company units of which one was a member. For purposes of index construction, the proportion of times

rather than having had previous interfirm mobility; and (f) support norms and values of lifetime commitments to their present firm.[6] A related cultural-relativist prediction is that, in Japan, the type of recruitment channel through which one enters the firm has performance consequences: hiring directly from schools on the basis of school recommendations is believed to maximize performance; hiring those from the labor force who are known to present employees of the firm is the next most desirable channel; and hiring through

Table 3

MULTIPLE REGRESSION ANALYSIS OF EMPLOYEE PERFORMANCE IN ELECTRIC AND SHIPBUILDING FACTORIES

Independent Variable	Electric Factory			Shipbuilding Factory		
	Beta	Beta	r	Beta	Beta	r
Sex	.26**	.28**	.54**			
Organizational Status	.22**	.25**	.54**	.15**	.14**	.35**
Knowledge of Procedures	.17**	.18**	.47**	.16**	.17**	.33**
Residence	.07**		−11**	.10**		.12*
Participation	.06**		.23**	.11**	.11**	.14**
Employee Cohesiveness	.06**	.09**	.13**	.01		.10*
Job Satisfaction	.05*		.39**	−01		.22**
Values	.04*		.31**	.09**		.19**
Paternalism	.04*		.09*	.04		.13**
Size of Community of Origin	−.02		.12**	−02		.03
Number of Previous Jobs	.02		.23**	.08**		.06
Promotion Chances	.01		.40**	.16**	.17**	.28**
Lifetime Commitment	−.00		.15**	.15**	.16**	.30**
Recruitment Channel				.06		.02
Age				.12**	.16**	.29**
Multiple R =	.63	.62		.53	.51	
R² =	.395	.382		.285	.261	
N =	784	855		440	440	

*Significant at the .05 level.   **Significant at the .01 level.

participated variable was coded never or sometimes, most times, always. Participation scores range from a low of 3 to a high of 9. Mean scores are 4.6 in the Electric Factory (s.d. = 1.2), and 4.4 in the Shipbuilding Factory (s.d. = 1.6). The index reliability coefficients are 0.40 in the Electric Factory and 0.64 in the Shipbuilding Factory.

[6]Our index of lifetime commitment contains four questionnaire items: (a) perception of the proportion of male employees who have decided to work in the present firm until retirement; (b) whether one wants to remain in the present firm oneself, or to quit; (c) what one thinks of an employee who voluntarily changes firms (the lifetime commitment responses are "his behavior is not 'Japanese,' disloyal, opportunistic"; an intermediate response is "I can understand his behavior"; and the nonlifetime commitment response is "I'd do the same if I had the chance"); and (d) should most males work for the same company until retirement? Lifetime commitment scores range from a low of 4 to a high of 12. The mean scores are 8.2 in the Electric Factory and 8.7 in the Shipbuilding Factory; the standard deviations are 1.5 and 1.6; respectively. The alpha coefficient of reliability is 0.38 in the Electric Factory and 0.59 in the Shipbuilding Factory.

the impersonal channels of the mass media and government vocational centers is thought to be the least desirable, from the viewpoint of maximizing performance.

We shall refer to this particular application of the cultural-relativist theory—Hypotheses 9 through 15—as the "integration theory of performance."

Structural theory, as we interpret it, asserts that the main determinants of performance are variables 1 through 8 above (especially those having to do with status and rewards, variables 1, 2, 3, 5, and 7), and that when these are held constant, the variables which measure the degree of the employee's social integration into the firm will have no independent influence on performance. In other words, while cultural-relativist theory hypothesizes a positive relationship between integration and performance, strucutral theory posits that performance varies independently of the employee's degree of integration into (or differentiation from) the firm.

Findings

Table 3 presents the multiple regression analysis results of testing our hypotheses. First, consider the Electric Factory. The zero-order correlations (column 3) are all statistically significant; however, performance is most strongly related to status (r = .54), sex (.54), knowledge of procedures (.47), perceived promotion chances (.40), and job satisfaction (.39).

In the first multiple regression run (Table 3, column 1), performance is regressed simultaneously on all 13 independent variables. When other variables are held constant, the best predictors of performance are sex (beta =.26; males higher performance than females), status in the organization (.22), and knowledge of procedures (.17). When these three variables are controlled, none of the other independent variables contributes more than marginally to explaining the variance in performance. In particular, job satisfaction, values, number of previous jobs, and promotion chances all have relatively strong zero-order relationships with performance; however, these are shown to have little independent effect on performance, once sex, status, and knowledge of procedures are taken into account. To explore these relationships further, a second multiple regression was run for the Electric Factory. This run used only those nine independent variables whose betas had significant F-values in the first run. It was found (Table 3, column 2) that four of these variables acting together—sex, status, knowledge of procedures, and employee cohesiveness—explained as much of the variance in performance (R = .62, R^2 = 382) as did all thirteen of the original set of independent variables. But before interpreting these results more substantively, let us summarize the parallel analysis done in the Shipbuilding Factory.

In the Shipbuilding Factory, the zero-order correlations (Table 3, column 6) indicate that performance is most strongly related to organizational status (r =.35), knowledge of procedures (.33), lifetime commitment (.30), age (.29), and perceived promotion chances (.28). When performance is regressed on the 14 independent variables (including age and recruitment channel, but excluding sex), a number of them are seen (column 4) to have a significant effect, though no single variable has a very strong effect when others are held constant. In this first multiple regression run, performance among the Shipbuilding workers is positively related to knowledge of procedures, status, promotion chances, lifetime commitment, age, participation, residence, primacy of work values, and number of previous jobs. To achieve a more parsimonious explanation, a second multiple regression was run using only the nine variables whose betas had a significant F-value. The results, shown in column 5, indicate that when other variables are held constant, six of these nine variables each contibutes something toward explaining the variance in performance. Together, these six had virtually as high a multiple R with performance (.51) as did all fourteen of the originally hypothesized set of independent variables (.53). Job satisfaction, which was related to performance at the zero-order level, was found to have no effect on performance *independent* of the effect of perceived promotion chances, age, knowledge of procedures, lifetime commitment, and the other best predictors.

To summarize, in both the Electric Factory and the Shipbuilding Factory, employee performance is maximized when employees have higher status in the company and know procedures more fully. Two other variables— age and sex—are each a best predictor of performance in the one factory where each analysis was run: older and male employees have higher performance ratings than younger and female employees. (Moreover, when age is substituted for status in the Electric Factory multiple regression, it emerges there, too, as one of the best predictors.) Three other variables are causally important in the Shipbuilding Factory, though not in the Electric Factory: promotion chances, participation, and lifetime commitment. Employees have better performance when they perceive their promotion chances as good, when they participate more often in company recreational activities, and when they support lifetime commitment norms and values. Finally, in the Electric Factory (though not in the Shipbuilding Factory), a causally important relationship exists between cohesiveness and performance. The higher one's cohesiveness with fellow employees, the higher one's performance.

Let us use the results of the second multiple regression run for each factory (Table 3, columns 2 and 5) as the criteria for confirming our theory. When cultural-relativist theory and structural theory make the *same* predictions concerning performance, these are confirmed 8 out of a maximum of 15 times (twice each for status, age, and knowledge of procedures; once each for sex and promotion chances). When the theories make *alternative* predictions, structural theory—which predicts that employee integration into the firm has no independent causal effect on performance when other structural variables are held constant—is confirmed 10 times (twice each for residence, paternalism, and number of previous jobs; once each for participation, cohesiveness, lifetime commitment, and recruitment channel), while cultural-relativist theory is confirmed only 3 times (once each for participation, cohesiveness, and lifetime commitment).

We conclude that when the two theories make alternative predictions about performance, structural theory fits the causal facts better than does cultural-relativist theory. Once certain structural variables (status, knowledge of procedures, etc.) have been taken into account, little is added to the explanation of performance by considering any of the informal ways in which the employee is socially integrated into the firm. Performance in these Japanese factories appears to be more the result of variables which operate universally in large-scale, complex organizations, rather than the result of a more culturally variable factor like the degree of the employee's informal social integration into the firm.

HUMAN RELATIONS THEORY AND PERFORMANCE

Another theory of performance we shall consider is human relations theory (Likert, 1967). Classical theories of administration and organization stress formal structure, while human relations theory stresses informal structure. Structural theory attempts a more integrated analysis of the formal and informal aspects of organizational structure. It emphasizes formal rewards—status, rank, promotion chances, etc.—rather than only informal rewards—cohesiveness, participation in informal recreational activities, etc. Structural theory also emphasizes objective status and power differentials, and the conflicts of interest that derive therefrom. In this area, as well as in the area of conflict between personal needs and organizational requirements, structural theory stands in contrast to human relations theory by virtue of its recognition that these facts of conflict are to some extent inevitable in organizations and cannot be eliminated by better communication.

With regard to the variables on which we have data, human relations theory, cultural-relativism or integration theory, and structural theory make some similar and some different predictions concerning performance. Human relations theory, like cultural-relativism theory (but unlike structural theory), asserts that performance is maximized to the extent that employees have: (a) high cohesiveness; and (b) frequent participation in company recreational activities. Like both other theories, human relations theory predicts (c) that performance is positively related to job satisfaction. Some versions of human relations theory posit a causal chain in which cohesiveness and participation influence job satisfaction, and these three variables, in turn, influence performance. This causal model appears in Figure 1, together with r's and *beta* weights for both the Electric Factory and the Shipbuilding Factory.

Among Electric Factory employees, job satisfaction is about equally influenced by cohesiveness and participation; however, performance is more strongly related to job satisfaction than to participation, and more strongly related to participation than to employee cohesiveness. The multiple R between performance and these three human relations variables (shown in Table 4) is .45, but job satisfaction alone predicts performance virtually as well (.42) as all three variables together.

In the Shipbuilding Factory, job satisfaction is more a result of employee cohesiveness than of participation, considering each independent variable when the other is held constant. As in the Electric Factory, performance is more strongly related to job satisfaction than to participation, and more

Figure 1

A HUMAN RELATIONS CAUSAL THEORY OF PERFORMANCE[a]

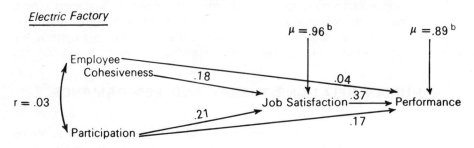

Electric Factory

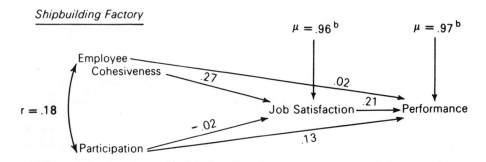

Shipbuilding Factory

[a]Relationship between cohesiveness and participation is Pearson product-moment r; all other relationships are path coefficients, which are the same as *beta* weights.

[b]μ = the estimate of the residual, i.e., the influence of all other variables than those stated, on the dependent variable. The assumption is that the total variation of each dependent variable (job satisfaction, performance) is completely determined by a linear combination of the specified independent variables and the residual, or error variables, μ. Since the independent variables and the residual variables are also assumed to vary independently of each other, $\mu = \sqrt{1-R^2}$ (Land, 1969).

strongly related to participation than to cohesiveness. In Table 4 we see that job satisfaction, participation, and cohesiveness all have significant but only weak zero-order correlations with performance. When all three of these central human relations variables act simultaneously on performance, they can explain only seven percent of the predictable variance.

These findings reveal that in only one of the two factories is even one of the three human relations variables moderately related to performance, either at the zero-order level or when the other two variables are held constant. This variable is job satisfaction in the Electric Factory. This gives only cold comfort to human relations theorists, however, for it has been shown elsewhere that job satisfaction in the Electric Factory is more a result of *organizational status* than of cohesiveness or participation (Marsh and Mannari, 1976: Table D.3). This means that the only successful predictor from human relations theory is itself a function of a variable—status—that is more often associated with a structural theory of organization than with

Table 4

MULTIPLE REGRESSION OF PERFORMANCE ON HUMAN RELATIONS VARIABLES IN ELECTRIC AND SHIPBUILDING FACTORIES

Electric Factory

Independent Variable	Standardized Partial Regression Coefficient	Zero-Order Correlation
Job Satisfaction	.37**	.42**
Participation in Company Activities	.17**	.25**
Employee Cohesiveness	.04	.12**

Multiple R = .45
R² = .204
N = .823

Shipbuilding Factory

Independent Variable	Standardized Partial Regression Coefficient		Zero-Order Correlation
	First run	Second run	
Job Satisfaction	.21**	.20**	.22**
Participation	:13**	.14**	.14**
Employee Cohesiveness	.02		.10*

Multiple R = .26   .26
R² = .066   .065
N = .427   .482

*Significant beyond the .05 level.
**Significant beyond the .01 level.

a human relations theory. In this sense, we conclude that structural theory provides a better explanation of performance than does human relations theory (Carey, 1967).

CONCLUSION

A measure of employee performance was developed for two Japanese factories, one in the household electric appliance industry and one in the shipbuilding industry. The index measures both objective (attendance, number of suggestions contributed, and awards for suggestions) and subjective (thinking about suggestions, desire to meet production goals) aspects of performance. To explain performance variations among employees in each factory, hypotheses from three theories were tested. Structural theory predicts that performance varies positively with one's status and relationship to the formal reward system of the firm. The version of the cultural-relativist theory considered in this study holds that performance varies positively with the degree to which (in Japan) the employee is informally socially integrated into the firm. Human relations theory sees performance as a positive function of job satisfaction, which in turn derives from one's cohesiveness with other employees and participation in company recreational activities.

Multiple regression analysis leads to the conclusion that, at most, our variables explain 40 percent of the variance in performance in either factory. Of the variance that is explained, the most important causes are those usually associated with structural theory; rather than cultural-relativist theory or human relations theory.

The main implications of these findings are twofold. First, the essentially weak explanatory power of human relations variables with regard to performance has been noted in research in the United States (Blau and Scott, 1962: 95–96; Brayfield and Crockett, 1955; Covello and Treiman, 1972; Vroom, 1964). Second, in the comparative study of organizations, a controversy continues over the relative importance of *universal structural* aspects of any organization and its members, and the *distinctive* ways in which organizations and their members are shaped by the *cultural settings* of particular societies. With regard to the determinants of performance in organizations, both these theoretical positions have their proponents. Our findings suggest that performance has more to do with such universal structural factors as status and knowledge of proceeding than with the "distinctively Japanese" pattern of alleged extreme integration of the employee into the firm. The latter position is disconfirmed in two ways: Japanese employees vary in the extent to which they are integrated into their firms; they are not uniformly highly integrated. And secondly their performance in relation to company goals does not depend primarily on the degree to which they are integrated into the firm.

REFERENCES

Abegglen, J. C.   *Management and Worker: The Japanese Solution.* Tokyo: Kodansha
   1974   International.

————.   "Organizational Change." In R. J. Ballon (ed.), *The Japanese Employee*:
   1969   99–119. Rutland, Vermont: Charles E. Tuttle.

————.   *The Japanese Factory.* Glencoe, Ill.: The Free Press.
   1958

Blau, P. M., and W. R. Scott.   *Formal Organizations: A Comparative Approach.*
   1962   San Francisco: Chandler.

Brayfield, A. H., and W. H. Crockett.   "Employee Attitudes and Employee Perfor-
   1955   mance." *Psychological Bulletin*, 52:396–424.

Carey, A.   "The Hawthorne Studies: A Radical Criticism." *American Sociological*
   1967   *Review*, 32:403–416.

Covello, V. T., and D. Treiman.   "Slippery Water and Other Gimmicks: A Critical
   1972   Review of Research on Worker Satisfaction and Organizational Effective-
          ness." Paper presented at the Mathematical Social Science Board Con-
          ference on Quantitative Social Theory and the Study of Formal Organiza-
          tions. Airlie House, Virginia.

Etzioni, A.   *Modern Organizations.* Englewood Cliffs, N. J.: Prentice-Hall.
   1964

Land, K. C.   "Principles of Path Analysis." In E. Borgatta (ed.), *Sociological*
   1969   *Methodology*: 3–37. San Francisco: Jossey-Bass.

Likert, R.   *The Human Organization.* New York: McGraw-Hill.
   1967

Marsh, R. M., and H. Mannari.   *Modernization and the Japanese Factory*. Princeton,
  1976   N. J.: Princeton University Press.
Price, J. L.   *Handbook of Organizational Measurement*. Indianapolis, Ind.: D. C.
  1972   Heath.
————.   *Organizational Effectiveness*. Homewood, Ill.: Richard D. Irwin.
  1968
Stinchcombe, A. L.   *Constructing Social Theories*. New York: Harcourt, Brace and
  1968   World.
Vroom, V. H.   *Work and Motivation*. New York: Wiley.
  1964

Section III

ORGANIZATION
EFFECTIVENESS
—UTILIZATION—

The two papers in this section are concerned with the problems associated with utilizing scientific knowledge to alter levels of organizational effectiveness. In the first paper, McGill underscores the need for empirical assessment of strategies designed to improve organizational effectiveness. Frohman, Sashkin, and Kavanagh, on the other hand, provide a systematic exposition of a comprehensive approach to the diagnosis and subsequent alteration of levels of organizational effectiveness.

Factors Accounting for Goal Effectiveness: A Longitudinal Study

JAMES H. STEWART
Saint Olaf College

INTRODUCTION

The effectiveness of an organization has been of concern to both researchers and practitioners—especially those who are also decision makers—for some years now. Despite such marked interest in the subject, however, much confusion still exists regarding the definition, theoretical approach, dimensions, and measurement of effectiveness (Hall, 1972: 96–102).

The purpose of this paper is to present a model of organizational effectiveness based on an open-systems perspective, and to test several hypotheses concerning goal effectiveness factors. We are interested in the values and goal priorities of policy leaders and how these affect goal effectiveness viewed within different time frames.

The model asserts that effectiveness is related to a variety of organizational objectives stemming from the functional requirements of the organization; hence, the definition of effectiveness must be multidimensional. The study illustrates the need for a benchmark from which to evaluate the progress or effectiveness of a single organization. Without an external criterion, it is impossible to make a comparative analysis of an organization's attainments. This can be done by studying similar organizations or the same organization over time. This author chose the latter.

The research subject is an organization of Catholic priests which began in the wake of Vatican Council II. The National Federation of Priests' Councils (NFPC) is a unique organization which combines social movement attributes with the characteristics of a professional association. The NFPC is a federation of 131 local councils. Of these, 99 are senates, 29 are associations, and 3 are religious order councils. The present governing body is made up of a 208-member unit named the House of Delegates. The principal goal of the organization is to press for changes in the Roman Catholic Church in the area of priests' rights and in social justice concerns. The NFPC is a change-oriented organization which is both deviant and illegitimate in the eyes of the National Conference of Catholic Bishops (NCCB).

There are significant differences between two types of affiliated councils. Senates are authorized in the dioceses by the bishops and serve at their pleasure; they exist to assist the bishops in such areas as the priestly role, diocesan government, personnel policy, and pastoral matters. The free associations, on the other hand, were established without the authorization or subsequent approval of their bishops; consequently, they work more independently from the bishops.

The differences between these two types of affiliates have caused a considerable amount of structural strain, both within the NFPC and in the NFPC's relations with the NCCB. The NFPC has been told by the NCCB that recognition will not be given to the NFPC with its current composition (Stewart, 1973).

A MODEL OF ORGANIZATIONAL EFFECTIVENESS

Previous research studies on effectiveness have employed the following conceptual frameworks: (a) goal achievement; (b) system resource, (c) organizational means and ends; and (d) functional requirements models (Ghorpade, 1971, 1970: 31–40). The last three approaches are specifications of the open-systems schema.

There are two components of the goal approach (Yuchtman and Seashore, 1967: 891–903). First, there is the "prescribed goal approach" which, according to them, "is characterized by a focus on the formal charter of the organization, or in some category of its personnel (usually its top management) as the most valid source of information concerning organizational goals . . ." (p. 892). Second, there is the "derived goal approach" in which the investigator, according to the same author, "derives the ultimate goal of the organization from his [functional] theory, thus arriving at goals which may be independent of the intentions and awareness of the members . . ." (p. 892).

The prescribed goal approach has been the most widely utilized by students of organization. Perrow (1968), Price (1968), and White (1960), among others, have employed the goal approach as a major tool in their assessment of organizational success.

Yuchtman and Seashore criticize the prescribed goal approach with respect to goal identification. They state that this component of the goal approach "has failed to provide a rationale for the empirical identification of goals as an organizational property . . ." (1967–897).

The derived goal approach (Parsons, 1960, 1956a, 1956b) is criticized by Yuchtman and Seashore with respect to its basis for the evaluation of effectiveness. They state that the derived goal approach "has no difficulty identifying the ultimate goal of the organization, since the latter is implied by the internal logic of the model, but the . . . model does not take the organization as the frame of reference . . ." (1967: 897).

The derived goal approach uses society, not the organization, as the frame of reference for evaluating organizational effectiveness. If the benefit of society is the basis on which effectiveness is evaluated, then the basis of evaluation is external to the organization, according to them.

Yuchtman and Seashore view the organization as an open system exploiting its environment in the acquisition of scarce resources. An organization is most effective when it "optimizes its resource procurement" (p. 898). This approach eliminates goals as a dimension of effectiveness and concentrates on the adaptation function. However, the authors admit that several of their 10 resource procurement factors could be considered as goals. Moreover, Price (1972: 8–10) points to the difficulty of measuring optimization.

The approach of Georgopoulos and Tannenbaum (1957) employed multiple criteria based on organizational ends and means. They claim that productivity, flexibility in terms of internal and external adaptations, and absence of tension and conflict within subgroups are dimensions of effectiveness and have applicability to most organizations. This strategy has been used by Bennis (1966) and Friedlander and Pickle (1968) to study these relationships within organizations—which are by constitution multifunctional. Price (1972) provides an excellent review of these major approaches to effectiveness.

The present state of research suggests that the development of some overall measure of effectiveness has not been fruitful. Researchers have increasingly employed a multidimensional approach (Guion, 1961; Katz and Kahn, 1966; Mahoney and Weitzel, 1969; Mott, 1972). To organizational output, adaptive functions, and operative goals, one must add consolidation factors, such as communication, collaboration, and cohesion (Stewart, 1970: 630–639). These dimensions will differ in their importance in light of such factors as time sequence, values of decision makers and clients, turnover of leadership, and structural factors, such as centralization. Seashore (1965) developed a hierarchy of criteria based on the means versus ends framework. Mahoney and Weitzel (1969) make use of this distinction in their multidimensional approach to effectiveness. They state that, "The research and development manager . . . use cooperative behavior, staff development, and reliable performance as high order criteria; and efficiency, productivity and output behavior as lower order criteria" (p. 362).

What is needed is a model that will first, specify the multiple dimensions and their specific measures of effectiveness, and second, be useful as a conceptual framework for comparative purposes. A framework of organizational effectiveness can be derived from systems requirements, which are related to the organization's internal and external environment. These familiar functional requirements are goal attainment, adaptation, integration, and latency (Caplow, 1964: 124–126; Parsons, 1956a, 1956b; Scott, 1959).

An organization has a natural history during which it moves through different phases of development (Hughes, 1958: 56–67). Four phases can be identified: foundation; consolidation; operations; and achievement of goals. There is no implication that these phases are discrete intervals, nor is unilinear development assumed. An organization must also successfully but differentially meet the four functional requirements to maintain itself and survive. One requirement demands more attention and emphasis at a certain time than another.

The problems of external adaptation, integration, and latency are

James H. Stewart

Figure 1

A SYSTEM EFFECTIVENESS MODEL

Career Stages	Functional Requirements	Objectives	Effectiveness
Foundation	*Adapation (external)	Acquisition	Acquisition
	*Adaptation (internal)	Power	Power
Consolidation	*Integration and *Latency (cohesion) Adaptation (internal)	Consolidation	Consolidation
Operation	*Adaptation (external)	Acquisition	Acquisition
	*Adaptation (internal) Integration and Latency (cohesion) Goal attainment	Power	Power
Attainment	*Goal attainment Adaptation Integration and Latency (cohesion)	Goal	Goal

Performance { Operation / Attainment

*Dominant (theoretically speaking).

related in a special way to the foundation and consolidation phases, while other adaptive functions and goal attainment are related to the operations and achievement phases. The operational and goal attainment functions may not be empirically distinguishable, except in cases of goal succesion (Sills, 1957). For our purposes, these two phases can be subsumed under the concept of performance.

Organizational effectiveness, then, can be framed in terms of the above objectives: acquisition, consolidation, power, and goal. Thus, effectiveness is defined as the extent to which a social system makes progress toward its acquisition, consolidation, power, and goal objectives (see Figure 1).

The four categories of objectives constitute a scheme whereby discussion of the separate dimensions can be arranged into a coherent framework. This affords us a tool of analysis to explore and identify the significant elements and processes that contribute to this or that form of organizational effectiveness. It likewise enables us to generate explanatory hypotheses about determinants of the effectiveness syndrome at different phases of organizational development. The criteria of this framework allow one to compare effectiveness over time in terms of subsystem units, similar systems, and the system itself. Since organizations are different in terms of size, functions, and environment, it is helpful to employ this model within an organizational classification scheme, such as Etzioni's (1961) compliance model.

In sum, I have argued that organizational effectiveness is multidimensional. Price (1972) and Seashore (1965) would view the acquisition, consolidation, and power objectives as means or penultimate goals. If the four objectives derived from Parsons' (1960) AGIL framework are viewed as necessary conditions for the functioning and survival of an organization, then their effectiveness is basically necessary. Consolidation effectiveness may not be as important as goal effectiveness; but it is just as necessary.

This paper is not concerned with the submodels of acquisition, consolidation, and power effectiveness. An empirical assessment of these dimensions has been provided elsewhere (Stewart, 1974). The interest here is in the goal effectiveness dimension.

According to Gross (1969, 1968), Price (1972: 5–6), and others, the focus on goal effectiveness research should be on: (a) the decision makers of the organization; (b) organizational goals as distinguished from the private goals of leaders and participants; (c) the actual goals in contrast to "official" goals of the organization; and (d) the intentions and activities of the leadership. I have utilized these guidelines in researching goal effectiveness, which is defined here as the extent to which an organization successfully realizes or makes progress toward its actual goals.

The strategy of assessing effectiveness from the top leadership perspective was adopted because the clients—as well as the NFPC's adversaries—are much less informed about its internal organization and its variable progress toward the establishment, priority, and attainment of actual goals. Consideration was given to the influence of decision-makers' intentions and activities in setting goals and their priorities; however, it was felt that these intentions and activities have an influence on goal effectiveness or progress. Values and interests are aspects of leadership intentions insofar as they shed light on the aims and directions of organizational leadership.

A value-oriented person expects rights or accepts duties in generalized terms independent of his particular relationship with another person or group. There are many types of values; however, our concern is with the basic rights of people, such as the freedom of conscience or right to lawful dissent. Interests refer to special rights and to an allocation of goods which particular individuals or groups desire (LaPalombara, 1964). Thus, we are concerned with how values, interests (as herein defined), and priority settings affect the effectiveness of different organizational goals. These goals, as will be shown, are of two types: commonweal and particularistic.

Movements for change will vary and take different directions, depending on whether the participants are value oriented or interest oriented. Turner and Killian (1957: 331–385) summarize this in stating that value-oriented

movements point in the direction of changing a social institution for the
greater common good. These organizations are concerned with societal
reform rather than personal reward. Movements of self-interest, which they
call power-oriented movements, are directed more toward gaining some
recognition or special status. The incentive of interest-oriented actors is
the approval of the people that they love, fear, or respect. Interest-oriented
actors take action; but such action must always be calculated in terms of
personal or group gains and losses. Their operating principle is to act with
caution and not ignore those who have the power (Neal, 1965: 45–54).
A study by Nelson (1964) supports the relationship between values and
interests and types of change. He found that individuals who defined the
Church in terms of the local congregation's interests were more resistant
to a Church merger than those who defined the Church in value terms, such
as the "Communion of Saints."

RESEARCH DESIGN

Data for this study were collected from two cross-sectional surveys
of the total population of the NFPC House of Delegates. The first questionnaire was mailed out to the delegates in January, 1970. Ninety percent of the
questionnaires were returned, yielding data on 201 delegates out of 224
in the population. The second questionnaire was administered in March,
1972, yielding a return of 89 percent. This represented 186 respondents
out of the total population of 208 delegates. Thus, the return rate of questionnaires in both studies is considered quite adequate to characterize the
parameters of the delegate population for both time periods.

The hypotheses in this study are based on the notions of "intentions"
and "activities" of organizational leadership mentioned above. By intentions
we mean the policy preferences of the leadership based on both their goal
priorities and their deeply internalized value and interest sets. By activities
we mean the actual policies adopted by the leadership in the form of resolutions passed over a seven-year period. Internal to these preferences and
priorities is the time sequence factor. Leadership preferences change and
policy makers are subject to turnover.

The NFPC, as reflected in its resolutions over the past seven years,
reflects the following pattern of policy change. The rights and interests of
priests dominated its activity from 1968 to 1972, then sharply dropped as
issues of major concern. On the other hand, the commonweal issues became
increasingly more important from 1972 onward. In the first period, 71 percent
of the resolutions were about priestly concerns and complaints, such as
personnel matters, while 29 percent were of a commonweal or social justice
nature. In contrast, the second period of the NFPC's history was dominated
by broader societal concerns (74 percent), compared with the particular
concerns (26 percent) of the priests (Stewart, 1974).

There are four basic hypotheses in this study:

1. *The goal priority of the leadership will be positively associated
   with goal effectiveness.*

The question arises, "how does one measure effectiveness or progress?" This author felt that the only way to measure normative goal effectiveness was to ask the leadership's assessment. There is an inherent danger here of a self-fulfilling prophecy, of course. In setting priorities, the leadership can easily slip into the error of placing higher evaluations on goals to which they have assigned higher priorities. Some degree of control was attempted in this study, however, For example, respondents reported very high effectiveness regarding the goal of optional celibacy. NFPC documents, as well as both secular and religious printed media, supported the leadership's assessment of the effectiveness of these goals.

2. *Value and interest orientations of the leadership will be positively but differentially associated with the multiple goals of the NFPC.*

More precisely, the basic value of human freedom to think and judge for oneself will be more associated with commonweal goals, while particular interests of priests will be more associated with priests' rights and privileges.

3. *Goal priority and value and interest orientations, taken together will be more strongly associated with goal effectiveness than will the first two hypotheses.*

4. *Over time, the value orientation of the leadership will become an increasingly important factor in explaining the assessment of goal effectiveness.*

One item was used to measure the value orientation of the leadership. The item questioned the degree to which the belief in freedom of conscience was personally meaningful. This basic right, while taken for granted by most Americans, has been quite crucial for priests in the light of changing attitudes toward episcopal and papal authority, especially regarding doctrine and Church law.

Interest-oriented persons, according to Neal (1965: 45–64), are always careful not to jeopardize their positions; thus, action is taken both with caution and consideration of legitimate authority. One item was employed which questioned the importance of the Catholic bishops' official recognition of the NFPC for its effective operation.

Priority was measured by asking the respondents to indicate the importance of each goal. Effectiveness was measured by asking the respondents to assess the progress for each goal. The value, interest, and priority items were set up on Likert-type scales and were dichotomized into high and low. The responses to progress of the goals were simply "good" or "poor." Spearman rho coefficients were used.

Four goals were utilized. These were based on the organization's documents and resolutions and seemed to be of wider concern than simply the interests of affiliates. These were called commonweal goals and were specified as: a representative voice for all priests, due process for all priests, social action programs, and experimental ministries. Two goals or issues, again based on the organization's documents, seemed to measure the particular interests of the NFPC affiliates: the development of professional standards and realistic discussions about the possibility of optional celibacy for priests.

FINDINGS AND DISCUSSION

First, descriptive data will be provided on the priority and effectiveness of actual goals of the NFPC (see Table 1). Inspecting the 1969 and 1972 columns, one discovers a general pattern in which higher priority goals are perceived to be the actual goals and likewise register the greater effectiveness. It is important to note that by 1972, all six goals were considered high priority.

When one looks at effectiveness over time, it varies. In absolute terms, the commonweal goals register greater effectiveness. Moreover, relatively speaking, the fact that the two commonweal goals of social action and experimental ministries register greater effectiveness in contrast with the particularistic goals is due in part to the controversy surrounding them. Development of professional standards would give priests more autonomy; optional celibacy would provide less regulation to one's personal life. The reason why the commonweal goals of social action and experimental ministries register greater progress is due in part to the fact that there are fewer restrictions in the environment to impede progress in this direction. In sum, effectiveness is affected in part by the constraints of Church authority and its unwillingness to adopt changes.

There is one other observation. The 1972 delegates assigned much higher priorities to the last four goals in Table 1 than did the 1969 delegates. It is important to note that these four goals register greater variation in effectiveness than the other goals. This again illustrates that organizations give priority to different goals at different times; consequently, goal effectiveness is differentially assessed. We will now discuss the factors accounting for goal effectiveness.

If the leadership places higher priority on some goals than on others, then barring outside constraints, one would expect more effort and probably more effectiveness toward the realization of the higher priority goals. The data in Table 2 again point to the need to consider external barriers.

Inspecting the Time-1 data, it is evident that there is only a slight relationship between priority and effectiveness. It is an old story: high expectations do not automatically translate into realizations. In 1969, the NFPC was both young and aggressive. Above all, the organization was autonomous from the bishops' control. Their demands for changes in the priestly life, role, social action, and ministry were viewed as a threat to episcopal power. The climate in the Church at that time militated against the achievement of external goals: that is, goals over which the Church had little or no control. The only organizational goal over which they had control was that of developing a representative voice, an internal goal. It was in regard to this goal that priority and progress had their strongest relationships in both Time-1 and Time-2.

Table 1

PRIORITY AND EFFECTIVENESS OF ACTUAL GOALS OF THE NFPC BY COUNCIL TYPE*
(BY PERCENTAGES)

	High Priority		Actually Pursued		Good Progress		Variations in Effectiveness
	1969 Total Delegates	1972 Total Delegates	1969 Total Delegates	1972 Total Delegates	1969 Total Delegates	1972 Total Delegates	
Commonweal Goals:							
Due Process	86	94	95	90	78	80	02
Representative Voice	80	93	91	86	67	71	03
Social Action Programs	63	92	68	82	30	50	20
Experimental Ministries	56	92	60	80	13	46	33
Particularistic Goals:							
Professional Standards	65	91	78	72	21	39	18
Optional Celibacy	54	80	71	75	25	35	10

*The N for 1969 Delegates is 203; for 1972, N is 186.

Table 2

RELATIONSHIPS BETWEEN PRIORITY OF GOALS AND GOAL EFFECTIVENESS

Progress of:	1969 Priority of the Goal	1972 Priority of the Goal
Becoming a representative voice	.337	.854
Developing experimental ministries	.206	.469
Launching social action programs	.193	.441
Developing structures of due process	.122	.382
Developing professional standards	—.124	—.028
Launching discussions on celibacy	—.213	—.163

There is, in general, a pattern of relationships between priority and effectiveness in the 1972 data. Priority is more strongly associated with goal effectiveness in each case; thus, the first hypothesis is supported. The relationship of priority and progress is the strongest (first three goals) where the priests met the least opposition from the bishops. Regarding the due process issue, the NFPC faced a great deal of opposition from the bishops because of certain historical events that occurred in 1969 and 1970 (Stewart, 1974). This opposition leveled off in 1972. The negative relationship between priority and progress for the two particularistic goals can be explained in part by the continued strong hostility of the bishops on these matters. In sum, the smaller the amount of external opposition, the greater the priority intentions of the leadership, and the more strongly they relate to goal effectiveness.

Table 3

RELATIONSHIP OF VALUE AND INTEREST FACTORS WITH GOAL EFFECTIVENESS

Goal Effectiveness	1969		1972	
	Value Factor	Interest Factor	Value Factor	Interest Factor
Commonweal Goals				
Due Process	.341	.304	.305	.198
Representative Voice	.390	.205	.415	.228
Social Action Programs	.322	.295	.370	.119
Experimental Ministries	.341	.320	.538	.318
Particularistic Goals				
Professional Standards	.230	.372	.103	.321
Optional Celibacy	.045	.375	.179	.361

Table 4

RELATIONSHIP OF VALUE AND INTEREST ORIENTATION AND
HIGH PRIORITY TO GOAL EFFECTIVENESS

Goal Effectiveness	High Priority 1969		High Priority 1972	
	Value Factor	Interest Factor	Value Factor	Interest Factor
Commonweal Goals				
Due Process	.642	.603	.719	.699
Representative Voice	.579	.574	.733	.721
Social Action Programs	.572	.537	.639	.622
Experimental Ministries	.554	.467	.238	.176
Particularistic Goals				
Professional Standards	.581	.725	.421	.457
Optional Celibacy	.445	.477	.598	.669

Turning to value and interest orientations, the second hypothesis is also supported. In both time periods, the general pattern holds that the value stance had greater influence on the effectiveness of commonweal goals, while the interest stance was more strongly associated with particularistic goal effectiveness (see Table 3).

As mentioned, value-oriented persons feel much more keenly about objectives that have societal worth or common good. Interest-oriented persons strive to secure rights for their own groups, being careful not to jeopardize their positions. People tend to work for the realization of matters which are congruent to their way of thinking and evaluating. Commonweal goals are more to the liking of the value-oriented delegates, as are the particularistic goals congruent to the interest-oriented delegates. The important point is that effectiveness is viewed differently by the organization's leaders, depending on their intentions and values.

In comparing both time periods, one sees a stronger relationship on the whole between the 1972 value oriented and commonweal goals in contrast with the 1969 counterparts. This pattern also holds, as can be seen in Table 4, when the priority factor controlling for value and interest orientation is correlated with goal effectiveness. This provides support for the fourth hypothesis. As mentioned previously, the activities of the leadership in terms of approved resolutions support the growing trend emphasizing value-related issues.

One finds even stronger associations between goal effectiveness and value and interest oriented, high-priority respondents. Table 4 supports the third hypothesis, and one observation should be made. Although the general pattern holds, namely, value—and high-priority respondents are more strongly related to progress of commonweal goals, while interest—

and high-priority respondents attain this relationship with progress of particularistic goals, the differences between these orientations on most goals and in both time periods are not great. The conclusion may be drawn from this that regardless of the motivation in assigning high priority to specific goals, be it values or interests, it is the motivation effect together with priority which accounts for goal effectiveness.

CONCLUSIONS

Although the model presented in this paper specifies four necessary dimensions of organizational effectiveness, this author feels that goal effectiveness is the most important. It is difficult to deal with the assessment of goal effectiveness in a normative organization because of the intangible nature of many of its goals. In this study, the approach has been to measure effectiveness from the leadership's perspective. As noted earlier, the four guidelines set forth by Price (1972) are of great utility despite the fact that there is, of course, the possibility of built-in bias.

One important methodological consideration which needs attention is the factor of opposition. Such opposition may be in the nature of public opinion, a competitor serving the same goals, or power brokers. In this study, it was the latter which constrained the realization of certain goals. A variety of NFPC documents were used to validate these constraints, as well as the leadership's subjective assessment of goal effectiveness. Gross (1969, 1968) has opened a fruitful avenue of research in considering the intentions and activities of the leadership in goal identification. This report is a venture in a different direction: namely, utilizing intentions as determinants of effectiveness. In this sense, the study falls in the Georgopoulos and Mann (1962) perspective.

REFERENCES

Bennis, W.   *Changing Organizations*. New York: McGraw-Hill.
1966
Caplow, T.   *Principles of Organization*. New York: Harcourt, Brace and World.
1964
Etzioni, A.   *A Comparative Analysis of Complex Organizations*. New York: The
1961   Free Press.
Friedlander, F., and H. Pickle.   "Components of Effectiveness in Small Organi-
1968   zations." *Administrative Science Quarterly*, 13:289–304.
Georgopoulos, B., and L. C. Mann.   *The Community General Hospital*. New York:
1962   Macmillan.
Georgopoulos, B., and A. S. Tannenbaum.   "A Study of Organizational Effectiveness."
1957   *American Sociological Review*, 22:534–40.
Ghorpade, J.   *Assessment Of Organizational Effectiveness*. Pacific Palisades, Calif.:
1971   Goodyear Publishing, Inc.
————.   "Study of Organizational Effectiveness: Two Prevailing Viewpoints."
1970   *The Pacific Sociological Review*, 13:31–41.
Gross, E.   "The Definition of Organizational Goals." *British Journal of Sociology*,
1969   20:277–294.
————.   "Universities as Organizations: A Research Approach." *American
1968   Sociological Review*, 33:518–544.

Guion, R. M. "Criterion Measurement and Personnel Judgments." *Personnel*
1961   *Psychology*, 14:141–149.
Hall, R. H.   *Organizations Structure and Process.* Englewood Cliffs, N. J.: Prentice-
1972   Hall.
Hughes, E. C.   *Men and Their Work.* New York: The Free Press of Glencoe.
1958
Katz, D., and R. Kahn. *The Social Psychology of Organizations.* New York: Wiley.
1966
LaPalombara, J. G.   *Interest Groups in Italian Politics.* Princeton, N. J.: Princeton
1964   University Press.
Mahoney, T. A., and W. Weitzel.   "Managerial Models of Organizational Effective-
1969   ness." *Administrative Science Quarterly*, 14:357–365.
Mott, P. E.   *The Characteristics of Effective Organizations.* New York: Harper and
1972   Row.
Neal, M. A.   *Values and Interests in Social Change.* Englewood Cliffs, N. J.: Prentice-
1965   Hall.
Nelson, G. I.   "Social Change in Rural Churches." Unpublished paper. Minneapolis,
1964   Minn.: University of Minnesota.
Parsons, T.   *Structure and Process in Modern Societies.* Glencoe, Ill.: The Free
1960   Press.
————.   "Suggestions for a Sociological Approach to the Theory of Organi-
1956a   zations: Part 1." *Administrative Science Quarterly*, 1:63–85.
————.   "Suggestions for a Sociological Approach to the Theory of Organi-
1956b   zations: Part 2." *Administrative Science Quarterly*, 1:224–239.
Perrow, C.   "Organizational Goals." In D. Sills (ed.), *International Encyclopedia*
1968   *of the Social Sciences*, Vol. II. New York: Macmillan Co. and The Free Press.
Price, J. L.   "Organizational Effectiveness." *Sociological Quarterly*, 13:3–16.
1972
————   *Organizational Effectiveness.* Homewood, Ill.: Richard D. Irwin and
1968   Sons, Inc.
Seashore, S. E.   "Criteria for Organizational Effectiveness." *Michigan Business*
1965   *Review*, 17:26–30.
Scott, F. G.   "Action Theory and Research in Social Organizations." *American*
1959   *Journal of Sociology*, 64:384–388.
Sills, D. L.   *The Volunteers: Means and Ends in a National Organization.* Glencoe,
1957   Ill.: The Free Press.
Stewart, J. H.   "When Priests Organize." Unpublished paper. Northfield, Minn.:
1974   Saint Olaf College.
————.   "Values, Interests and Organizational Change: The National Federation
1973   of Priests' Councils." *Sociological Analysis*, 34:281–295.
————.   "Conceptual Analysis of Organizational Effectiveness." Unpublished
1970   Ph.D dissertation. Notre Dame, Ind.: University of Notre Dame.
Turner, R. H., and L. M. Killian.   *Collective Behavior.* Englewood Cliffs, N. J.:
1957   Prentice-Hall.
White, C. M.   "Multiple Goals in the Theory of the Firm." In K. M. Boulding and
1960   W. A. Spivey (eds.), *Linear Programming and the Theory of the Firm*:
           181–201. New York: Macmillan.
Yuchtman, E., and S. E. Seashore.   "A System Resource Approach to Organizational
1967   Effectiveness." *American Sociological Review*, 32:891–903.

Assessing the Effectiveness of Organization Development (OD) Programs

MICHAEL M. McGILL
Southern Methodist University

With rapidly growing frequency, organizations are engaging in discrete organizational change efforts aimed at increasing organization effectiveness. The effectiveness of these "effectiveness improvement" efforts, typically referred to as Organization Development (OD) programs, has only recently come into question—and the answers are not readily at hand.

Does OD show? Does it work? How do we find out if it works? When? Who finds out? What do we do with what we find? These embarrassing evaluation questions are raised with increasing frequency as OD is presented to growing numbers of professional and practitioner audiences. The questions are embarrassing not because they are new, but because despite their frequency and publicness, those of us involved in organizational change (as either consultants or clients) have no ready answers.

Why don't we know more about evaluating the effectiveness of OD? After all, as an established field of study and practice, OD is some 15-years old now. In that 15 years, OD efforts have been initiated in literally hundreds of organizations. Large support groups of professionals and practitioners have emerged to spread the word. In the literature, taxonomies of the many approaches to OD reflect the maturity of the field. Yet despite all this activity in and around OD, the question of effectiveness remains sub rosa. Why?

One explanation for the absence of concrete responses to the questions surrounding OD may lie in what we have elsewhere called the "monolithic myth" of OD (McGill, 1973). There has been a belief, popular among consultants and clients alike, that OD is one thing, a single unitary process. In fact this is not true. Observation of the field shows OD to be many things, with varying values, assumptions, and approaches. Evaluation of effectiveness in the face of such variety is difficult at best. OD is revealed to be something other than that which was expected, and standards of evaluation drawn from the monolithic model are found to be inapplicable.

Another explanation for this prolonged disregard for effectiveness

123

issues in OD centers around corporate competition and concerns for privacy. If OD aids organizational performance and effectiveness, it may provide just the competitive edge a company needs. A company would, therefore, be understandably reluctant to reveal its successes. On the other hand, the response to an unsuccessful OD effort may be "the less said the better." This rationale for the apparent inattention to evaluating OD would have us believe that evaluation does occur—but it is an internal and very private affair and not for public discussion. There is some evidence to suggest that, with regard to at least a few OD efforts, this is indeed the case.

A third often heard reply to these questions is: "We will evaluate the program when it's done, but that may be some years from now." Such responses imply that to evaluate OD before the effort has run its course would be premature and promiscuous. OD is by definition a long-term process, and if evaluation hasn't occurred to date it is because it is not yet time to evaluate.

Yet another rationale for the relative absence of effectiveness data is advanced by those who argue that much of OD rests upon response to nonplanned interventions, such as market conditions and organizational politics. The effects of these variables are difficult to assess and, therefore, render most evaluation efforts meaningless.

While these responses (and others not mentioned here) may be appropriate with regard to specific incidents of OD evaluation or the absence thereof, they contribute little toward a response to the more general questions regarding effectiveness. Does OD work? How do we find out if it works? When? Who finds out? What do we do with what we find out? Conventional responses to these queries, such as those above which stress privacy or timing, appear at best to be defensive and at worst, flippant. The questioner is left with his original concerns and some added confusion, matched probably by the concerns and confusion of his consultant or client respondent.

It is the thesis of this paper that the primary cause of the confusion and lack of clarity in evaluating the effectiveness of OD stems from: (1) the inappropriate application of an ends-means perspective to the activities of OD; and (2) the consequent reliance on summative evaluation designs. We develop this argument by beginning with a closer look at the current state of the art of evaluating OD.

OD is one of the newest of the "applied social sciences" and owes much of its own development to developments in that broader field. An important dimension of this legacy, which has come to characterize OD as much as it has characterized the applied social sciences in general, is the sharp distinction drawn between the *ends* to be achieved and the *means* to those ends. Writings on the application of science to the solution of social problems and, more specifically, to the solution of organizational problems, typically presupposes some such scheme which delineates between diagnosis of system needs (determination of ends) and intervention to provide resolution (implementation of means). The OD consultant who adopts such a scheme often sees himself as a social technician of sorts (we even speak of the "social technology of OD"). He takes some goal diagnosed as desirable, either set for him by the organization or one which he sets for himself, and selects a means of intervening in the organization to bring about the desired end.

This ends-means approach to assessing the effectiveness of OD activities has a long tradition in the sciences, both physical and social, and the implications of such a perspective for evaluation are similarly well established. Postulation of ends-means implies linear relationships, causal and chronological, after this fashion:

Diagnosis Intervention o————————————o Diagnosis End

$$T_1 \qquad \text{Time} \qquad T_n$$

Evaluation in such a scheme clearly asks: Has the end been achieved? Has the OD program done what it set out to do? Evaluation is a terminal function. When the intervention has run its course, progress against the overall objective is measured. We call evaluation orientations of this sort "summative," since they follow action and appraise the final result.

Perhaps the most familiar example of summative evaluation is found in assessing management training programs. Typically, training needs are identified and a program is designed to meet those needs over a specified time period. At the conclusion of the program, participants are tested in some fashion to see whether the diagnosed needs were met. If such an evaluation scheme is appropriate for assessing management training programs, it seems logical to use this scheme to evaluate OD. It seems logical, that is, until one looks more closely at OD.

It is our proposition that the summative evaluation orientation is ill-suited to OD. It confuses rather than clarifies critical concerns, and it frustrates rather than facilitates effective evaluation efforts. A few examples of evaluation problems arising from the application of this summative orientation may substantiate this observation.

First, it must.be understood that OD is predominantly *process* as opposed to *product oriented*. This process orientation means in the first instance that terminal points become obscure, both in occurrence and in content. Consider, for example, a diagnostic survey which yields goal statements and in the process, albeit unintentionally, alters members' ways of looking at the organization and their own organizational experiences. Is the end, a renewed goal statement, then a means? What is measured against what? Perhaps a more general example is to be found in the technological, social, and structural changes long viewd by OD consultants as primary means for pursuing organizational ends. Yet, technological, social, and structural changes often become valued in and for themselves and are pursued as ends. Ends and means in organizations cannot be as easily separated as that scheme would imply, and the difficulties of application are of critical consequence for evaluation. The question, "Does OD work?" becomes exceedingly complex when we must also determine where diagnosis ends and intervention begins. When are ends means and means ends?

Second, there is the issue of who does the evaluating of OD effectiveness. The conceptualization of OD diagnostic and intervention activities as ends and means implies a consultant acting *upon* organizational phenomena to bring about the desired ends, these phenomena including organization members. This further implies a position of power from which the consultant can intervene and effect movement toward diagnosed ends, and a position of distance from which he can objectively assess progress toward the goal. While such an implied intervention/evaluation model may have been true for traditional applied social scientists' roles, today's OD consultant more often finds himself acting *with* rather than *upon* organizational phenomena. He stands *within* rather than *outside* or *above* the organization. He *shares with* rather than *imposes upon* the organizational membership diagnosis and intervention roles. Is he to share evaluation well? Are the initiators and respondents of diagnosis and intervention at the same time the evaluators and those to be evaluated? To the aforementioned issue of *what* is to be the summative perspective, now adds the question of *who* is to measure.

Finally, we turn to the question of what is to be done with the results of evaluation. In summative evaluation, data gathered at the termination of the program is used to reflect on the effectiveness of the program in toto. The data, coming as it does at the conclusion of intervention, cannot be used to improve that intervention process, only the next one (assuming there is a next one). Summative evaluation requires investing in an OD program full term and learning, only at the end of the program, if that investment was warranted or where it might have been improved.

It is important to note that the evaluation problems and paradoxes we have mentioned are inherent not in OD, but in the application of the ends-means dichotomy (with its attendant summative evaluation scheme) to the activities of OD. It is our position that the critical evaluation questions being raised about OD cannot be answered within this perspective; they can only be further complicated and obfuscated. Effectively addressing evaluation of OD requires an alternative perspective on OD activities and on the assessment of those activities. Such a perspective we introduce here.

The alternative to the ends-means, diagnosis-intervention dichotomy has as its foundation a conception of organizational change phenomena as "processes" rather than "things." As Lewin (1946) observed, a scheme for altering these processes must have as its central properties those of the social phenomena it purports to study. Therefore, in OD, a sharp distinction between diagnosis and intervention is not forced because they do not exist in sharp distinction to one another. Rather, diagnosis and intervention are viewed as sequential, each inherent in the other. Each intervention is both a step toward realizing goals and a method for isolating another diagnostic variable. OD thus becomes a cyclical process of: (1) carefully appraising data which describes the existing situation; (2) probing the readiness of the organization to take the proposed step; (3) small-scale pretests of interventions; (4) appraisal; (5) intervention; and (6) appraisal—which in turn is the first step in a still further intervention. In this model of OD, both ends and means constantly undergo revision on the basis of growing past experience.

Such a perspective on OD, one which treats ends and means as inherently inseparable, also implies the need for an alternative to summative

Figure 1

PROBLEM IDENTIFICATION

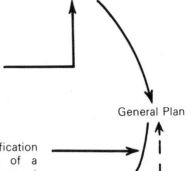

Identification of those attitudes, behaviors, and/or circumstances which account for where the organization is and/or prevent its moving forward.

Evaluation of problem identification data leads to formulation of a general plan of action, laying out what needs to be done in order to achieve intervention objectives.

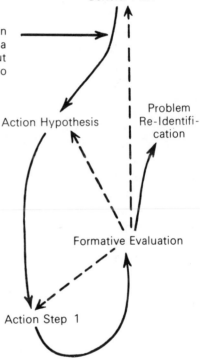

Action Hypothesis

Action Step 1

Formative Evaluation

These processes occur almost simultaneously. From the General Plan, a specific desirable goal is selected and a procedure or action defined for achieving that goal (*Action Hypothesis*). The *Action Hypothesis* leads to an *Action Step*, which is then executed, revealing data which reflects not only upon the specific *Action Hypothesis* tested, but on the viability of the orginal problem identification, general plan, etc. Thus the execution of the *Action Step* initiates *Formative Evaluation*, which in turn generates a second cycle of Problem Identification, etc.

evaluation schemes. The strategy of evaluating progress against the goals upon termination of the means can be applied only to the smallest, most minute segments of the OD process. This is because the standard of measurement, the ends, are in relatively constant flux. Where all OD activity is viewed as both ends and means, each activity must be evaluated as well as the whole, and the resulting data must be fed back into the process. Evaluation in this context must be a continuous function designed to assess the consequences of every action for the focus and nature of each succeeding action and the process as a whole. We call such an evaluation design *formative evaluation*; it occurs simultaneously with action and serves program improvement.

Figure 1 describes the steps in formative evaluation and the relationship of these steps to OD.

How is each activity to be evaluated? In order for formative evaluation to be effective, the consultant and client must be rigorous in generating hypotheses regarding potential actions and their effectiveness. These "Action Hypotheses" predict that certain desirable consequences will result from specific actions in the change effort. The criteria of "desirable consequences" emerge from both the consultant and the client. These criteria may be effectiveness (degree of goal attainment), or efficiency (cost/output ratio), or both, whatever seems important to the organization. This flexibility alone insures better evaluation and better use of evaluation data.

"Action Hypotheses" are the crux of effective OD evaluation efforts. As these hypotheses are "tested," they reveal what works in OD and often why. In so doing, the real evaluation questions about OD theory and practice are answered, to be fed back into the process to *contribute* to OD by shaping what is to come rather than to solely condone or condemn what has gone before.

We can now respond to the evaluation questions raised in our initial paragraphs from the perspective of OD. Let us take them in reverse order. *First*, what do we do with what we find out about OD? In formative evaluation designs, data from evaluation helps to shape the OD process as it proceeds; the data is used as it emerges. *Second*, who finds out? The consultant and client working together assess their own diagnosis and intervention activities and use their assessments to shape the program. *Third*, when do we evaluate OD? Constantly, at every point in the program. *Fourth*, how do we find out if it works? We generate hypotheses regarding our actions and test those hypotheses with data observed as we take action.

Finally, we come to the crux of the entire issue: Does OD work? Is it effective? I do not feel that we can categorically say either yes or no in response to this question. I do know that formative evaluation with its "Action Hypotheses" allows us the opportunity to find out what in OD works and what doesn't, and, equally important, why. It remains to be seen whether those of us concerned about evaluating OD will grasp this opportunity, or shape other evaluation opportunities, or, regrettably, continue to wallow in the frustration and evasion of current evaluation designs. It seems that we have little choice. If we believe in what we are doing, it is long past time to find out if we are really doing anything that shows.

REFERENCES

Lewin, K.   "Action Research and Minority Problems." *Journal of Social Issues,*
    1946   2:148–163.
McGill, M.   "Discarding the Monolithic Myth in OD." Paper presented at the Ameri-
    1973   can Society for Public Administrators (ASPA) conference. Los Angeles,
             Calif.

Action-Research as Applied to Organization Development

MARK A. FROHMAN
R. G. Barry Corporation
Columbus, Ohio

MARSHALL SASHKIN
Wayne State University

MICHAEL J. KAVANAGH
State University of New York
at Binghamton

The field of organization development (OD) has gained increasing popularity in recent years. Certain "prepackaged" OD programs, such as Grid OD (Blake and Mouton, 1968), recent variants of MBO (Beck and Hillmar, 1972), and laboratory training programs (Schein and Bennis, 1965), have attained particular prominence and use—for at least four reasons. First, some OD practitioners may have a favorite development technique; therefore, they do not consider using other action strategies. For example, a particular OD consultant may have had experiences which lead him to conclude that all organization members need to receive training in openness, self-examination of assumptions and values, and feedback of others' perceptions of them. As a result, he may consistently prescribe sensitivity training to improve the operation of an organization.

A second reason is based on the desire of some OD consultants to specialize in certain specific OD activities. Thus, one consultant may concentrate on the application of team training in situations where some diagnosis has indicated the need for such a program.

Third, extensive diagnosis of an organization takes time, and a client—feeling some degree of pain and, therefore, pressure for help and action—is often unwilling to accept any delay in action. Thus, the client may call upon a management consultant who will promptly analyze the problem and provide immediate recommendations for its solution.

Finally, the client may argue that he *knows* what the problem is and does not require the investment of time, money, and manpower to undertake diagnostic research for purposes of action planning; after all, a consultant is called in to help "improve" the organization, not to spend time "researching" what is already known.

These arguments all have some merit. As a result of the demands, needs, and resources of the consultant or the client, a direct application of some prepackaged OD program may be decided upon. Furthermore, this may achieve satisfactory results. However, several potentially negative outcomes are associated with the reasoning presented above.

One negative consequence is that many people view OD in a very limited way. The notion that a weekend sensitivity session or a one-week Grid program comprises the entire OD effort seems ingrained in many executives. As a result of this limited management perspective, many OD programs are doomed to failure from the beginning in that the OD effort is approached piecemeal, or nonsystemically. For example, many Grid programs and laboratory training sessions are run for a limited number of persons, exluding either whole departments or the top-management levels of an organization (Sykes, 1962). Nonsystemic OD efforts show a clear pattern of failure (Greiner, Leitch, and Barnes, 1968), and their effects seem to quickly "wash out" (Fleishman, 1953).

A second negative consequence is a tendency toward overconcern with the *content* of the organizational change to the exclusion of the *processes* involved. For example, members of the organization may be enthralled by the Managerial Grid diagram and consequently ignore the important interpersonal and task behaviors being subjected to the change activity. Or, a top-management group planning a major reorganization may focus on the quality and elegance of the new organizational structure chart and ignore the implications of the change relative to the interrelationships and role perceptions of the people in the organization.

A final consequence of the prepackaged approach is that many OD efforts are *nonadaptive;* that is, once a commitment is made to use a specific OD technique or program, the organization may retain it even though the effects of the attempted change may be minimal or, even worse, in a negative direction. This lack of flexibility in many OD programs results from approaching the organization as a static rather than a dynamic entity. Even though the organization itself may change over time as the result of an OD effort, many prepackaged programs are not designed to change with the changing circumstances in the organization.

This paper will describe a model of organizational development called action-research OD. It is aimed at correcting the above deficiencies (a nonsystemic approach, overemphasis on content, and lack of adaptive flexibility). The reader is, therefore, cautioned that the present report is *not* aimed at a comparative analysis of the processes and outcomes of different OD approaches. There is a great need for such information, of course. Sashkin, Morris, and Horst (1973) have provided a theoretical analysis, and Bowers (1973) has presented some research data; however, little work has yet been accomplished in this area.

In presenting the action-research OD approach, it will be necessary to first define action-research and its application to the field of organization development. The stages and processes involved in action-research OD will then be identified and examined in terms of studies involving this approach.

ACTION-RESEARCH

The term "action-research" is not new. Historically, it can be traced to the work of Collier (1945), and of Lewin (1946) and his students (Lippitt, 1950). Others (Corey, 1953; French and Bell, 1973) have provided historical descriptions of the development of the action-research model. Action-research describes a particular process model whereby behavioral science knowledge is applied to help a client (usually a group or social system) solve real problems and not incidentally learn the processes involved in problem solving. At the same time, it generates further knowledge in the field of applied behavioral sciences. Collier (1945), discussing Indian affairs in the United States, described action-research as follows:

> in the ethnic field, research can be made a tool of action essential to all other tools, indeed, . . . it ought to [be] the master tool. But we had in mind a particular kind of research, or if you will, particular conditions. We had in mind research impelled from central areas of needed action. . . . Since the findings of the research must be carried into effect by the administrator and the layman, and must be criticized by them through their experience, the administrator and the layman must themselves participate creatively in the research, impelled as it is from their own area of need (p. 275).

The action-research model is based on collaboration between the behavioral scientist-researcher and the client. They collaborate in exploring problems and generating valid data concerning the problems (research activity); in examining the information to understand the problems and develop action plans for their solution; in actually implementing these plans; and in generating data regarding the effects of the action. Thus, the accurate evaluation of results can be accomplished. Evaluation of results may (and generally would) be followed by further problem diagnosis, action planning, action implementation, and evaluation. By means of repetitions of this cycle, real problems are resolved and the client learns to use a science-based model of problem solving.

There is, however, a second aspect to the research process defined by the model, as noted by Lewin (1946). In addition to providing effective solutions to specific client problems and developing new problem-solving skills for the client, a successful action-research project generates new behavioral science knowledge which is fed back into the professional. bank of information and used by other behavioral scientists. This new knowledge is obtained through the research activity of the applied behavioral scientist. It may deal with general laws about human behavior, or the type of problems with which the client is confronted, or the process of consultant-client collaboration. In any case, it addresses issues broader than the specific problems faced by the client.

ACTION-RESEARCH AND ORGANIZATION DEVELOPMENT

There are a variety of approaches to organization development. We disagree with French and Bell (1973), who state that the action-research model is basic and common to all effective OD efforts. Action-research OD is one of a variety of OD approaches. In general, OD involves the application of behavioral science knowledge in organizations, through client-consultant collaboration, for the purpose of creating effective and lasting changes in the system (*i.e.*, adaptive responses to organizational problems). While there is some overlap between our descriptions of action-research and OD, there are also some elements present in one but not the other. Table 1 summarizes these similarities and differences.

Let us now see how the approaches described in Table 1 might be united, or how action-research can be tied to an OD approach. The action-

Table 1

COMPARISON OF DESCRIPTIVE FACTORS
IN ACTION-RESEARCH AND IN ORGANIZATION DEVELOPMENT

Organization Development	Both	Action-Research
* May involve data-based diagnosis of organization problems; * Is aimed at producing effective and lasting system change; * Often involves application of a preplanned "package" of actions; * May involve training the client in the application of effective processes of change; * May or may not include evaluation of results— effects and effectiveness of efforts—in concrete terms; * Often does not result in new behavioral science knowledge.	* Involve the planned application of behavioral science knowledge based on consultant-client collaboration; * Involve the use of groups; * Recognize that any action with respect to a client system is an intervention and may have some effect on the client system.	* Emphasizes data-based diagnosis of system problems; * Is aimed at solving system problems as a means of improving problem solving skills of the client; * Rarely involves application of a preplanned "package"; specific actions generally are developed on the basis of specific problems; * Emphasizes training the client in effective problem solving skills and processes; * Generally involves evaluation of results as a basis for further diagnosis of problems, action-planning, and action implementation; * Usually does result in new behavioral science knowledge.

Table 2

SUMMARY OF PHASES IN ACTION-RESEARCH

Action-Research Phase	Emphasis	Aim
Scouting	Research	Arriving at a decision of whether or not to enter;
Entry	Action	Establishing a collaborative relationship, initial problem exploration, and selecting data collection/feedback methods;
Data Collection	Research	Developing measures of organization variables and processes;
Data Feedback	Action	Returning data to the client system for discussion and diagnosis;
Diagnosis	Research	Understanding the state of the system and problems;
Action Planning	Action	Developing specific action plans— including determining who will implement the plans and how the effects will be evaluated;
Action Implementation	Action	Implementing specific change plans;
Evaluation	Research	Determining effects and effectiveness of action implementation, leading to futher efforts or to termination.

research approach as applied to OD involves data collection interventions by an OD practitioner in collaboration with the client. Thus, working together, they can obtain useful information which will enable them to jointly: develop and implement action plans for change in the client system; evaluate the effects and effectiveness of these action plans; and based on these evaluations, create and implement further action plans. The ultimate aims of the changes are increased organizational effectiveness and the development of internal organizational resources for creating adaptive, problem-solving change. The total process is based on the interlocking, interdependent, and interactive processes of research (data collection and evaluation) and action (directed intervention and implementation of change).

Phases of Action-Research OD

We have described action-research as a cyclical-sequential model, proceeding through several phases of research and action. These phases are briefly listed and defined, in the context of OD practice, in Table 2.

In some respects, our phases are similar to other models (*e.g.*, Lippitt, Watson, and Westley, 1958). We will discuss each phase in some detail.

Scouting. As Lippitt, Watson, and Westley (1958) note, the change agent, consultant, or OD practitioner generally has an implicit "descriptive-analytic theory," a frame of reference (or bias) which he uses to arrange and interpret information about the organization, and which has implications regarding the interventions he will choose to make in the client system. It is important that the OD practitioner consciously understands his own analytic framework, and equally important that the elements of the framework which are of significance to the client be made explicit to the client. Thus, the practitioner-client relationship is collaborative from the beginning. The practitioner exposes his assumptions, biases, and values and receives feedback from the client about how the above factors fit or fail to fit the frame of understanding of the client system members. The concept of scouting is drawn from a model developed by Kolb and Frohman (1970). In the scouting phase, the OD practitioner develops an initial "fix" on the significant characteristics and problems of the client system. He then makes an initial application of his "descriptive-analytic theory" to organize and understand these facts. The general information of interest to the OD practitioner at this point includes various characteristics of the client system (e.g., product or service, structure, size, technology, demographic character-istics of organization members, types of customers, external environmental relationships, prior OD experience) and descriptions of the problem(s) initially perceived by the client. Obtaining these data constitutes the major work of the scouting phase. Such data will play a major role in the client and consultant mutually deciding whether they will enter into a formal relationship and, if so, at what point in the organization the entry will be made.

Entry. The process of establishing a collaborative and open OD practitioner-client relationship and clearly defining the expectations of the parties (Frohman, 1968) is the major focus of the entry phase. The major emphases at this point are establishing the credibility of the OD practitioner and making certain that those in power positions in the client system openly sanction the OD activity. The lack of such open sanction is a nearly certain guarantee that the OD effort will fail (Clark, 1972). In such an event, any OD actions which occur are likely to be carried out in a nonsystemic manner.

Data Collection. The "prediagnostic" examination of problems during scouting and entry is collaborative in nature and useful for exploring the implications of collecting data about the client system and the problems it faces. Note that such prediagnosis during the first two phases is primarily the product of the OD practitioner. The third phase, data collection, involves client system members to a greater extent—first, in selecting a method and deciding how it will be used, and second, in the actual collection of infor-mation (which will inevitably involve client system members via interviews, questionnaire responses, and observations of their behavior, or some com-bination of these methods). French and Bell (1973) provide a set of excellent reference tables on data gathering for diagnosis, typologized by system level and by the organizational process of major concern, and including types of information which should be obtained and common methods for doing so.

The first three phases are focused primarily on research activities but, nonetheless, involve certain action interventions which may have some impact on the client system. Some research data, which will be reviewed (Frohman and Waters, 1969), suggest that entry and data collection in and of themselves have little, if any, impact on the client system. These early phases are within the broader phase of social-system change that Lewin (1947) called "unfreezing," or developing a need for change and establishing a client-consultant change relationship (Lippitt, Watson, and Westley, 1958). These are necessary (but not sufficient) conditions for effective organizational change.

Data Feedback.   If diagnosis of problems and action planning are to be collaborative activities (as prescribed by the action-research model), the OD practitioner must fully share with the client the data which are gathered. There are a variety of options for accomplishing this, which we will not detail here. Most, however, involve some form of group or work-team meeting. It is during the data feedback phase that interventions may have some real impact on the client system (Bowers, 1971b; Frohman, 1970), although such effects do not seem to be of major significance.

Feedback provides the client with information about the client system, information which is useful in determining the strengths and weaknesses of that system. Therefore, this fourth phase, data feedback, is intimately tied with the next phase, diagnosis. It is quite artificial to treat them separately; however, there are two reasons for doing so. First, the feedback of data to the client is the first activity of the OD practitioner which is *primarily an action intervention* in the client system, as opposed to the phases described earlier and the next phase, which primarily involve research activities (Brown, 1972). Second, we want to describe the action-research OD process as clearly as possible, and this separation may aid the reader in following and understanding the nature and logic of the model. In practice, data feedback and diagnosis often occur at the same time.

The artificiality of the clear-cut separation of phases is further highlighted by considering the interdependent and interactive nature of the phases. Data collection and data feedback are obviously interdependent; one must collect data if one is to share those data with the client. The phases are also interactive; hence, the feedback targets will, in part, determine the types of data to be collected, while the data obtained will, in part, determine the best presentation or feedback methods.

Diagnosis.   The focus of the process shifts back to research as the client system members and the OD practitioner jointly use the data to define and explore organizational problems and strengths. This diagnostic process is very different from the general meaning of "diagnosis." The medical-clinical model defines diagnosis as an activity by the consultant (or physician), who is solely responsible for the specific diagnostic conclusions. In action-research OD, diagnosis is a joint activity of the consultant and the client (Sashkin, 1973). Note that this collaborative diagnosis is no less data based than the traditional form—it is the collaborative nature of the process that is critically different.

An adequate diagnostic process will lead directly to implications for the actions needed to resolve the problems. However, a conclusion that further data are needed for accurate diagnosis is quite possible, in which case the action-research process will "recycle" to the data collection phase. Finally, this research phase of diagnosis is directly and interactively linked to the subsequent action phase (action planning), just as the research phase of data collection is closely linked to the following action-oriented phase (data feedback).

Action Planning. This and the next phase shift the focus of the action-research OD model back to action. The involvement of the client is increased during this phase in that the client participates in planning change activities. At this point, the role of the OD practitioner becomes one of a process helper and a trainer, rather than a consultant-expert. If the OD practitioner solves the client's problems as an "expert," an effective change might take place; but the client will learn little of the skills or processes involved in dealing with problems in the organization—a major goal of many OD programs. Thus, it is at this point that the OD practitioner's aim of developing internal problem-solving skills and resources becomes operationalized.

In accomplishing this aim, the OD practitioner walks a tightrope: he must help in the presentation (feedback), interpretation (diagnosis), and exploration (action planning) of specific data, but he must avoid being cast in the role of expert problem solver. Specific action plans must be created by the client with the assistance of the OD practitioner, not presented to the client by the expert-consultant.

Action Implementation. This and the preceding two phases fall with the broader phase of social-system change that Lewin (1947) called "moving." By altering certain social forces and removing or introducing others, the social system may be moved toward a new state or "quasi-stationary equilibrium," in Lewin's terms.

The action implementation phase involves the most actively directed OD efforts. One cannot, however, be very specific as to the actual content of the changes. This is because the content of the action implementation phase, the specific actions taken and changes made, depends on the situation and the nature of the problems diagnosed. Thus, the variety of possible action steps is wide in range. Some OD practitioners have produced catalogs of action interventions which can serve as useful reference sources (Fordyce and Weil, 1971; Pfeiffer and Jones, 1972a, 1972b, 1971, 1970); however, the specific plan chosen must be based on situational determinants. Regardless of the content chosen, the primary concern here is with the process of implementation. In this process, the model again specifies active collaboration between client and OD practitioner.

The actions taken may depend greatly on the skills and resources of the OD practitioner, or may be developed almost entirely by the client. Essentially, this means that the professional action-oriented resources of the OD practitioner are not ignored; but the decision to use the change agent in specific ways is reached jointly—by the client *and* the consultant. Thus the OD practitioner may develop and implement a team-training laboratory for certain groups in the client system. A decision to do so, however, would be based on *collaborative* diagnostic and action-planning activites; such action would not be taken on the basis of a consultant recommendation, but rather on the basis of mutual problem exploration, need definition, and examination of various alternative actions. An example of an action implementation carried out primarily by the client would be the decision to institute weekly cross-department coordination and problem-solving meetings. The consultant might offer assistance in conducting such meetings, but the primary action would be accomplished by the client. The decision to implement this specific action would have been made in the same way as the earlier example—through a process of client-consultant collaboration.

The development of action plans requires attention to two major factors. The first is that the action plan must contain an adequately detailed description of what is to be done, who is to do what part, and when. The second factor, too often omitted in OD practice, is that there must be *continual monitoring* of the effects of the action intervention. This must be done throughout the action-research OD process, and most particularly with regard to the specific problem-solving actions planned and implemented in this and the preceding phases of the process. Thus, the model ends with a direct link back to research—the evaluation phase.

Evaluation. The action plan should specify, in detail, evaluation procedures to be implemented during and following the preceding phase. All too often consultants and OD practitioners seem satisfied with little more than guesses as to the effects and effectiveness of actions in and on the client system. But thorough evaluation is an absolute necessity, for both the consultant and the client, for several reasons. First, a data-based evaluation will indicate to the consultant whether the specific change efforts have been successful. Second, the same data will be needed by the client system as a basis for further diagnosis and action planning (recycling). Third, the empirical data will help the client and the OD practitioner determine when it is appropriate that their relationship be ended. And finally, only a well-designed evaluation phase can determine whether and when the primary, overall goal of the OD effort has been achieved: the development of internal client system resources with skills for creating effective, adaptive, problem-solving change in the future.

"Refreezing" (Lewin, 1947) has been one term used to describe this primary goal. Unfortunately, it carries the connotation of a fixed, unchanging, and unchangeable end state. Moreover, Lewin's use of the term was in reference to the attainment and continuation of specific changes, rather than to the development of increased and more efective adaptability on the part of the client system. Frohman's (1970) term, "integration," seems more appropriate but lacks descriptive detail. Lippitt, Watson, and Westley's (1958) term, "stabilization and generalization of change," is more descriptive but omits the focus on evaluation and recycling. An extension of this term to "stabilization of specific, effective changes and generalization of the action-research OD process" seems to best describe the desirable end-state of action-research OD.

Action-Research OD Processes

The reader should be aware that the preceding discussion on the phases of action-research OD represents the content of this approach. Earlier, one possible general deficiency of organization development activities was identified as a concern with content to the exclusion of process. The OD practitioner could, for example, follow the phases outlined but still fail to use the action-research OD model because he omitted the critical processes or attended to these processes without possessing the required skills to do so effectively. The real strength of the action-research OD approach is its emphasis on the processes involved in the client-consultant relationship. Thus, the identification of critical processes characteristic of action-research OD is perhaps more important than a comparison or integration of the elements of the two approaches described in Tables 1 and 2.

There are five processes or methods of operation basic to and continuous throughout the application of the action-research model. These are not tied to a specific time or phase, but all five share a common element—a *problem-solving orientation*. Even though the processes can be identified clearly and discussed independently, it is obvious that in practice they do not operate independently. The commonality of problem orientation binds them to one another. Each process will be briefly defined, but no order or priority is implied by the listing.

Client-Consultant Collaboration. The previous descriptions of the phases consistently emphasized the process of collaboration between client and consultant in each phase and in all activities. This process is most critical in diagnosis and action planning, where older models prescribed decision making primarily by the consultant. Of course, this is where the OD practitioner may most easily fall into the trap of becoming the expert problem solver on content issues, rather than the process trainer. The OD practitioner, through this close client collaboration, aims not only to help the client solve immediate problems but, more significantly, to help the client learn a generally useful problem-solving process. To some extent, the OD practitioner is a model for the client. Acceptance of his behavior as desirable to model is facilitated by collaboration between the two parties. In other words, effective internalization of modeled behavior (Kelman, 1958) depends upon a base of referent power (French and Raven, 1959), which is developed and enhanced through the collaborative relationship.

In addition to the reasons previously discussed relative to the phases of the action-research OD model, the collaborative process is also crucially important in establishing client system involvement in the OD effort. While involvement is necessary to attain the overall aims of the OD effort, it is also required to successfully accomplish many of the specific activities of each phase. For example, the OD effort must respond to relevant demands and characteristics of the client system. This requires collecting accurate and adequately detailed data about the client system, an activity greatly facilitated by client involvement.

Client Learning for Internal Resource Development. By helping the client understand the action-research OD approach, the OD practitioner becomes a trainer. Through this training, the client learns to use the action-research OD model and develops the internal skills for effective use of the model on a continuing basis. Client learning is an important process element in each phase of the model. To a large extent, the OD practitioner trains by *modeling*, although other learning approaches are also likely to be involved (conceptual instruction, guided skill practices, etc.). In the broadest sense, the client system learns to use the action-research OD approach by *doing*; this is an experiential learning process. It is important to note that this client-learning process has its major emphasis on problem solving and is not merely an academic exercise or an attempt to make "sensitivity trainers" of the organization's membership.

Monitoring and Evaluation.   Action-research is data based, which means that "tracking"—empirical monitoring and evaluation of the effort—is continuous throughout, not just limited to the evaluation phase. The particular problems and objectives generated as a result of the client-consultant collaboration provide the focus for the monitoring and evaluation. In terms of client learning, this continuous evaluation provides data-based feedback, a requirement for effective learning. Furthermore, this evaluation demonstrates to the client, in specific, concrete terms, the value (or lack of value) of the OD effort or any specific portion of the program. The monitoring and evaluation function is useful for the consultant as well, for through it he learns more about the action-research OD process and its application and generates information which may be added to the bank of professional knowledge (academic and applied).

Interaction and Link Between Research and Action.   It has been previously noted that there is an interdependence and interaction among the various phases of the action-research OD process. This reflects the fact that the model, by genesis oriented toward solving problems in the client system (Collier, 1945), is based on the reciprocal interlinking of research and action interventions. This makes explanation of the model difficult, particularly in separating the phases and processes for definition and discussion. Scientific methods of data gathering and analysis are tied to reality with the persistent questions, "What does this information mean, and what implications does it have in terms of *actions*?" The interventions of the OD practitioner may be seen as primarily research or primarily action oriented; however, the effects of research as action are not ignored (Brown, 1972), and actions invariably contain a research element in the design for evaluating their effects.

Flexibility.   Finally, the action-research OD approach is characterized throughout by a high degree of flexibility, of ready modifiability. This process is obviously related to the prior two processes and is aimed at resolving one of the deficiencies of many OD efforts (described earlier as a lack of adapt-ability). For example, recycling is one aspect of flexibility. Data gathering may yield information which implies a need to return to the client in order to modify the feedback plan, or to obtain further data which will better fit the initial feedback model. The feedback process may result in a request for further or different data analysis or presentation. Diagnostic discussion may identify a need for more or other data, or for further feedback using the same or a different feedback model. It should be clear that recycling can occur at any point in the process, thus requiring a high degree of flexibility in the application of the model.

Flexibility also means that the range of research methods and action interventions open to the OD practitioner is essentially unlimited. Survey, interview, and observational research methods are all among the options; none is automatically excluded or prescribed. In a similar manner, many different actions are possible—so many, in fact, that it is not feasible to itemize here even those which are part of the OD practitioner's standard repertoire. We might note, however, that actions could even involve the application of a specific OD program, such as Grid OD (Blake and Mouton, 1968), sensitivity training (Bradford, Gibb, and Benne, 1964), or management by objectives (Beck and Hillmar, 1972). Again, the "problem-centeredness" of the model, applied to the organization as a dynamic entity, requires flexibility in its application.

To this point, we have dealt with three major questions: (a) What is action-research? (b) What is action-research OD? and (c) What are the critical processes in action-research OD which differentiate it from other OD models? However, the most important question must still be addressed: Do OD efforts have better prospects of success when they are based on and conducted using the action-research model? This question could be approached deductively, since it is evident that any OD program could be selected and implemented within the context of the action-research model. Therefore, action-research would seem to offer a higher probability of satisfactory results as compared with prepackaged programs. However, as with all logical answers to practical questions, the next, more significant questions must be: (a) Does the model operate as described in this paper? and (b) Does it really work (*i.e.*, yield effective results) in OD applications?

To answer these final questions we must turn to some empirical research. Rather than reporting and discussing the numerous older studies involving action-research, only some of which have an organizational focus, the following review will concentrate on recent research, examining four studies conducted in the past five or six years. All of these studies involved, to some extent, a particular form of research data-gathering and feedback methodology known as the "survey feedback" approach. It seems worthwhile, then, to briefly review one large-scale study examining the effects of the survey and feedback methodology as the basis of an OD approach, compared with several other packaged OD programs. This will help us understand how survey and feedback methods operate when implemented as a means of data gathering and data feedback within the action-research OD approach.

RESEARCH ON THE GENERAL IMPACT OF SURVEY AND FEEDBACK

The impact of survey and feedback on work groups relative to other strategies has been investigated by Bowers (1973, 1971a, 1971b). Using data from longitudinal multicompany studies, he compared changes (on leadership and climate variables) associated with five different OD programs. The condition of these variables was measured by questionnaire before and after the action plans were implemented. The five OD strategies compared were: (a) survey feedback; (b) interpersonal process consultation; (c) sensitivity training; (d) task process consultation; and (e) data handback. For each action strategy, about 100 or more work groups were studied.

No full and current description of the survey and feedback method is easily accessible, although several reference sources exist (Bowers and Franklin, 1972; Mann, 1957; Neff, 1965; Taylor and Bowers, 1972). In brief, the approach, as currently used (Bowers and Franklin, 1972; Taylor and Bowers, 1972), involves the application of fairly sophisticated survey research methods in the development and use of an organizational survey throughout a client system. The data is analyzed, summarized, and fed back to the client in a series of small-group discussions. In these discussions, the change agent assists the manager or supervisor in conducting a discussion of the data and the problems they indicate, and in exploring relevant issues in greater detail. In this way, all members of the client system will eventually be exposed to the data gathered and will participate in the problem diagnosis.

Thus, the survey feedback OD package used by Bowers (1973) is, in effect, a data-based diagnostic package. The survey instrument is essentially standardized (Taylor and Bowers, 1972), and this particular data-gathering and feedback model is applied to a client without consideration of alternative methods. We must be clear, then, that the present discussion is for the purpose of examining this particular methodology in comparison with other packaged options; the survey feedback model, as used here, is not an example of action-research OD.

We need spend little time describing the sensitivity training approach; it is well known and standard reference sources are available (Bradford, Gibb, and Benne, 1964; Schein and Bennis, 1965). Interpersonal process consultation (Schein, 1969) emphasizes developing the ability of groups within the client system to work together and handle their own interpersonal relationship problems and concerns effectively.

Task process consultation focuses almost singularly on task objectives. Extensive exploration of the job-related strengths and weaknesses in a group is the major thrust of the consultant. A premise of this OD technique is that interpersonal processes and dynamics are relevant only as they relate to task accomplishment. This method seems related to (or an extension of) the operations research approach (Bennis and Peter, 1966). The last technique, data handback, is actually no treatment at all. As Bowers (1971a, 1971b) describes it, surveys were taken and written reports were sent to the client, but no consultant activity occurred. Therefore, this fifth condition served as a base-line comparison for the other four.

Based on a detailed analysis comparing changes stemming from these five techniques, Bowers (1971a) concludes: "treatments differ in their productive potency. Interpersonal process consultation and those treatments which are data-based, particularly survey feedback, seem to have an advantage over either laboratory training or a more task-oriented form of process consultation" (p. 52). Later he notes, "Data handback while generally positive in impact, seems to have had little capability for handling the climate change problem and suffers somewhat as a result" (p. 53).

Thus, using a variety of statistical methods, Bowers found that a survey and feedback technique ranked high in overall effectiveness in prompting change in climate conditions and leadership behavior, as compared with four alternate approaches. Again, we emphasize that *none* of the OD efforts described by Bowers can be considered action-research OD in the sense that we have defined it. "Each setting consisted of a more or less universal application of an intervention package" (Bowers, 1971b: 55). In no case was any meaningful diagnostic activity undertaken to determine the type of OD action most appropriate. Bowers' reports are, of course, of great value, representing the only large-scale comparative study of differing OD methods ever conducted. Much knowledge has thus been gained regarding both the general application of packaged OD programs and their comparative utilities, including the particular value of survey and feedback as a diagnostically oriented packaged program. Bowers' work, however, tells us little about the part that survey feedback methodology may play in the context of the action-research model. The following studies are successively more clearly directed toward this critical issue.

FOUR STUDIES IN ACTION-RESEARCH OD

*Study I: Action-Research Using Survey
and Feedback Methods*

Bowers' (1973, 1971a, 1971b) work demonstrates that survey feedback as a diagnostically oriented OD package can lead to positive changes in an organization that exceed the outcomes of other types of OD packages. However, the question of greater concern is whether survey feedback as part of a total action-research OD effort can produce organizational changes exceeding what might be accomplished with the survey feedback package alone. This can best be tested by systematically varying OD strategies which range from only a survey and feedback process through several degrees of client-consultant involvement in diagnosis, action planning, and implementation. Frohman (1970) examined the effects of different organizational change strategies in four comparable units (units A, B, C, and D) within one sales region of a national corporation. Three units , A, B, and C, were composed of eight to ten work groups, while unit D was the top management group.

In unit A, the OD effort was limited solely to survey and feedback of data. Unit B received survey and feedback, as well as a follow-up questionnaire on progress (filled out by work-group managers) and a meeting with the consultant to discuss specific ideas for further action steps. Unit C was exposed to the survey and feedback effort; in addition, the consultant spent several hours with each manager (prior to the group survey feedback meeting held by that manager) discussing questions and problems raised by the data. Unit D, the top-management group of the sales region, received substantially the same treatment as unit C but, in addition, the consultant attended monthly staff meetings and offered help in understanding and improving the process of those meetings. Note that only for units C and D do the change efforts come close to meeting the requirements for an action-research OD program by making the process of *client-consultant collaboration* more fully operational. In addition to having the strongest client-consultant collaboration, unit D also had the greatest emphasis on the process of *client learning for internal resource development*. In fact, the manipulated strength of these two processes increased steadily from unit A (essentially zero) to unit D.

Pre- and post-treatment questionnaires were administered in each unit, nine months apart, allowing measurement of changes in perceptions of supervisory behavior, peer behavior, and group processes. The results were not exactly as expected, but they were extremely consistent over all variables measured and were highly significant. Unit D, the top-management group, showed a sizable improvement in supervisory and peer behaviors and group processes, shifting toward Likert's (1967, 1961) "System 4" ideal. Unit C also showed consistent improvements, although not as great as unit D. Unexpectedly, unit B showed a slight deterioration on most variables, while unit A evidenced a slight but distinct improvement. Overall, for almost every one of the 14 dependent variables measured, the 4 units could be ranked in terms of change, from greatest to least, as D, C, A, and B.

In discussing these results, Frohman (1970) concluded that, under the proper conditions, survey feedback alone could be enough to prompt organizational improvement, perhaps because of a "Hawthorne effect" (Roethlisberger and Dickson, 1939). In trying to understand the negative results for unit B, some additional evidence indicated that unreasonably high expectations had been aroused for this unit as a result of the consultant's post-survey intervention. The brief nature of this intervention did not permit further development of the ideas and improvements discussed. The consequent inability to carry out the ideas generated apparently led to a rejection of the entire feedback program, thus the negative impact.

Here we see a situation where survey and feedback intervention alone resulted in mildly positive consequences, much as was the case for Bowers' (1971a) "data handback" method. When combined with some further, more directed interventions, based on the data obtained, the outcome was mildly negative. The importance of this finding for the too-frequent practice of minimal follow-up for organizational surveys seems apparent, particularly when contrasted with the strongly positive effects in units C and D. Perhaps management should not be surprised with the negative reactions of employees when confronted with another survey following this minimal follow-up approach (low in subsequent client-consultant collaboration). The results from units A and B demonstrate quite clearly that data collection and feedback are action interventions. Brown's (1972) later work also validates this conclusion. Based on Bowers' results regarding data handback and Frohman's results with a similar procedure, one might tentatively conclude that data collection and feedback, when used alone, has mild positive effects. However, further intervention by the OD practitioner, followed by abdication of his involvement at a point in the process before the client is prepared to assume the major portion of involvement, seems to have some negative consequences.

The more positive effects in units C and D, however, suggest that the survey feedback method—in conjunction with extensive on-site consultant follow-up and guidance—holds promise as a major OD approach (Bowers and Franklin, 1972). The greater emphasis on the processes discussed as critical to the action-research OD model seem to have produced significantly more positive effects for the specific organizational units involved. Of course, it is possible that the changes in unit D were primarily due to a high degree of problem awareness and motivation to change within this top-management group—an "unfrozen" state—combined with a strong power base for change. Thus, any intervention at all might have produced similar results in unit D. However, the findings discussed above, which suggest that data collection and feedback alone is a rather weak, diffuse intervention (not greatly strengthened even when combined with some further, minimal OD-practitioner intervention), indicate that Frohman's analysis and conclusions are more convincing than this alternative explanation which could not explain the positive results for unit C.

Finally, the reader should realize that the contrasting conditions in this study clearly illustrate the distinction regarding content versus process changes. The data collection and feedback techniques in units A and B represent an emphasis on content changes to the exclusion of processes involved. However, the approaches in units C and D are oriented toward both the processes and content of the change effort, a critical ingredient of action-research OD.

*Study II: Action-Research at
the Top-Management Level*

One common factor in the research studies already discussed (Bowers, 1973; Frohman, 1970) has been the practice of external researcher-change agents working with a large number of organization members at all levels of the system. This second action-research study (Frohman and Waters, 1969) differs from the first in that the primary emphasis was on developmental work with only the top-management group. This focus on top management had two objectives: to develop the top executives into a coordinated, smoothly functioning team and to develop the individuals in the top group as internal development resources for their own subordinates and for lower levels. Thus, this study is similar to the previous one in that it is problem oriented, but it is somewhat different in that its primary thrust is toward the action-research OD process identified as *client learning for internal resource development*. As in units C and D of Frohman's other (1970) study, survey feedback played a major part in the OD effort; however, it was by no means the only tool used in this action-research program.

The organization involved was one region of a national fire and casualty insurance company, employing about 360 people. The top-management group consisted of the regional head, a resident vice president, and the latter's eight direct subordinates—this included the personnel manager, who was to be a key figure in the change effort.

The activities of the outside consultant can be divided into three categories (Waters, 1969): (a) examining group processes in top-management meetings, (b) sharing and discussing survey feedback data at all levels of the organization, and (c) skill training sessions for top management. There were three further aspects to this OD program. First, the consultant adopted a general strategy of focusing on problems and issues raised by members of the top group regarding their own "work-life space." Thus, the specific content of the consultant's activities depended on the situation and was not determined by a tightly preplanned or packaged program, emphasizing the "problem-centeredness" and *flexibility* of the action-research OD model. Second, the role of the personnel manager was modified from its traditional nature to that of a "coach-counselor," who could collaborate closely with individuals at all organizational levels. Third, the top-management group participated in a team development laboratory in order to reinforce new attitudes and behaviors and improve interpersonal relationships. Obviously, these last two aspects were aimed specifically at *client learning for internal resource development*.

The program was designed to include thorough research evaluation of its processes and outcomes, another important aspect of any action-research OD effort. Two other regions of the parent firm which did not receive consultant assistance were used as comparison controls, and identical forms of data were collected in all three regions. These data included before and after measures of organizational structures, processes, and performance.

The survey instrument was composed of 18 indices constructed to measure supervisory leadership, peer leadership, group processes (such as influence and decision making), and satisfactions (*e.g.*, with job, pay, peers). It was completed by employees in all three regions. Improvement, in comparing the before and after measures, was considered to be change toward more participative-consultative management. The respondents had identified this as the direction they wanted to move in at the start of the OD program. Thus, we see the importance of early *client-consultant collaboration* in executing the action-research OD model.

For the total employee sample, the results indicated a general decline in the 18 organizational indices for *each* of the three regions; but the average decline was more than twice as great in the comparison regions as in the experimental region. Fifteen of the eighteen changes showed the experimental region superior. Looking at the direct target, the top-management group in the experimental region, there was improvement on all 18 indices and 8 of the changes were statistically significant. The top teams of the comparison regions showed a general decline on the 18 measures, comparing their before and after scores. Thus, the action-research effort appears to have contributed to slowing a general decline in organizational "health," and significantly reversing this decline for the top-management group in the target region.

Performance indicators (sales, retention, growth, underwriting gain) clearly showed the experimental region superior to the others. For all nine regions in the company, the average percentage change was zero on all four factors. While the control regions did slightly worse than the overall average, particularly on sales (seven percent decrease), the experimental region did considerably better, particularly on sales (twelve percent increase). At this point, one should again note the weakness of data collection as the only intervention. The collection of survey data in the two control regions had little, if any, positive impact on those organizations. Conversely, it is possible that data collection had negative impact; but this seems quite unlikely since the two control regions differed very little on the four performance indicators relative to six regions in which no data were collected.

A third type of data for program evaluation was provided by taped, in-depth interviews with each member of the top-management group. Content analysis of these tapes showed that these individuals perceived the changes indicated by the survey data and performance measures (Frohman and Waters, 1969).

This study illustrates the importance of top-management support and involvement. While some OD practitioners, such as Beckhard (1969), believe that top-management support and involvement (in the "management of change") is a necessary condition for effective OD, others, such as Beer and Huse (1972), have questioned this. It seems most likely that top support is a necessary but not sufficient requirement for successful OD work, which must involve more of the organizational membership. This study was aimed primarily at two percent of the members of the organization, the top-management group, and this action-research program was clearly associated with improved organizational health and performance relative to comparison units. From these results, it seems that top management can not only support and encourage OD, but can serve as internal resource catalysts for change and act to facilitate change downward through the system.

Another aspect of this study was the use of the personnel manager as the direct internal "linker" between all organizational levels and the outside consultant team. The key role of the individual who obtains knowledge and skills from resources external to an organization and conveys this information to those who can use it within the system is only beginning to be understood (Havelock, *et al.*, 1969). In an action-research strategy, the "linker" role seems to be especially critical in the entry, action planning, and action implementation phases. Furthermore, with personnel managers apparently tending to adopt the role of internal OD practitioners (Beckhard, 1969), the focus on how this role was used in the Frohman and Waters' study is of significant interest.

There are two other features of this particular action-research program which are important. First, action-research is based on a continuous cycle of research and action interventions and is, therefore, relatively more *flexible* than prepackaged programs, such as Grid OD. In this case, the consultant was able to respond appropriately as diagnostic information from the surveys became available. Thus, he became more and more attuned to the emerging needs and demands of the system and, as he observed and charted the top team's functioning, he intervened with what he felt were appropriate training actions. Obviously, considerable competence and understanding of group processes are necessary for the success of such an action-research strategy, as well as a sizable investment of time.

The second important feature was that the team development lab played an important part in the program because of its timing and focus. The consultants believed that the top group was at the point where sensitive interpersonal issues could surface and be discussed. Through work on group skills and management styles, a climate had evolved that greatly facilitated and enhanced the openness and confrontation of the lab setting. Thus, coming at the end of the OD program, the lab not only reinforced previous learnings but also dealt with new issues on the interpersonal level. This increased the impact of the program and the effectiveness of top managers as they worked with each other and their subordinates in applying their learnings. Contrasting this with the prepackaged approach using laboratory training as the first (and sometimes only) step to "open-up" the participants may in part account for the often-encountered negative image of OD practitioners (Levinson, 1972).

Study III: Action-Research
in a School System

Up to this point, we have discussed action-research based OD programs which have shown considerable evidence of success. While programs which are not successful probably are less likely to be reported, it is true that programs which fail or show no remarkable (or significant) success can be as useful (if not more so) in understanding the action-research model (and OD in general) as those which succeed. Miles, *et at.* (1969), report on a survey and feedback approach to OD in a small school system which, at best, had equivocal results. Describing the sequence of events which followed the survey, they state:

> summarized data displays were fed back first to the top administrative group which engaged in diagnosis and problem solving. Then each building principal repeated this process with his faculty in a series of meetings ... [then] cross-building "task forces" were set up to work on problems noted in the feedback sessions, and their proposals were considered for action by the administrative group (Miles, *et al.*, 1969: 463–64).

The research design had been carefully constructed to mitigate contaminating factors and to yield quantitative data focusing on power equalization, communication, and norms in the school system. The results "did not show more than chance fluctuation in the 36 indicators studied for the administrative group and the 43 examined for the teachers" (p. 446).

From the report of Miles and his colleagues, we can derive several possible causes for their lack of success. First, there were no action implementations in this program. The feedback data were discussed but no specific plans were made to implement the results of these discussions, thus illustrating a failure to use the *reciprocal interlinking of research and action intervention*, the very heart of the action-research OD model. Second, due to the lack of consultant follow-up on action planning and implementation, it seems likely that the feedback program was seen as an isolated event with no general relationship to the organization or its processes, illustrating the *nonsystemic* deficiency identified earlier. Third, the top administrators were given little time to fully understand and use the data before lower levels became involved, *i.e.*, weak *client-consultant collaboration*. Finally, the researchers themselves note that their measures may have been "somewhat insensitive to change" (Miles, *et al.*, 1969: 466). The importance of reliable, valid, and *sensitive* measures of organizational factors (*e.g.*, role perceptions, leadership style) for the purposes of planning, implementing, and evaluating change within action-research strategies (and OD research in general) hardly needs emphasis in light of the tremendous importance of data-based *monitoring and evaluation* of changes in the action-research OD model.

It seems clear that the effect on the total client system was minimal, which is probably due to the first two problems mentioned above concerning the weakness of the data feedback intervention. The survey feedback approach, as used here, was chosen as a means for developing a power equalization change (Leavitt, 1965) with respect to teachers and administrators. However, from the research reviewed in this paper, it does not seem that survey feedback is, in itself, a very powerful intervention technique. The intended link from survey feedback, through diagnosis, to action planning was blocked by the administrative group, both at the teacher-principal interface and at the principal-top administrator interface, primarily due to the nonsystemic nature of the effort and its failure to link action to research.

After this initial negative experience with this organization, the OD practitioners, on the basis of the poor data results, attempted to revise the approach by modifying their program to focus on the administrative group. At this point, they did attend to the critical link between action and research, and used the flexibility of the action-research model to shift the thrust of the program. While the survey and feedback method was continued in the renewed effort, there was a change toward team development for the administrative group aimed at improving the problem-solving and interpersonal processes of that group.

Later reports (McElvaney and Miles, 1971, 1969) document the effects of these changed OD efforts. Again, no substantial changes were found in the system, although teachers did report seeing greater innovativeness and a more open climate in the district. Interview data showed changes in the functioning of the top administrative group, with improvement in interpersonal processes and working relationships. This was reflected by greater openness in airing feelings and opinions and better communication in general.

McElvaney and Miles (1971) suggest that due to the continued support and involvement of the OD practitioners, the basic processes concerning the way the top team functioned were altered, thus laying a "foundation for more effective functioning in the future" (p. 135). They admit, however, to the possibility that "the program was a momentary perturbation in the functioning of a stable system and . . . no really fundamental shifts occurred . . ." (p. 133).

It remains to be seen whether this effort will ultimately result in system changes in the direction of increased organizational effectiveness and adaptive functioning. In any case, the study very well documents our initial description of OD problems, as well as the phases and processes of the action-research model as applied to OD.

Study IV: Action-Research OD on a Turnover Problem

So far, we have reviewed action-research programs where the initial research aim was to identify strengths and weaknesses of the organization. There is another type of action-research strategy which also fits the model. Such a strategy involves designing the data collection phase and, therefore, orienting the action phase toward understanding and resolving a specific organizational problem or weakness.

An action-research strategy which is initiated because of some problem identified by the members of the organization has at least three advantages. First, it provides a starting point from which to select or develop data collection procedures and instruments. Second, if the specific problem (*e.g.*, poor product quality or interdepartmental conflict) affects a number of people, then the diagnostic work is more readily accepted. Consultant activities which address specific concerns held by a number of persons in the organization are seen as more relevant and less wasteful of time. Third, OD activity based on a client's specific problem seems more conducive to developing a collaborative relationship between OD practitioners and organization members. Although they may have very different backgrounds and interests, both parties are talking about the same thing and are together to reach a specific common goal. The sharing of vocabulary and goals has been shown to facilitate effective development work (A. Frohman, 1970)

On the other hand, OD practitioners who use an action-research strategy around a specific problem must be conscious of two traps. First, the problem identified by the organization may not, in fact, be the real cause of difficulty in the organization; it may only be a symptom. For example, interdepartmental conflict may be the result of a history of unequal mobility in the two departments or competitiveness between the department heads. A well-constructed diagnostic phase (Levinson, 1972; Sashkin, 1973), as well as the establishment of an open and clear action-research "contract" between client and consultant, may overcome this problem. A second trap lies in the possible deemphasis of action planning and implementation. Often, a great deal of satisfaction results from well-done research, especially when identification of an appropriate developmental plan is derived from the research data with relative ease. Indeed, this is a general problem concerning the use of survey methods and sophisticated data analysis. Overconcern with data and analysis of relevance to academically-oriented research in general may lead the OD practitioner to lose sight of the interventionist role. However, as suggested by the work we have reviewed here, it is critical that there be help in applying new ideas and management techniques and a follow-up of the progress made by the persons attempting to use them. Thus, research to identify the causes of difficulties must not be overemphasized at the expense of taking action to correct problems.

Weisbord, Frohman, and Johnston (1971), and Frohman, Weisbord, and Johnston (1971) reported an OD program which, while avoiding the traps discussed above, illustrates quite well the application of an action-research model with an initial and continued specific problem focus. These consultants were asked to help solve a turnover problem in a large food service company. The organization had an overall average yearly turnover rate of approximately 100 percent (in 1969), which cost the firm well over $10 million annually in terms of direct replacement and training costs; the *full* cost, which would include lost performance and management time spent dealing with the effects of the turnover problem, was considerably greater.

The consultants initially observed that many units had consistently high turnover rates, while other units were considerably lower; they therefore directed their first efforts toward researching the differences between high- and low-turnover units. To start this diagnostic phase, they developed contacts with line managers in the region selected for the research, emphasizing *client-consultant collaboration* at the onset. This was followed by preliminary interviews with a sample of employees to identify issues that the workers felt were important. In addition, the interviews served to familiarize the consultants with the organization. The next step was the design of a survey questionnaire. The specific items were developed by line managers and staff persons, as well as the consultants (who drew ideas from their interviews and their experiences with other clients). This sequence illustrates how entry activities emphasizing collaboration link into a collaborative data collection process.

The information collected in this research phase included demographic data on employees (*e.g.,* age, tenure), type of union contracts, type of client contracts, and labor and material costs, among other data. This information was correlated with the rate of turnover in each organizational unit of the region and within each of seven job classes. In addition, a survey of management practices, co-worker relations, training and advancement procedures, working conditions, and attitudes was administered in each of the high- and low-turnover units, and comparisons were made. The results were quite clear; there was little association between turnover rates and any of the demographic or business data variables, but the comparison of survey data from high- and low-turnover units showed some striking differences:

> employees in low turnover units feel they had a better orientation and training, more helpful and friendly unit managers, better cooperation with co-workers, better working conditions, and more chances to advance than those in high turnover units. In addition, they show better attitudes toward pay and greater satisfaction with their jobs (Frohman, Weisbord, and Johnston, 1971:4).

After the survey research phase, the consultants turned to reporting the data to organization members and, in conjunction with members of the client system, developing change strategies on three fronts: (a) management training (which involved a series of four workshops, the first three with unit managers—focused on problem diagnosis, problem solving, and skill training, and including the application of a survey and feedback approach for all units involved—and the final workshop involving top management in the development of collaborative relations with subordinate managers and the creation of managerial performance evaluation procedures); (b) administrative improvement (*e.g.*, turnover reporting system and manpower planning); and (c) policy changes (*e.g.*, recruitment sources and training methods). This demonstrates the *reciprocal interlinking of research and action* that is critical to the success of the action-research OD approach. After completing the feedback and action planning, the next step was to implement the planned strategy in one district on an experimental basis, using another district as a comparison control. The control district received no help from the consultants.

Subsequent to the completion of the change plan in the first district, the action strategies were modified and implemented in another district on the basis of initial results. This illustrates the *monitoring and evaluation* process. Again, a comparison district was identified. The second action plan took into consideration the actual experience and immediate results obtained in the first district, and therefore provided a stronger set of interventions (demonstrating *flexibility* in the action-research OD process).

A final evaluation of the effects of the program was made in 1973, examining the changes in turnover rates for the two districts (1971 versus 1972) and comparing the 1972 rates with the turnover rates in the comparison control districts. This analysis (contained in a confidential final evaluation report) showed striking and highly significant changes. In the first experimental district, turnover was reduced by 52 percent, with 7 of 8 units in the district showing reductions ranging from 16 to 122 percent. In the second experimental district, turnover decreased by 58 percent, with 17 of 19 units showing reductions ranging from 11 to 150 percent. Comparison of the 1972 turnover rate for the experimental districts (42 percent, overall) with that of the control districts (95 percent, overall) showed that the improvements in the experimental districts were highly significant ($p < .001$).

In summary, this action-research program started with a specific problem, turnover, with clear profit and loss implications for the organization. Its importance to this paper is that it clearly shows that the various phases and processes of the action-research OD model are equally adaptable to this type of situation. The problem was studied using data about the business structure, performance, and human organization. The collected information then served as a basis for developing an action strategy for a specific problem. Action changes were collaboratively planned and implemented, and the effects were carefully monitored. Interim evaluation resulted in program changes and modifications. An extensive final evaluation analysis documented the effects and effectiveness of the change effort. All of the action-research OD phases we identified earlier are apparent in this case. Of the five action-research OD processes, we see clear evidence of the operation of four—client-consultant collaboration, monitoring and evaluation, the interaction of action and research, and flexibility. Only evidence for client system learning is lacking.

DISCUSSION AND CONCLUSION

Our review has not followed the traditional format of the extensive

literature overview, summarization, and analysis. Rather, we have attempted
to answer three major questions by means of illustration. First, can the
phases and processes described earlier actually be identified in the studies
reviewed? Second, are the three OD problems we initially defined effectively
dealt with in these studies through the use of the action-research OD
approach? Third, what generalizations can be made about action-research
OD on the basis of the studies examined above?

Action-Research OD: Phases and Processes

Phases. Table 3 analyzes the four studies in terms of the action-
research OD phases defined in Table 2. Clearly, we have little indication of
whether the first two phases, scouting and entry, were carried out in the
depth and sequence postulated. In part, this lack may be due to the common
omission of such descriptions from research reports. Yet, the importance
of scouting and entry is emphasized by Kolb and Frohman (1970) and
documented in such reports of failure as that given by Clark (1972), in which
the client-consultant relationship was never adequately defined and
legitimated. The remaining phases, as can be seen in Table 3, occur in much
the order given in Table 2. It would seem that the only real discrepancies
of sequence occurred in Study II, which involved some degree of preplanned action (*i.e.*, action not based on the diagnosis but planned in advance
of the data collection), and in Study III, where a diagnosis was made prior
to full data collection.

More critical than sequence, however, is the question of whether
the phases actually *occurred*, particularly action planning and diagnosis.
In Study I, the action-planning phase does not clearly fit our model. Partly,
this is because the broad scope of action by the consultant was preset by
the research design. Yet it would also seem that there was considerable
planning done jointly, by the clients and consultant, following the diagnostic
phase. The nature and extent of action planning in Study II is not certain,
except that there *was* an element of preplanned action. The diagnostic
process, too, is uncertain from our description of Study II. As suggested
earlier, in Study III it seems likely that an early diagnosis, made on the basis
of incomplete data, played some part in the subsequent problems of that
OD effort.

Overall, Table 3 shows that the action-research OD framework, the
eight phases, can be used to chart the actual flow of the four studies over
time. While we see a few discrepancies, the major problem is our lack of
sufficient detail in the reports of these studies, and the lack of space to
review in sufficient detail the data that do exist.

As has been mentioned before, we do not imply that the eight phases
always occur in the order presented here. To follow this sequence rigidly
would be inconsistent with the advocacy of flexibility in the action-research
OD program. However, whereas effective action-research sequences do
often demonstrate back-tracking and recycling of steps, the major thrust—
as seen in these four studies—is to accomplish these eight phases in an
organized fashion.

Processes. Table 4 reviews the four studies in terms of the five

Table 3

PHASES OF ACTION-RESEARCH OD AS SEEN IN FOUR RESEARCH STUDIES

PHASE	STUDY I (Frohman, 1970: units C & D)	STUDY II (Frohman & Waters, 1969)	STUDY III (Miles, et al., 1969; McElvaney & Miles, 1971, 1969)	STUDY IV Weisbord, et al., 1971; Frohman, et al., 1971)
Scouting	not reviewed;	not reviewed;	not reviewed;	problem-centered;
Entry	not reviewed;	not reviewed;	not reviewed;	clear "contract";
Data Collection	extensive, planned;	extensive, planned;	extensive, planned;	extensive, planned;
Data Feedback	intensive, planned;	intensive, planned;	intensive, planned;	intensive, planned;
Diagnosis	explicit, collaborative;	not reviewed;	explicit, made prior to full data collection and feed-back;	explicit, formal;
			recycled to diagnosis;	diagnosis; semicol-laborative;
Action Planning	some preplanned consultant action, also considerable collaboratively planned action following diagnosis;	moderate degree of action preplanned by the consultants;	collaborative following diag-nosis, but done without commit-ment to action implementation;	detailed plan following diagnosis; semicol-laborative;
			new focus of action chosen;	
Action Implementation	specific actions not reviewed;	several specific actions noted; implemented as planned;	none, originally; recycled to diagnosis;	specific actions reviewed;
			some specific actions noted;	
Evaluation	pre- and post-measures, experi-mental comparison variations.	multiple methods, pre- and post-measures, control comparisons.	pre- and post-measures, no control, measures believed some-what inadequate	tentative, "tracking" evaluation used for modification; final evaluation extensive, using controls.
			multiple methods, pre- and post-measures.	

Table 4

ACTION-RESEARCH PROCESSES IN FOUR RESEARCH STUDIES

PROBLEM-CENTERED PROCESSES	STUDY I (Frohman, 1970; units C & D)	STUDY II (Frohman & Waters, 1969)	STUDY III (Miles, et al., 1969; McElvaney & Miles, 1971, 1969)	STUDY IV (Weisbord, et al., 1971; Frohman, et al., 1971)
Collaboration	extensive throughout; documented;	extensive throughout; documented;	not evident systemically;	emphasized in diagnosis and action planning;
Client System Learning	emphasized by consultants;	major explicit aim of the effort;	some indicated for top group;	uncertain;
Monitoring and Evaluation	monitoring primarily informal; extensive final evaluation;	monitoring throughout; extensive final evaluation;	formal monitoring and evaluation emphasized throughout;	formal monitoring and evaluation throughout; extensive final evaluation;
Interaction of Action and Research	very great due to use of survey and feedback method;	very great due to use of survey and feedback method;	very great due to monitoring procedures;	very great; research-based diagnosis led to action; research monitoring action led to modification;
Flexibility	most evident in treatment of unit D.	emphasized by consultants.	major factor, indicated by re-cycling.	clearly indicated.

processes underlying action-research OD. While certain of the studies seem to place greater emphasis on one or another of the five processes, it is clear that these processes were major factors in all four studies, with two exceptions. In Study III, collaboration was evident with the top administrative group but not with lower-level groups, although the effort was directed toward systemic change. This may be one reason for the lack of major systemic change, although the second strategy adopted (extensive work with the top group) may ultimately result in such change, as the researchers suggest, much as was the case in Study II. The process of client learning for internal resource development is uncertain in Study IV. This may be due to the great emphasis on one specific problem, which could result in a lower degree of generalizable client system learning.

Of course, the differential emphasis on certain processes is exactly what we might have expected, considering the nature of the action-research OD model. While all five processes are significant, a problem-centered orientation suggests that the individual OD practitioner (or team) must focus on these processes in terms of client system needs. All five basic processes must be attended to, but emphasis must be placed on those of particular relevance to the problems of a particular client in a particular situation.

Action-Research and OD Problems

We initially defined and reviewed three problems which seem common to the practice of OD: (a) the confusion of specific action interventions with an OD program, or the tendency toward a nonsystemic approach; (b) an overemphasis on content interventions or actions with consequent deemphasis on OD processes; and (c) the lack of flexibility or adaptability to changing client system needs which may result from commitment to one specific OD package. We suggested that the action-research OD approach avoided these problems, and the four studies reviewed seem to demonstrate adequately that this approach does not, in fact, share these three deficiencies.

The first three studies all aim explicitly at systemic change, while the fourth maintains a systemic approach although focused on a specific problem. The work of Frohman and Waters (1969) in developing the problem-solving abilities of a top-management group such that this group would have the skills needed to implement change throughout their organization is a good example of how a systemic approach can be operationalized.

It is clear that all four studies maintain a balanced concern with both the specific content of action interventions *and* the processes producing and supporting systemic change. All four studies shared, for example, an explicit collaborative orientation, although this process was emphasized more in Studies I and II. All four studies also shared a great concern for monitoring the process of change, using this process to determine the effects of specific content interventions and plan modifications or major changes in these intervention actions.

Shaping action interventions to the needs of the client system is evident in all of the studies. Most clearly, perhaps, this occurred in Study III, where a major redirection of the change effort was undertaken on the basis of a thorough reanalysis of the state of the client system. In Study I (units C and D), in Study III (consulting with the top group), and in Study IV (assessing the causal factors behind a particular organizational problem), we see efforts made to respond to the needs of the client system. Even at a "microintervention" level we can see flexibility in operation, as demonstrated in Studies I and II. In both cases, the practitioner did not approach team training with a prepared program; rather, he listened to the group involved and attempted to provide specific training help based on the particular needs of the group. Thus, these action-research OD applications did not contain implicit solutions, or a "package in search of problems." They were, of course, very much problem centered in terms of a flexible approach based on the phases and processes of action-research OD.

We do not contend that an action-research OD approach will automatically avoid all problems common to OD practice. There are, for example, problems and issues we have not touched on or examined in any depth (Argyris, 1961). However, this approach does seem to avoid the "traps" discussed above by making more likely adaptive responses to client system needs, by focusing explicit attention on content and process, and by beginning with and retaining a systemic approach to and perspective on organizational change.

Action-Research OD: Generalizations

From our review of action-research OD, we can derive several general observations regarding OD practice within this model. These observations pertain to client-consultant relationship issues which may arise from the use of this approach, to the knowledge and skills of the OD practitioner, to OD technology, and to the general role of action-research in OD.

First, it is easy to see from the number of steps outlined and the complex interactions of the basic processes that action-research OD is not a quick strategy. Rather, it may require considerably greater time compared with other approaches. Thus, an action-research OD approach requires a high level of willingness on the part of the client organization to delay "instant action" and to handle the uncertainty of not having a clear-cut action proposal at the time the consultant is hired. In many results-oriented bureaucratic organizations with short-term perspectives and methods, such commitment may not be at all readily attainable; yet, the effective use of the action-research model demands the application of time-consuming research methods by the OD practitioner. Diagnostic information generated in this way may bring to light further problems which require recycling through the action-research OD phases. Action plans which develop from the diagnosis may also bring to light new data which suggests recycling. In brief, one requirement for effective application of an action-research OD approach is patience on the part of the client, a willingness to wait for action efforts rather than jumping into some preplanned program, and an understanding and acceptance of the time span commitments that may be necessary.

Second, drawing on our analysis of studies by Frohman and his colleagues (Frohman, 1970; Frohman and Waters, 1969; Frohman, Weisbord, and Johnston, 1971), the importance and effect of top-management support and involvement is evident. Without such support, the commitment of lower levels to expend time and effort on data collection, feedback sessions, joint diagnosis, and action-planning meetings is unlikely. Top-management involvement is very likely at the point of evaluation, for the question of whether the effort has been worthwhile then becomes most relevant; but if such involvement is limited solely to evaluation of results, the probabilities would favor rather minimally effective outcomes. We are referring here to the issues of client needs assessment and a systemic approach, which become serious issues when a major subsystem—top management—is minimally involved. While top-management involvement probably is not, in general, sufficient to produce effective organizational change, it does seem to be one necessary condition for the achievement of such change.

Third, the OD practitioner using an action-research approach must, no less than the client, be prepared to endure—and deal with—resistance and delay at various points in the effort. The consultation skills needed to deal with false starts in entry and resistance which may occur (particularly in the action-planning, implementation, and evaluation phases) place considerable demands on the OD practitioner. Basically, the consultant must reflect in his actions the flexibility of the approach—the patience to stick with it and the skill to do something about it. Waters' (1969) report highlights the significance of consultant skills and flexibility.

Fourth, we must briefly reiterate the earlier discussion of the dual role of the action-research OD practitioner; that is, a practitioner must be familiar with and possess the knowledge and skills required for both research (data collection, diagnosis, and evaluation) and action (entry, action planning, and implementation). The effective fulfillment of this dual role calls for a person educated and skilled in research methods and conceptual analysis, as well as intervention techniques and technology. Collecting and reporting survey data does not constitute an action-research OD program; neither does the development of "gut-level" feelings about the state of the system followed by "appropriate" action interventions. Our definitional framework and the research reports reviewed show that the effective application of an action-research OD approach requires the unusual combination of knowledge and skill in research and in action intervention, a combination which may require a consultant team rather than one OD practitioner.

Fifth, it is clear that action-research OD necessitates the use of research methods which provide an accurate monitoring of what goes on in the client system in terms of the initial state of the system, the process of the program, and the effects of action. Without adequate data collection and evaluation methods, such monitoring cannot be accomplished. To some extent, there have been efforts to develop reliable and valid standardized instruments (Taylor and Bowers, 1972); however, much further work is needed on the development of measures (both static and longitudinal) of organizational variables.

Finally, although it would seem that action-research offers an extremely sound basis for OD practice, we see this more as a promise than as present reality. One aim of the action-research model, as noted by Lewin (1946), is the development of new scientific knowledge about the use of this model in dealing with various social problems (as well as general knowledge about the causes and treatment of such problems). OD practitioners and researchers have only begun to systematically study the effects of different action strategies in similar and different organizations (Bowers, 1973). As was initially noted, this report does not attempt any comparative analysis of OD approaches. While some work has been accomplished at a theoretical level (Sashkin, Morris, and Horst, 1973), the promise of action-research as an OD approach cannot be fully achieved until more *applied* research of this sort is accomplished. Thus, we suggest that researchers and OD practitioners would profit greatly by adopting, in their work strategy, the same problem-solving orientation inherent in the action-research model.

A Concluding Note

As a final note, we might comment that the development of an empirically based action-research model, which we feel the present analysis goes a long way toward achieving, is an indication of the growing maturity of OD as a profession. Bennis (1969) has raised a number of cogent problems facing OD, and we believe that as of 1976 considerable progress has been made regarding some of those issues. Bennis states that OD "systematically avoids the problem of power, or the *politics* of change" (p. 78). The McElvaney and Miles (1971, 1969) study makes a beginning in dealing with issues of power. "Most [OD] cases that finally reach print focus almost exclusively on the T-group as the basic strategy of intervention" (Bennis, 1969: 78). In none of the cases reported here was sensitivity training a basic strategy; in only one case were T-groups involved at all (Bowers, 1973). Bennis says, "I have yet to see an [OD] program that uses an interventional strategy other than an interpersonal one" (p. 78). We have described one such example in the study reported by Frohman, Weisbord, and Johnston (1971), and Weisbord, Frohman, and Johnston (1971). Bennis notes an "overall disinterest in long-term research projects" (p. 81). Bowers' (1973) and Taylor and Bowers' (1972) work is the result of a long-term program conducted in not one but several organizations.

Bennis describes a number of further problems, some on which progress has since been made and others on which progress is sorely needed. We do, however, see definite progress on what may be the most significant of all the issues he raises. That is, this paper demonstrates one step in the development of a "tradition of *adding knowledge cumulatively* to the general theory of practice" (Bennis, 1969: 80).

REFERENCES

Argyris, C.   "Explorations in Consulting-Client Relationships." *Human Organization*,
1961   20:121–133.
Beck, A. C., Jr., and E. D. Hillmar.   *A Practical Approach to Organization Develop-*
1972   *ment through MBO*. Reading, Mass.: Addison-Wesley.
Beckhard, R.   *Organization Development: Strategies and Models*. Reading, Mass.:
1969   Addison-Wesley.

Beer, M., and E. F. Huse.   "A Systems Approach to Organizational Development."
1972   *Journal of Applied Behavioral Science*, 8:79–101.
Bennis, W. G.   *Organization Development: Its Nature, Origins, and Prospects.*
1969   Reading, Mass.: Addison-Wesley.
Bennis, W. G., and H. W. Peter.   "Applying Behavioral Science for Organizational
1966   Change." In H. W. Peter (ed.), *Comparative Theories of Social Change.*
         Ann Arbor, Mich.: Foundation for Research on Human Behavior.
Blake, R. R., and J. S. Mouton.   *Achieving Corporate Excellence through Grid
1968   Organization Development.* Houston: Gulf.
Bowers, D. G.   "OD Techniques and their Results in 23 Organizations: The Michigan
1973   ICL Study." *Journal of Applied Behavioral Science*, 9: 21–43.
————.   "Development Techniques and Organizational Change: An Overview
1971a   of Results from the Michigan Inter-Company Longitudinal Study." Techni-
         cal Report to the U. S. Office of Naval Research. Ann Arbor, Mich.: Center
         for Research on Utilization of Scientific Knowledge, Institute for Social
         Research, University of Michigan.
————.   "Development Techniques and Organizational Climate: An Evaluation
1971b   of the Comparative Importance of Two Potential Forces for Organizational
         Change." Technical Report to the U.S. Office of Naval Research. Ann
         Arbor, Mich.: Center for Research on Utilization of Scientific Knowledge,
         Institute for Social Research, University of Michigan.
Bowers, D. G., and J. L. Franklin.   "Survey Guided Development: Using Human
1972   Resources Measurement in Organizational Change." *Journal of Contempo-
         rary Business*, 1:43–55.
Bradford, L. P., J. R. Gibb, and K. D. Benne.   *T-Group Theory and Laboratory
1964   Method.* New York: Wiley.
Brown, L. D.   " 'Research Action': Organizational Feedback, Understanding, and
1972   Change." *Journal of Applied Behavioral Science*, 8:697–712.
Clark, A. W.   "Sanction: A Critical Element in Action Research." *Journal of Applied
1972   Behavioral Science*, 8:713–731.
Collier, J.   "United States Indian Administration as a Laboratory of Ethnic Relations."
1945   *Social Research*, 12:275–276.
Corey, S. M.   *Action Research to Improve School Practices.* New York: Bureau of
1953   Publications, Teachers College, Columbia University.
Fleishman, E. A.   "Leadership Climate, Human Relations Training, and Supervisory
1953   Behavior." *Personnel Psychology*, 6:205–222.
Fordyce, J. K., and R. Weil.   *Managing With People.* Reading, Mass.: Addison-
1971   Wesley.
French, J. R. P., Jr., and B. Raven.   "The Bases of Social Power." In D. Cartwright
1959   (ed.), *Studies in Social Power.* Ann Arbor, Mich.: Institute for Social
         Research, The University of Michigan.
French, W. L., and C. H. Bell, Jr.   *Organization Development.* Englewood Cliffs,
1973   N. J.: Prentice-Hall.
Frohman, A. L.   "The Development of Impact of a Joint Goal Setting Technique
1970   for Conflict Resolution." Unpublished doctoral dissertation. Cambridge,
         Mass.: Sloan School of Management, Massachusetts Institute of Techno-
         logy.
Frohman, M. A.   "An Empirical Study of a Model and Strategies for Planned Organi-
1970   zational Change." Unpublished doctoral dissertation. Ann Arbor, Mich.:
         The University of Michigan.
————.   "Conceptualizing a Helping Relationship." Mimeographed paper.
1968   Ann Arbor, Mich.: Center for Research on Utilization of Scientific Know-
         ledge, Institute for Social Research, University of Michigan.
Frohman, M. A., and C. A. Waters.   "Building Internal Resources for Organizational
1969   Development." Paper presented before the staff of the Institute for Social
         Research, The University of Michigan. Ann Arbor, Michigan. November.

Frohman, M. A., M. R. Weisbord, and J. Johnston. "Turnover Study and Action
1971   Program." Unpublished report. Merion Station, Pa.: Organization Research
        and Development Co.
Greiner, L. E., D. P. Leitch, and L. B. Barnes. "The Simple Complexity of Organi-
1968   zational Climate in a Governmental Agency." In R. Tagiuri and G. H. Litwin
        (eds.), *Organizational Climate*. Boston: Division of Research, Graduate
        School of Business Administration, Harvard University.
Havelock, R. G., A. Guskin, M. A. Frohman, M. Havelock, M. Hill, and J. Huber.
1969   *Planning for Innovation*. Ann Arbor, Mich.: Center for Research on Utili-
        zation of Scientific Knowledge, Institute for Social Research, The University
        of Michigan.
Kelman, H. C. "Compliance, Identification, and Internalization: Three Processes
1958   of Attitude Change." *Journal of Conflict Resolution*, 2:51–60.
Kolb, D. A., and A. L. Frohman. "An Organization Development Approach to
1970   Consulting." *Sloan Management Review*, 12:51–65.
Leavitt, H. J. "Applied Organizational Change in Industry: Structural, Technological,
1965   and Humanistic Approaches." In J. G. March (ed.), *Handbook of Organi-
        zations*. Chicago: Rand McNally.
Levinson, H. "The Clinical Psychologist as Organizational Diagnostician." *Pro-
1972   fessional Psychology*, 3:34–40.
Lewin, K. "Frontiers in Group Dynamics." *Human Relations*, 1:5–42.
1947
————. "Action Research and Minority Problems." *Journal of Social Issues*,
1946   2:34–46.
Likert, R. *The Human Organization*. New York: McGraw-Hill.
1967
————. *New Patterns of Management*. New York: McGraw-Hill.
1961
Lippitt, R. "Value-Judgment Problems of the Social Scientist Participating in
1950   Action-Research." Paper presented at the annual meeting of the American
        Psychological Associational, September.
Lippitt, R., J. Watson, and B. Westley. *The Dynamics of Planned Change*. New
1958   York: Harcourt, Brace and World.
Mann, F. C. "Studying and Creating Change: A Means to Understanding Social
1957   Organization." In C. Arensberg (ed.), *Research in Industrial Human
        Relations*. Publication No. 17. New York: Industrial Relations Research
        Association.
McElvaney, C. T., and M. B. Miles. "Using Survey Feedback and Consultation."
1971   In R. A. Schmuck and M. B. Miles (eds.), *Organization Development
        in Schools*. Palo Alto, Calif.: National Press.
————. "The School Psychologist as a Change Agent: Improving a School
1969   System through Survey Feedback Methods." In G. B. Gottsegen and
        M. G. Gottsegan (eds.), *Professional School Psychology*. New York:
        Grune and Stratton.
Miles, M. B., H. A. Hornstein, P. H. Calder, D. M. Callahan, and R. S. Schiavo. "The
1969   Consequence of Survey Feedback: Theory and Evaluation." In W. G.
        Bennis K. D. and R. Chin (eds.), *The Planning of Change*, 2nd. ed. New York:
        Holt, Rinehart, and Winston.
Neff, F. W. "Survey Research: A Tool for Problem Diagnosis and Improvement
1965   in Organizations." In A. W. Gouldner and S. M. Miller (eds.), *Applied
        Sociology*. New York: The Free Press.
Pfeiffer, J. W., and J. E. Jones. *A Handbook of Structured Experiences for Human
1972a   Relations Training*, rev. ed., vol. 1 Iowa City: University Associates Press.
————. *The 1972 Annual Handbook for Group Facilitators*. Iowa City: University
1972b   Associates Press.
————. *A Handbook of Structured Experiences for Human Relations Training*,
1971   . . vol. 3. Iowa City: University Associates Press.

—————. *A Handbook of Structured Experiences for Human Relations Training*,
1970   vol. 2. Iowa City: University Associates Press.
Roethlisberger, F. J., and W. J. Dickson. *Management and the Worker*. Cambridge,
1939   Mass.: Harvard University Press.
Sashkin, M. "Organization Development Practices." *Professional Psychology*,
1973   4:187—194 ff.
Sashkin, M., W. C. Morris, and L. Horst. "A Comparison of Social and Organi-
1973   zational Change Models: Information Flow and Data Use Processes."
         Psychological Review, 80:510—526.
Schein, E. H. *Process Consultation: Its Role in Organization Development*. Reading,
1969   Mass.: Addison-Wesley.
Schein, E. H., and W. G. Bennis. *Personal and Organizational Change through*
1965   *Group Methods*. New York: Wiley.
Sykes, A. J. M. "The Effect of a Supervisory Training Course in Changing Super-
1962   visors' Perceptions and Expectations of the Role of Management." *Human
         Relations*, 15:227—243.
Taylor, J. C., and D. G. Bowers. *The Survey of Organizations: A Machine-Scored*,
1972   *Standardized Questionnaire Instrument*. Ann Arbor, Mich.: Institute for
         Social Research, The University of Michigan.
Waters, C. A. "Building Internal Resources for Organization Development."
1969   In Executive Study Conference, *Managing Organizational Effectiveness*.
         Princeton, N. J.: Educational Testing Service.
Weisbord, M. R., M. A. Frohman, and J. Johnston. "Action-Research on Turnover
1971   as an OD Entry Strategy." Paper presented at the Fall, 1971 meeting of
         the OD Network. Minneapolis, Minn.

Section IV

**ORGANIZATIONAL
EFFECTIVENESS
—RELEVANCE—**

Organizational Effectiveness: The Problem of Relevance

S. LEE SPRAY

The general goal of this volume is to reduce the gap between theoretical knowledge and practical action. Embedded in this goal are two specific objectives. The first objective is to provide a portrait of contemporary social science knowledge concerning organizational effectiveness. The second objective is to assess the value of this body of knowledge to organizational practitioners. To achieve the first objective, leading scholars in the field were asked to prepare original papers dealing in some way with organizational effectiveness. The nine papers in this volume represent the impressive response of the social scientific community to this request. To achieve the second objective, the scholars were asked to present their papers at a conference to which both concerned social scientists and organizational practitioners were invited to attend and engage in discussion of the papers. In addition, three leading organizational practitioners, Mr. Cal Batton, Vice President of Hoover Worldwide Corporation, Dr. William S. Kieser, Board of Governors, Cleveland Clinic Foundation, and Charles Warner, Jr., Goodyear Executive Professor, Kent State University (1974-75), served on a panel focusing on the utilization of scientific knowledge in the area of organizational effectiveness.

The format and composition of the conference were well suited to the accomplishment of the specific objectives: ideas were clearly explicated and the utility of the knowledge was systematically assessed. While it is perhaps premature to suggest that the movement in the direction of realizing the general goal was produced by the dialogue, it is clear that the conference did serve to highlight the problems involved in narrowing the gap between theory and practice. Equally important is the fact that the proceedings of the conference contained, often by implication, a number of suggestions for developing a more meaningful integration of research and practice. In light of these developments, the purposes of this paper are twofold. The first is to identify major obstacles currently blocking the realization of the general goal of narrowing the gap between the generation of theoretical

165

knowledge and its utilization. The second purpose is to utilize the dialogue and discussion generated in the conference as the foundation for proposing a strategy to facilitate the utilization of theories of organizational effectiveness by organizational practitioners

With regard to the difficulties involved in integrating scientific knowledge and practical action, the major problems revolve around the qualitatively different criteria of relevance utilized by organizational scientists and organizational practitioners. As the papers in this volume indicate, the scientific assessment of organizational effectiveness is an extremely complex subject. The experienced practitioner is also aware that any situation is complex, if one takes note of all, or even many, of the interrelated phenomena involved. What is needed in such a situation, of course, is some "criterion of relevance" which serves to direct attention to a limited and manageable number of concepts and relationships.

The segment of reality covered by the concept of organizational effectiveness is large enough to make the need for selective principles to guide attention particularly acute for the organizational scientist. Organizational researchers have responded to this pressure in a variety of ways, resulting in the generation of a multiplicity of competing approaches and divergent analytical traditions in the study of different types of organizations. However, this diversity of perspectives should not be allowed to obscure the fact that, at the present time, there is a growing theoretical unity and coherence in the study of organizational effectiveness: a unity based on a systems model of organizational functioning. This is not to deny the fact that many studies of organizational effectiveness do not start with an explicitly systems view of the organization. Nor is the intention to deny the validity or utility of making distinctions between such approaches as the "goals" and "natural systems" perspectives or "open" and "closed" systems. Rather, the intent is to place these distinctions in proper perspective. That is, to view these diverse approaches as essentially family squabbles within the scientific community, as disputes over the appropriate way to use criteria of relevance inherent in the systems model of organizational effectiveness and not as fundamental disagreements over the source of criteria.

To be specific, a model can be viewed as a kind of ideal type. As such, a model is a collection of characteristics of a complex phenomenon abstracted from the actual empirical context of their existence. The characteristics abstracted and grouped together represent what an investigator considers important about the entity under investigation. Thus, a model serves to define worthwhile objects of study rather than describe the empirical characteristics of the objects. Organizational scientists have used the systems model in this way by deriving worthwhile objects of study from the primitive definition of a system. That is, a system is defined as any set of elements which share one or more relationships. From this definition, a host of worthwhile objects of investigation are deduced, including problems of self-maintenance, interdependence, environmental adaptation, the creation of harmonious relationships among units, and mobilization of resources toward the realization of systems goals.

It is true that many studies of the determinates of organization effectiveness do not start with an explicit systems view of the organization. However, the alternative models proposed—the decision-making model, the criterion approach, the structural approach—tend to agree with the systems model in their results: the emphasis is placed on flexibility, adaptability, and dynamics as the prerequisities of organizational efficiency. In studies explicitly based on a systems model, these same factors are viewed as properties of enduring social systems. This leads directly to the conclusion that, whether explicitly recognized or not, the systems model serves as the basic organizing framework for most theoretically grounded studies of organizational effectiveness. Thus, in this volume, Marsh and Mannari examine the relationship between employee performance and features of the reward system, the cultural system, and the interpersonal system found in Japanese firms. Similarly, Srivastva and Salipante investigate the ways in which such processes as information feedback, interpersonal skills, and innovation influence the relationship between autonomy and organizational effectiveness.

It is also true that the concept of "system" is used in different ways by different investigators of organizational effectiveness. Some organizational scientists tailor the systems approach to give priority to a specific problem. In this volume, Price uses a systems approach to examine the relationship between personnel turnover and organizational effectiveness while Stewart utilizes a systems perspective to examine the relationship between the values and orientations of policy leaders and goal effectiveness. Other organizational scientists relate organizational effectiveness to the enduring properties of a social system. Evan's paper in this volume, in which he proposes measures of systemic processes as a means for assessing organizational effectiveness, represents such an approach.

Clearly, the contemporary literature supports the view that the systems model prefigures the range of factors organizational scientists attend to in studying organizational effectiveness. The taken-for-granted eminence of the systems model is further revealed in issues raised by social scientists during the conference. Specifically, dialogue among organizational scientists revolved around such "worthwhile" objects of study as the following:

1. What is the relationship between decisions concerned with short-run internal efficiency of an organization and decisions concerned with the long-term survival of an organization?
2. What are the methodological consequences of predicting organizational performance from individual data?
3. Shouldn't we really pay attention to how the issues of internal organizational efficiency and external social utility get resolved in the public context?
4. Is it not possible that in labor intensive organizations you enhance the economic objectives of the firm by enhancing internal social processes?
5. Is there anything in the literature that indicates how variable

measures of organizational effectiveness are at different time
periods in the life of an organization?

6. How far down an organization do you have to go to obtain a
   reliable measure of group characteristics, such as average job
   satisfaction?

7. Isn't it possible to statistically relate data that organizations
   themselves collect to structural characteristics measured by
   social scientists?

8. In view of existing studies, what percent of the variance in satisfaction is accounted for by level of autonomy?

9. How do we determine the system's needs for change and stability at a particular point in time?

While these questions do not exhaust the range of topics discussed at the
conference, they do reflect the flavor of the dialogue occurring among
organizational scientists: that is, the criteria of relevance used by the academicians led to discussion of such "classic" system issues as the conceptual
and methodological problems involved in using data gathered from individuals to characterize various states of system level variables. The need for
empirical referents to highly abstract system level concepts was another
classic topic popular with the academicians. At no point in the conference,
however, did organizational scientists offer serious challenges to the
validity or utility of relying on a systems framework for attempting to understand organizational effectiveness. The reason for this is not surprising. The
importance and insightfulness of the issues raised clearly attests to the
heuristic value of the systems model, that is, the common reliance on
criterion of relevance derived from systems models clearly facilitates communication and understanding among organizational scientists. However,
the existence of this socially shared view of organizational reality contains
a number of implications raising the possibility that preoccupation with the
system model may not facilitate communication between organizational
scientists and practitioners. Specifically, the existence of a dominant
framework among organizational scientists contains implications for both
the evaluation and transmission of existing knowledge about organizational
effectiveness.

With regard to the evaluation of extant knowledge concerning organizational effectiveness, the common reliance on a systems model results in
the production of "objective" standards for transforming observations into
data. Both observations and data are, of course, reflections of someone's
experience. The term *observation* is generally used to refer to any bit of
information pertaining to an object of observation. It may be reported as
an instance of a larger, more abstract, class of phenomena, or it may be
reported in the form of a unique event. An "observation" is transformed
into a "datum" when it is reported as a position on or with respect to some
theoretical variable. It follows from this point of view that a particular
observation may represent many different positions on a variety of different
theoretical variables at various levels of abstraction. Thus, the utility of the
systems model is twofold. First, it provides a set of rules for classifying

observations with reference to a matrix of theoretical variables at ever higher levels of abstraction until variables are produced which can be combined into general cause-and-effect relationships. Second, it specifies the level of abstraction required for generalization to be achieved, as well as providing an *a priori* determination of the particular variables which will ultimately be contained in the developed theory.

The emphasis in the contemporary organizational literature on such system properties (Taylor, 1970) as the nonadditivity of relationships, mutual interdependence, equilibrium and intervening processes or mechanisms, (*e.g.*, servo-mechanisms) clearly indicates that criteria of relevance derived from the systems model is widely used by organizational scientists. However, the extent to which guidelines derived from systems theory constitute "objective" standards for determining the validity of sensory experience is debatable. Campbell has already cautioned us in this volume to remember that objective criteria are simply subjective criteria once removed. In the present context, this means that the existence of a common set of evaluative criteria may simply reflect the fact that organizational scientists have had highly similar educational experiences which qualify them for membership in a "community of scholars" who are highly likely to develop similar constructions of organizational reality. Organizational practitioners also develop standards for evaluating observations and procedures for classifying their experiences in an organizational context. As Wilson (1973) has suggested, to take for granted that the standards of evaluation utilized by organizational scientists are objectively valid implies that the use of other evaluative criteria merely reflects a technical lag which subsequent scientific developments will eventually overcome. From the organizational scientists' standpoint, the use of commonly agreed upon criteria derived from a systems model is the rational way to proceed. However, from the organizational practitioners' point of view, it may be just as rational to make choices premised on past experiences, awareness of current alternatives, and anticipation of future situations. The practitioners' point of view has been conveniently summarized by Pfiffner in the following manner:

> The failure of the administrator to gather all available data and to list every possible alternative is not due only to mechanical limitations of the human mind, as some members of the classical school of rationality have suggested. It is due rather to the fact that the administrator has learned to be selective and to utilize cumulative knowledge just as the scientist has. This combined with the realization that there may be more than one satisfactory solution, has led to the utilization of common sense short-cuts. The administrative decision maker is constantly striving to reduce the number of alternatives, but by means other than the laborious covering of ground already trodden by others (Pfiffner, 1960:130).

The fact that the evaluative criteria utilized by organizational scientists and organizational practitioners do not match does not necessarily mean that the former is more objective than the latter. It is just as feasible to claim that the under-utilization of scientific evaluations in organizations is the scientist's problem as it is to suggest that the gap between theory and practice is the practitioner's problem.

The dominance of the systems model not only leads organizational scientists to assume that the only knowledge worthy of transmission to practitioners is knowledge related to systems processes and problems, it also structures the way in which scientists attempt to transmit the knowledge to organizational practitioners. As Zetterberg has demonstrated (1962), organizational scientists characteristically assume that, for effective communication to occur, they have to transmit the knowledge they have accumulated about publicly recognized problems to officials formally mandated to deal with them. The corollary assumption made by organizational scientists is that the substantive content of the knowledge they generate must match the substantive content of the manifest issues faced by the practitioner. The problem here, of course, is that this process of communication is effective only to the extent that the day-to-day problems handled by the practitioner are accurately reflected in his publicly visible position and set of responsibilities.

Given these considerations, it would appear that there are a number of potential impediments to effective communication between organizational scientists and organizational practitioners. It comes as no surprise, therefore, to find that the reactions of the panel of organizational practitioners to the conference proceedings included a number of critical observations about both the content and methods of transmission of scientific knowledge. For those who wish to feed more academic knowledge to organizational practitioners, the following comments made by panel members are instructive.

1. Businessmen are too busy with day-to-day problems to get deeply involved with fundamentals. I think it is useful to generate a body of knowledge about organizational problems around how you apply this knowledge to business needs.
2. What has been discussed in the past two days is primarily relevant to large organizations where people don't know each other. If this knowledge could be translated into methods that could be used in smaller businesses, it would make a tremendous contribution to national productivity.
3. This has been an interesting introduction to an area of scientific investigation which I think has some interesting possibilities.
4. To talk about organizational efficiency is like talking about cancer: you are probably wasting your time talking about the overall picture.
5. In terms of efficiency, I think we should be concentrating our attention on the smaller units that make up the organization. This is particularly true since we don't have the luxury of spending a whole lifetime talking about these issues if we are going to get anything done.
6. By the time this conference appears in print, this will all be irrelevant, as far as being of use to people who need it now.
7. What people have talked about at this conference has a long way to go in terms of being translatable into something we can

use. I don't mean that the work isn't excellent. I just mean that
it is hard to understand and make practical.

8. The only practical techniques I heard were not directed
at solving the problems of overall organizational effectiveness
but rather directed to the individual in the organization. I think
this is the most profitable area for us to tackle.

9. One of the basic problems I am confronted with can be stated
very simply: How many people do we need to get the job done?

10. One of our problems is bridging cultural gaps between our
operations in various areas of this country as well as in other
countries. We need some way to anticipate and understand why
productivity varies greatly from one operation to another.

11. Assuming that something fruitful and specific comes out of the
mass of research that is being done in organizational effectiveness, then the problem is bringing about change.

12. If you do come up with an answer to the question of
determinates of organizational effectiveness, is that answer
going to be valid, in terms of how we can use it in industry?

13. To measure change in patient recovery rate by type of medical
case may be an index of organizational efficiency, or effeciency
of that procedure; on the other hand, it may not stand up
to scientific analysis.

14. I think these variables are legitimate—these are a few of the
items built into any corporate system. But what is the ultimate
application of these factors, in terms of providing criteria for
comparing various units of any large corporation?

15. We do have standard measures of productivity and they reveal
sizable variations among our many plants. My problem is
to determine why some plants are below the desired standard
and then figure out ways to reorganize the unit to raise
productivity to standard.

When the criteria of relevance contained in this list of comments offered by
organizational practitioners is juxtaposed with the criteria of relevance
contained in the list of issues raised by the organizational scientists what
emerges is a vivid, earthy illustration of the analytical distinction, made
long ago by Mannheim (1940) between functional and substantive rationality. For Mannheim, "functional rationality" referred to "the organization
of activity of the members of society with reference to objective ends"
while "substantive rationality" referred to "the capacity to act intelligently
in a given situation on the basis of one's own insight into the interrelations
of events." (Mannheim, 1940: 58). It was Mannheim's view that increasing
industrialization led to progressive supplanting of substantive rationality
with functional rationality. The ultimate result, in his view, was a marked
reduction in the capacity to exercise independent judgment. While this
latter prediction may be debatable, Mannheim's observations do serve to
capture the points of disparity between the concerns of organizational
scientists and organizational practitioners contained in the two lists of

comments. The "functionally rational" concerns of the organizational scientists revolved around a specialized body of systematically connected information and theory, but in contrast, the "substantively rational" concerns of organizational practitioners revolved around everyday problems and reasoned independent judgment. The practitioners were quite willing to utilize scientific knowledge in dealing with problems of organizational effectiveness, but they were obviously not willing to accept the organizational scientists' criteria of evidence as the only sure ground of knowledge. Consequently, only a small portion of all the theory and research presented at the conference was considered to be relevant and practically useful by the practitioners, although all of them agreed that all of the information they acquired was generally enlightening.

CONCLUSION

In light of what has gone before it now appears fallacious to assume that the gap between theoretical knowledge and practical action can be significantly reduced by simply bringing scientific experts and practitioners together to discuss a particular substantive area. At least this appears to be true for the substantive problem of assessing organizational effectiveness. This is not to suggest that such conferences are a waste of time. On the contrary, such conferences enlighten both scientists and practitioners, and it should be noted, the sources of enlightenment come from both groups of participants. However, enlightenment does not directly contribute to the solution of immediate practical problems. Consequently, the "engineering" potential of a scholarly conference is distinctly limited. The discovery of this fallacy implies a moral of some significance.

It is now obvious that an analytic distinction can and must be made between the accumulation of expert knowledge and its applications.* Though the body of knowledge focusing on the determinates of organizational effectiveness may be scientific, objective, and theoretically sound, the utilization of this knowledge is shaped by criteria of relevance derived from "substantive rationality." Having separated theory building from theory utilization, it is now possible to explore the ways in which they might be meaningfully interrelated. The traditional strategy for interrelating theory and practice is based on the "expert-elite" model of information dissemination. This model is heavily weighted in favor of systematically connected facts or ideas generated by an elite segment of the public—a variety of experts—and marketed as the only valid knowledge. At the same time, the model implicitly discredits the opinions and attitudes of the public by characterizing them as being disconnected, distorted, and inaccurate. Members of this tradition who wish to introduce more scientific knowledge into the applied world tend to find their relevant knowledge base located in the academic world, and consequently, the direction of movement is from the academic office to the work site.

---

*Freidson (1970) has made the same point with reference to the profession of medicine.

An alternative, more egalitarian strategy would be to give more recognition and weight to knowlege which grows out of practitioners' experiences.* The role of the expert in this model would be twofold. First, the expert would engage in a systematic attempt to understand the day-to-day issues actually facing the organizational practitioner. Second, the expert would then engage in a systematic search of the extant scientific knowledge to determine whether or not a solution to the problem could be deduced from established theoretical principles. In this approach, the knowledge base would reside in the organization and the direction of movement would be from substantive knowledge to theory.

There are a number of advantages to the second or "pluralistic" approach. First, it would encourage, indeed demand, the continual development and testing of theoretical models. The papers in this volume represent the kind of work that would be simulated by this approach. Second, it would eliminate the atmosphere of conflict and/or deference which frequently characterizes the relationship between scientists and practitioners at the present time. The approach would also lessen the opportunity for experts to generalize their authority and control beyond the legitimate boundaries of their expertise. By relying on solutions derived from established principles, the approach would also provide a much needed antidote to the present tendency to substitute popularization for precision in the utilization of social science theory concerning organizations. Equally important is the fact the approach would serve to retard the proliferation of monistic sets of maxims currently being marketed as the cureall for any and all organizational ills. Finally, the approach might serve as a first step in the direction of alleviating what has become recognized as one of the central problematic elements in modern society: the place of the expert in an (at least nominally) democratic society.

REFERENCES

Freidson, Eliot. *Profession of Medicine*. New York: Dodd, Mead and Company.
1970
Pfiffner, John. "Administrative Rationality." *Public Administration Review*, 20:130.
1960
Taylor, Howard F. *Balance in Small Groups*. New York: Van Nostrand.
1970
Mannheim, Karl. *Man and Society in an Age of Reconstruction*. London.
1940
Wilson, H. T. "Rationality and Decision in Administrative Science." *Canadian*
1973   *Journal of Political Science*, 6:2.
Zetterberg, Hans L. *Social Theory and Social Practice*. New York: The Bedminster
1962   Press.

---

*The foundation of this strategy resides in Zetterberg's (1962) generally neglected proposal for a re-direction of applied sociology.

BIBLIOGRAPHY

The bibliography contains only works published since 1970.*

Aaker, D., and G. Day. "Corporate Responses to Consumer Pressures." *Harvard*
1972   *Business Review*, 50 (6):114–124.

Aiken, M., and J. Hage. "The Organic Organization and Innovation." *Sociology*,
1971   5:63–82.

Akinbode, I. A. "Attitudes and Performance as Indicators of Organizational Orien-
1973   tation." *Human Organization*, 32:371–378.

Aldrich, H. E. "Technology and Organizational Structure: A Re-examination of the
1972   Findings of the Aston Group." *Administrative Science Quarterly*, 17:26–43.

Allison, P. D., and J. A. Stewart. "Productivity Differences Among Scientists'
1974   Evidence for Accumulative Advantage." *American Sociological Review*,
        39:596–606.

Ansoff, H. I., and R. G. Brandenburg. "A Language for Organization Design:
1971   Part I." *Management Science*, 17:B705–B716.

————. "A Language for Organization Design: Part II." *Management Science*,
1971   17:B717–B731.

Aram, J. D., C. P., Morgan, and E. S. Esbeck. "Relation of Collaborative Inter-
1971   personal Relationships to Individual Statisfaction and Organizational
        Performance." *Administrative Science Quarterly*, 16:289–296.

Badawy, M. K. "Bureaucracy in Research: A Study of Role Conflict of Scientists."
1973   *Human Organizations*, 33:123–133.

Barrett, J. H. *Individual Goals and Organizational Objectives*. Ann Arbor: Institute
1970   for Social Research, University of Michigan.

Beck, A. C., Jr., and E. D. Hillmar. *A Practical Approach to Organization Develop-*
1972   *ment Through M. B. O.* Reading, Mass.: Addison-Wesley.

Beer, M. "The Technology of Organization Development." In M. D. Dunnette (Ed.),
In   *Handbook of Industrial and Organizational Psychology*. Chicago: Rand
Press   McNally. .

Beer, M., and E. F. Huse. "A Systems Approach to Organization Development."
1972   *Journal of Applied Behavioral Science*, 8:79–101.

Bennis, W. G. "Towards a Truly Scientific Management." In J. Ghorpade (Ed.),
1971   *Assessment of Organizational Effectiveness*. Pacific Palisades, Calif.:
        Goodyear.

Betz, F. and I. I. Mitroff. "Representational Systems Theory." *Management Science*,
1974   20:1242–1252.

Bonjean, C. M. and M. D. Grimes. "Bureaucracy and Alienation: A Dimensional
1970   Approach." *Social Forces*, 48:365–373.

Borman, W. C., and M. D. Dunnettee. "Selection of Components to Comprise a
1974   Naval Personnel Status Index (NPSI) and a Strategy for Investigating
        Their Relative Importance." Final Technical Report, ONR Contract N00014–
        73-C-0210, NR156–020. Minneapolis: Personnel Decision, Inc.

Bowers, D. G. "Development Techniques and Organizational Change: An Overview
1971   of Results from the Michigan Inter-Company Longitudinal Study." Techni-
        cal Report to the U. S. Office of Naval Research.

————   "Development Techniques and Organizational Climate: An Evaluation
1971   of the Comparative Importance of two Potential Forces for Organizational
        Change." Technical report to the U. S. Office of Naval Research.

————. Techniques and Their Results in 23 Organizations: The Michigan ICL
1973   Study." *Journal of Applied Behavioral Science*, 9:21–43.

Bowers, D. G., and J. L. Franklin. "Survey Guided Development: Using Human
1972   Resources Measurement in Organizational Change." *Journal of Contemp-*
        rary Business, I:43–55.

---

*This bibliography was prepared by John Roberts.

175

Britt, D., and O. R. Galle. "Industrial Conflict and Unionization." *American Sociolo-*
1972   *gical Review*, 37:46—57.
Brown, L. D. "Research Action: Organizational Feedback, Understanding, and
1972   Change." *Journal of Applied Behavioral Science*, 8:697—712.
Burke, R. J. "Methods of Managing Superior-Subordinate Conflict: Their Effective-
1970   ness and Consequences." *Canadian Journal of Behavioral Science*,
         2(2):124—135.
Burke, W. W. "Organizational Development." *Professional Psychology*, 4:194—199.
1973
Campbell, J. P., M. D. Dunnette, R. D. Avery, and L. W. Hellervik. "The Development
1973   and Evaluation of Behaviorally Based Rating Scales." *Journal of Applied
         Psychology*, 57:15—23.
Campbell, J. P., M. D. Dunnette, E. E. Lawler, and K. E. Weick. *Managerial Behavior,*
1970   *Performance, and Effectiveness.* New York: McGraw-Hill.
Campbell, J. P., D. A. Bownas, N. G. Peterson, and M. D. Dunnette. "The Measure-
1974   ment of Organizational Effectiveness: A Review of Relevant Research
         and Opinion." Final Report 1974, Navy Personnel Research and Develop-
         ment Center Contract N00022—73—C—0023, Minneapolis: Personnel
         Decisions, Inc.
Carpenter, H. H. "Formal Organizational Structural Factors and Perceived Job
1971   Satisfaction of Classroom Teachers." *Administrative Science Quarterly*,
         16:460—465.
Carroll, S., and H. Tosi. *Management by Objectives.* Homewood, Ill.: Irwin-Dorsey.
1973
Chervany, N. L., and G. W. Dickson. "An Experimental Evaluation of Information
1974   Overload in a Production Environment." *Management Science*, 10:1335—
         1344.
Child, J. "Organizational Structure, Environment, and Performance: The Role of
1972   Strategic Choice." *Sociology*, 6:1—22.
————. "Organizational Structure and Strategies of Control: A Replication of the
1972   Aston Study." *Administrative Science Quarterly*, 17:163—177.
————. "Strategies of Control and Organizational Behavior." *Administrative
1973   Science Quarterly*, 18:1—17.
Child, J., and R. Mansfield. "Technology, Size and Organization Structure."
1972   *Sociology*, 6:369—393.
Childs, M., and H. Wolfe. "A Decision and Value Approach to Research Personnel
1972   Allocation." *Management Science*, 18: B—269—B—278.
Christal, R. E. "JAN: A Technique for Analyzing Individual and Group Judgment."
1973   Lackland Air Force Base: 6570th Personnel Research Laboratory, Aerospace
         Medical Division, PRL—TDR—63—3, ASTIA Document AD—403 813.
Conrath, D. W. "Communications Environment and Its Relationship to Organi-
1973   zational Structure." *Management Science*, 20: 586—603.
Corwin, R. G. "Strategies for Organizational Innovation: An Empirical Comparison."
1974   *American Sociological Review*, 37: 441—454.
Dermer, J., and J. P. Siegel. "The Role of Behavioral Measures in Accounting for
1974   Human Resources." *The Accounting Review*, 49:88—97.
Dooley, J. E. "Decisions on Social and Technological Tasks Incorporating Expression
1974   Preference and Environmental Insult." *Management Science*. 20:912—920.
Dubin, R., J. E. Champoux, and L. W. Porter. "Central Life Interests and Organi-
1975   zational Commitment of Blue-Collar and Clerical Workers." *Administrative
         Science Quarterly*, 20(3):411—421.
Eitzen, S. D., and N. R. Yetman. "Managerial Change, Longevity, and Organi-
1972   zational Effectiveness." *Administrative Science Quarterly*, 17:110—117.
Fanshel, S., and J. W. Bush. "A Health-status Index and Its Application to Health-
1970   services Outcomes." *Operations Research*, 18:1021—1066.
Fenn, D., and D. Yankelovich. "Responding to the Employee Voice." *Harvard
1972   Business Review*, 50(3):83—91.

Flamholtz, E. "Should Your Organization Attempt to Value Its Human Resources?"
1971   *California Management Review*, 14(2):40–55.
————. "A Model for Human Resource Valuation: A Stochastic Process with
1971   Service Rewards." *The Accounting Review*, 46:253–267.
————. "Toward a Theory of Human Resource Value in Formal Organizations."
1972   *The Accounting Review*, 47:666–679.
Folgi, L., C. L. Hulin, and M. Blood. "Development of First Level Behavioral Job
1971   Criterion." *Journal of Applied Psychology*, 55:3–8.
Fordyce, J. K., and R. Weil. *Managing with People*. Reading, Mass.: Addison Wesley.
1971
Franklin, J. L. "A Path Analytic Approach to Describing Caused Relationships
1973   Among Social Psychological Variables in Multi-Level Organizations."
        Technical Report for Office of Naval Research, University of Michigan,
        Institute for Social Research.
Freeman, John, Henry. "Environment, Technology, and the Administrative Intensity
1973   of Manufacturing Organizations." *American Sociological Review*, 38:
        750–763.
Freeman, John. "Growth and Decline Processes in Organizations." *American
1975   Sociological Review*, 40:215–228.
Frederiksen, N., O. Jensen, A. Beaton, and B. Blaxom. *Prediction of Organizational
1972   Behavior*. New York: Pergamon.
French, W. "Organization Development: Objectives, Assumptions, and Strategies."
1972   In N. Margulies and A. P. Raia (Eds.), *Organizational Development:
        Values, Processes, and Technology*. New York: McGraw-Hill.
French, W., and C. H. Bell, Jr. *Organization Development: Behavioral Science
1973   Intervention for Organization Improvement*. Englewood Cliffs, N. J.:
        Prentice Hall.
Friendlander, F., and S. Greenberg. "Effect of Job Attitudes, Training, and Organi-
1971   zational Climate on the Performance of the Hard-core Unemployed."
        Journal of Applied Psychology, 55:287–295.
Fullan, M. "Industrial Technology and Worker Integration in the Organization."
1970   *American Sociological Review*, 35:1028–1039.
Geoffrion, A. M., J. S. Dyer, and A. Feinberg. "An Interactive Approach for Multi-
1972   Criterion Optimization, with an Application to the Operation of an Academic
        Department." *Management Science*, 19:357–368.
Georgopoulos, B. S., and A. S. Tannenbaum. "Study of Organizational Effective-
1971   ness." In J. Ghorpade (Ed.), *Assessment of Organizational Effectiveness*.
        Pacific Palisades, Calif.: Goodyear.
Gerwin, D. and W. Christoffel. "Organizational Structure and Technology: A
1974   Computer Model Approach." *Management Science*, 20:1531–1542.
Ghiselli, E. E. *Exploration in Managerial Talent*. Pacific Palisades, Calif.: Goodyear.
1971
Ghorpade, J. "Study of Organizational Effectiveness: Two Prevailing Viewpoints."
1970   *The Pacific Sociological Review*, 13:31–41.
————. *Assessment of Organizational Effectiveness*. Pacific Palisades, Calif.:
1971   Goodyear.
Glazer, E. M., and T. E. Backer. "A Clinical Approach to Program Evaluation."
1972   *Evaluation*, 1(1):54–59.
Glassman, R. B. "Measuring the Degree of Organization." *Organization and
1975   Administrative Sciences*, 6(1): 33–36.
Glennon, R. "Issues in the Evaluation of Manpower Programs." In P. Rossi, and
1972   W. William (Eds.), *Evaluating Social Programs: Theory, Practice, and
        Politics*. New York: Seminar Press.
Goodman, R. A. "Organizational Preference in Research and Development."
1970   *Human Relations*, 23:279–298.
Greene, C. N., and D. W. Organ. "An Evaluation of Causal Models Linking the
1973   Received Role with Job Satisfaction." *Administrative Science Quarterly*,
        18:95–103.

Hackman, J. R., and E. E. Lawler.   "Employee Reactions to Job Characteristics."
1971   *Journal of Applied Psychology*, 55:259–286.

Hall, D. T., and E. E. Lawler.   "Job Characteristics and Pressures and the Organi-
1970   zational Integration of Professionals." *Administrative Science Quarterly*,
        15:271–281.

Hall, D. T., and R. Manfield.   "Organizational and Individual Response to External
1971   Stress." *Administrative Science Quarterly*, 16:533–547.

Hall, R. H.   *Organizations, Structure, and Process*. Englewood Cliffs, N. J.: Prentice
1972   Hall.

Hall, W.   "Corporate Strategic Planning—Some Perspectives for the Future."
1972   *Michigan Business Review*, 24(1):16–21.

Hatry, H. P.   "Measuring the Effectiveness of Nondefence Public Programs."
1970   *Operations Research*, 18:772–784.

Herman, J. B., and C. L. Hulin.   "Studying Organizational Attitudes from Individual
1972   and Organizational Frames of Reference." *Organizational Behavior and
        Human Performance*, 8:84–108.

Hinings, C. R., and G. L. Lee.   "Dimensions of Organization Structure and Their
1971   Context: A Replication." *Sociology*, 5:83–95.

Hirsch, P. M.   "Organizational Effectiveness and the Institutional Environment."
1975   *Administrative Science Quarterly*, 20(3):327–344.

House, R. J., and J. R. Rizzo.   "Toward the Measurement of Organizational Practices:
1972·   Scale Development and Validation." *Journal of Applied Psychology*,
        56;388–396.

————.   "Role Conflict and Ambiguity as Critical Variables in a Model of Organiza-
1972   tional Behavior." *Organizational Behavior and Human Performance*,
        7:467–505.

Humble, J. W. (Ed.).   *Management by Objectives In Action*. New York: McGraw-
1970   Hill.

Indik, B.   "Toward an Effective Theory of Organization Behavior." *Personnel
1970   Administration*, 31(4):51–57.

Inkson, J. H., D. S. Pugh, and D. J. Hickson.   "Organization Context and Structure:
1970   An Abbreviated Replication." *Administrative Science Quarterly*,
        15:318–329.

Ivancevich, J. M., and J. H. Donnelly.   "Leader Influence and Performance."
1970   *Personnel Psychology*, 23:539–549.

————.   "Relation of Organizational Structure to Job Satisfaction, Anxiety-
1975   Stress, and Performance." *Administrative Science Quarterly*, 20(2):
        272–280.

Kast, F. E., and J. E. Rosenzweig.   *Organization and Management: A Systems
1970   Approach*. New York: McGraw-Hill.

Katz, D., and R. Kahn.   "The Concept of Organizational Effectiveness." In J. Ghorpade
1971   (Ed.), *Assessment of Organizational Effectiveness*. Pacific Palisades,
        Calif.: Goodyear.

Kavcic, B., V. Rus, and A. S. Tannenbaum.   "Control, Participation, and Effectiveness
1971   in Four Yugoslav Industrial Organizations." *Administrative Science
        Quarterly*, 16:74–87.

Kimberly, J. R.   "Environmental Constraints and Organizational Structure: A Compa-
1975   rative Analysis of Rehabilitation Organizations." *Administrative Science
        Quarterly*, 20(1):1–9.

Kimberly, J. R., and W. R. Nielsen.   "Organization Development and Change in
1975   Organizational Performance." *Administrative Science Quarterly*, 20(2):
        191–206.

Korman, A. K.   "Organizational Achievement, Aggression, and Creativity: Some
1971   Suggestions Toward an Integrated Theory." *Organizational Behavior and
        Human Performance*, 6:590–613.

Lammers, C. J.   "Self Management and Participation: Two Concepts of Democrati-
1974   zation in Organization." *Organization and Administrative Sciences*, 5(4):
        17–33.

Landy, F. J., and R. M. Guion. "Development of Scales for the Measurement of
1970   Work Motivation." *Organizational Behavior and Human Performance,*
        5:93–102.
Levine, E. L., and R. A. Kutzell. "Effects of Variations in Control Structure on Group
1971   Performance and Satisfaction: A Laboratory Study." *Proceedings of the
        79th Annual Convention of American Psychological Association:* 475–476.
Lieberson, S., and J. O'Connor. "Leadership and Organizational Performance."
1972   *American Sociological Review,* 37:117–130.
Macleod, R. K., "Program Budgeting Works in Nonprofit Institutions." *Harvard
1971   Business Review,* 49(5):46–56.
Margulies, N., and A. P. Raia. (Eds.), *Organizational Development: Values, Process,
1972   and Technology.* New York: McGraw-Hill.
Marsh, R. M., and H. Mannari. "Japanese Workers' Responses to Mechanization
1973   and Automation." *Human Organizations,* 32(1):85–93.
Mattessich, R. "The Incorporation and Reduction of Value Judgements in Systems."
1974   *Management Science,* 21(1):1–9.
McMatton, A. M., and S. F. Camilleri. "Organizational Structure and Voluntary
1975   Participation in Collective-Good Decisions." *American Sociological Review,*
        40:616–644.
McNeil, K., and J. D. Thompson. "The Regeneration of Social Organizations."
1971   *American Sociological Review,* 36:624–637.
Meyer, M. W. "Size and the Structure of Organizations: A Causal Analysis." *American
1972   Sociological Review,* 37(4):434–440.
Meyer, M. "A Note on Expertness and the Supervisory Component of Organizations."
1973   *Human Organizations,* 32(4):379–384.
————. "Organizational Domains." *American Sociological Review,* 40:599–615.
1975
Mott, P. E. *The Characteristics of Effective Organizations.* New York: Harper and
1972   Row.
Mulder, M., J. Ritsema, and R. deJong. "An Organization in Crisis and Non-Crisis
1971   Situations." *Human Relations,* 24:19–41.
Odiorne, G. S. *Training by Objectives.* New York: Macmillan.
1970
Odiorne, G. S. *Personnel Management by Objectives.* Homewood, Ill.: Irwin.
1971
Pennings, J. M. "The Relevance of the Structural-Contingency Model for Organi-
1975   zational Effectiveness." *Administrative Science Quarterly,* 20(3):393–410.
Porter, L. W., W. J. Crampon, and F. J. Smith. "Organizational Commitment and
1972   Managerial Turnover." Technical Report No. 13, University of California,
        Irvine, Individual Organizational Linkages Research Project.
Powell, R. M., and J. L. Schlaeter. "Participative Management: A Panacea?"
1972   *Academy of Management Journal,* 14:165–173.
Price, J. L. *Handbook of Organizational Measurement.* Indianapolis, Indiana:
1972   D. C. Heath.
————. "The Study of Organizational Effectiveness." *Sociological Quarterly,*
1972   13:3–15.
Prien, E. P., and W. W. Ronan. "An Analysis of Organization Characteristics."
1971   *Organizational Behavior and Human Performance,* 6:215–234.
Pritchard, R. L., and B. S. Karasick. "The Effects of Organizational Climate on
1973   Managerial Job Performance and Job Satisfaction." *Organizational
        Behavior and Human Performance,* 9:126–146.
Reufli, T. W. "Behavioral Externalities in Decentralized Organizations." *Manage-
1971   ment Science,* 9:B–649–B–658.
Rivlin, A. M. *Systematic Thinking for Social Action.* Washington, D. C.: The Brook-
1971   ings Institution.
Ronan, W. W., and E. P. Prien. "An Analysis of Organizational Behavior and Organi-
1973   zational Performance." *Organizational Behavior and Human Performance,*
        9:78–99.

Rosen, N.   "Open Systems Theory in an Organizational Subsystem: A Field Experi-
1970   ment." *Organizational Behavior and Human Performance*, 5:245–265.
Sashkin, M.   "Organization Development Practices." *Professional Psychology*,
1973   4:187–194.
Samuel, Y., and B. F. Manheim.   "A Multidimensional Approach Toward a Typology
1970   of Bureaucracy." *Administrative Science Quarterly*, 15:216–228.
Schneider, B.   "Organizational Climate: Individual Preferences and Organizational
1972   Realities." *Journal of Applied Psychology*, 56:211–217.
Schneider, B., and C. Bartlett.   "Individual Differences and Organizational Cli-
1970   mate: II. Measurement of Organizational Climate by the Multitrait-multi-
         rater Matrix." *Personnel Psychology*, 23:493–512.
Seidler, J.   "On Using Informants: A Technique for Collective Quantitative Data
1974   and Controlling Measurement Error in Organization Analysis." *American
         Sociological Review*, 39:816–831.
Snyder, D.   "Institutional Setting and Industrial Conflict: Comparative Analysis
1975   of France, Italy, and the United States." *American Sociological Review*,
         40:259–278.
Souder, W. E.   "Autonomy, Gratification and R and D Outputs: A Small-Sample
1974   Field Study." *Management Science*, 20(8): 1147–1156.
Stewart, J. H.   "Conceptual Analysis of Organizational Effectiveness." Unpublished
1970   Ph.D Dissertation. Notre Dame, Indiana, University of Notre Dame.
Stogdill, R. M.,   "Dimensions of Organization Theory." In J. D. Thompson and
1971   V. H. Vroom (Eds), *Organizational Design and Research*. London: Henry
         M. Snyder and Co., Inc.
Swinth, R. L.   "Organizational Designs for Complex Problem Solving." *Management
1971   Science*, 18:B–69–B–80.
Tannenbaum, R., and S. Davis.   "Values, Man, and Organizations." In N. Margulies
1972   and A. P. Raia (Eds.), *Organizational Development: Values, Process, and
         Technology*. New York: McGraw-Hill.
Taylor, J. C., and D. G. Bowers.   *Survey of Organizations*. Ann Arbor, Mich.: Institute
1972   for Social Research.
Turban, E., and M. L. Metersky.   "Utility Theory Applied to Multivariate System
1971   Effectiveness Evaluation." *Management Science*, 17:B–817–B–828.
Van de Ven, A. H.   "Group Decision Making and Effectiveness: An Experimental
1974   Study." *Organization and Administrative Sciences*, 5(3):1–10.
Wanous, J. P., and E. E. Lawler.   "Measurement and Meaning of Job Satisfaction."
1972   *Journal of Applied Psychology*, 56:95–105.
Weisbrod, M. R., M. A. Frohman, and J. Johnston.   "Action Research on Turnover
1971   as an O. D. Entry Strategy." Paper presented at the Fall, 1971 meeting of
         the O. D. Network, Minneapolis, Minnesota.
Weitzel, W. F., T. A. Mahoney, and N. F. Crandall.   "A Supervisory View of Unit
1971   Effectiveness." *California Management Review*, 13(4):37–43.
Whitely, R., and P. Frost.   "The Measurement of Performance in Research." *Human
1971   Relations*, 24:161–178.

Subject Index

Name Index

NOTES

NOTES

NOTES

NOTES